Growth Triangles in Asia

A New Approach to Regional Economic Cooperation

Edited by
**Myo Thant, Min Tang, and
Hiroshi Kakazu**

Published for the Asian Development Bank by
Oxford University Press

Oxford University Press

Oxford New York
Athens Auckland Bangkok Bombay
Calcutta Cape Town Dar es Salaam Delhi
Florence Hong Kong Istanbul Karachi
Kuala Lumpur Madras Madrid Melbourne
Mexico City Nairobi Paris Singapore
Taipei Tokyo Toronto
and associated companies in
Berlin Ibadan

Oxford is a trade mark of Oxford University Press

First published 1994
Second impression 1995

Published for the Asian Development Bank by Oxford University Press

British Library Cataloguing in Publication Data
available

Library of Congress Cataloging-in-Publication Data

Growth Triangles in Asia, a new approach to regional economic
cooperation / edited by Myo Thant, Min Tang, and Hiroshi Kakazu.
p. cm.
"Published for the Asian Development Bank by Oxford University Press."
Includes bibliographical references (p.   ).
ISBN 0-19-586600-2
1. Asia--Economic Integration.   I. Thant, Myo, 1957– .
II. Tang, Min, 1953– .   III. Kakazu, Hiroshi, 1942– .
IV. Asian Development Bank.
HC412.G713 1994
337.1'5--dc20   *94–28885*
CIP

Printed in Hong Kong

Published by Oxford University Press (China) Ltd.
18/F Warwick House, Taikoo Place, 979 King's Road, Quarry Bay, Hong Kong

Table of Contents

iv   Table of Contents

Page

Preface

The attainment of higher and faster rates of growth through regional economic cooperation has been one of the most elusive but enduring objectives in Asia. For a variety of reasons, successful economic cooperation — as distinct from cooperation for political ends — has been rare. Toward the end of the 1980s, however, the growth triangle approach to regional economic cooperation began to emerge conceptually as well as in practice.

Growth triangles are a unique Asian solution to the operational problems of regional integration among countries at different stages of economic development and with different social and economic systems. Yet they have developed more or less spontaneously, with little systematic examination of their benefits or costs. The need for a critical assessment was addressed through a technical assistance grant for the Workshop on Growth Triangles in Asia, provided by the Asian Development Bank in collaboration with the International University of Japan. The papers in this volume are revised versions of papers presented at the workshop, which was held in February 1993 at the ADB headquarters in Manila, Philippines.

The workshop focused on three growth triangles. The most established is the Southern China Growth Triangle, consisting of Hong Kong, Taipei,China, and South China. The Johor-Singapore-Riau (JSR) Growth Triangle, consisting of Singapore, the southern part of the Malaysian state of Johor, and Riau province of Indonesia has been operating since 1992. The third triangle is one being planned in the Tumen River Delta area, which includes the northern provinces of the People's Republic of China, Siberia in Russia, and the Democratic People's Republic of Korea.

The studies in the book *Growth Triangles in Asia: A New Approach to Regional Economic Cooperation* were prepared by scholars who are well known for their expertise and experience in the field. The discussions at the workshop also benefited greatly from the presence of observers from bilateral and multilateral development agencies, senior government officials, and other scholars. A significant feature of the workshop was the presence of senior officials from the United Nations Development Programme, who made available hard-to-obtain information and details of the Tumen River Delta area project.

The papers in this volume attempt to: (i) analyze the underlying economic foundations for regional economic cooperation in the form of growth triangles; (ii) examine the different approaches taken by the members of each growth triangle; (iii) explore the possibilities of extending the growth triangle approach to other areas of the region; and (iv) identify the need, scope, and modalities for future studies in this area.

Myo Thant and Min Tang of the ADB's Economics and Development Resource Center, and Hiroshi Kakazu of the International University of Japan designed, supervised, and coordinated the studies. Jon Miller edited the volume, and Cesar Dizon provided editorial assistance. Ludy Pardo provided invaluable technical assistance and coordinated the production of the book. Zeny Acacio, Helen Buencamino, Clair Dalaguit, Mina Jacinto, Liza Marcial, Eva Olanda, Sari Razon, and Dinna Real provided secretarial services. The assistance of Beth Leuterio is also noted. Special thanks are owed to J. Malcolm Dowling for his support, assistance, and encouragement at every stage of the project. Lastly, the ADB's Printing Unit typeset the manuscripts.

Mitsuo Sato

MITSUO SATO
President
Asian Development Bank

Overview

Promotion of regional economic cooperation to attain high rates of growth is an old objective among Asian developing countries. Actual achievements have, however, been limited and even in the case of the Association of Southeast Asian Nations (ASEAN), the most well established regional cooperation venture in Asia, the successes have been limited primarily to political matters. Towards the end of the 1980s, however, different versions of a new type of regional economic cooperation began appearing in Asia independently of each other. While there were differences, two common features of these regional groupings were the participation of two or more countries, and the inclusion of only parts of these countries. The groupings were given various names but the term "growth triangles" gradually emerged as a popularly acceptable generic term.

Increased economic cooperation on a regional basis was accompanied by renewed academic interest in the subject among individual economists. This interest led to the Workshop on Growth Triangles in Asia which was jointly sponsored by the Asian Development Bank (ADB) and the International University of Japan (IUJ). The Workshop was held on 24–26 February 1993 in Manila, Philippines. The Workshop reviewed the different experiences of three growth triangles in Asia: the Southern China Growth Triangle, the Johor-Singapore-Riau Growth Triangle, and the Tumen River Area Development Programme in Northeast Asia. The Workshop examined the process by which the triangles were established and their ability to promote economic development, and analyzed outstanding issues and obstacles to further development. To achieve these objectives, eleven noted regional scholars and experts on growth triangles were invited to present papers. While most of the experts were economists, they represented different intellectual traditions and had varying mandates. In common, they provided a detailed study of a particular triangle but differed in terms of the issues they focussed on. The papers and presentations benefited greatly from the presence of discussants and observers from international development agencies and representatives from the public sector.

The papers in this volume are the revised papers from the Workshop. The volume is unique in at least three respects. First, while there have been papers and even books dealing with individual growth triangles, it is the first book to analyze the experiences of three growth triangles in Asia. Second, the papers provide different perspectives and insights for each of these triangles. Finally, many of the papers contain information which are not readily accessible. The conclusions provided by the papers contribute to an improved understanding of the potentials and limitations of growth triangles and may serve as a basis for improving existing triangles as well as designing new ones.

The studies in this volume are given a general thrust and perspective by Min Tang and Myo Thant in their paper on conceptual and operational considerations. The authors conclude that the growth triangle is an appropriate form of regional cooperation for many Asian countries. Growth triangles are more export oriented than trading blocs and are a means of maintaining competitiveness in exports. Their attractiveness is also due to the fact that they can be established at relatively low cost within a short period of time. Growth triangles also localize the impacts of liberalization. Successful regional cooperation can be extended while negative consequences can be contained in the immediate triangle area. Countries may also be attracted to growth triangles by the possibility of utilizing the triangle to serve as a means of protecting themselves from trade blocs and increasing protectionism in other parts of the world. The authors, however, note that despite the growth triangles' potential, several conditions must be satisfied if the full potential is to be met. A prime requirement is the existence of economic complementarity between the members of the triangle. Differentials in factor endowments should be of such magnitude that cooperation between countries or parts of countries is mutually beneficial. Geographical proximity is necessary to reduce transaction and transport costs, and to take advantage of cultural and linguistic affinities. Furthermore, members must be politically committed and willing to forego some measure of sovereignty. Physical infrastructure must also be sufficiently well developed to keep transaction costs low. Finally, benefits must be distributed as equitably as possible among the constituent members of the triangle.

Five papers are devoted to the different aspects of the Southern China Growth Triangle which is the most well established one. An overview of this triangle is presented by Edward K.Y. Chen and Anna Ho. The authors note that the emergence of the triangle has been driven predominantly by private sector agents seeking to exploit the existence of factor price differentials. Complementarities in the comparative advantages of Guangdong and Fujian provinces in the People's Republic of China (PRC), Hong Kong, and Taipei,China have also been a strong driving force. Moreover, government support, geographical proximity, and cultural affinities have facilitated cooperation. The triangle, however, differs from regional groupings such as the European Community. First, the formation of the Southern China Growth Triangle is not formal, as no official negotiations took place between the member economies. Second, integration within the triangle is largely vertical. Trade within the triangle comprises more of intra-industrial and commodity trade than trade in final goods.

Economic cooperation has brought each economy significant benefits, including rapid economic growth and higher income in Guangdong and Fujian provinces, the development of an offshore manufacturing sector and an advanced service sector in Hong Kong, and the upgrading of the export and manufacturing sectors in Taipei,China.

This growth triangle, however, needs to address certain key issues if it is to develop further. Infrastructure development and administrative reform will have to be undertaken to solve the problems associated with the rapidly growing traffic of both people and vehicles across the PRC-Hong Kong border. Faced with the emergence of other special development zones in the PRC as well as elsewhere, the Southern China Growth Triangle will increasingly have to compete for capital resources. The growth triangle is also vulnerable to global market conditions particularly in the United States and Europe.

Foreign investment which has driven the growth of the Southern China Growth Triangle is discussed by Pochih Chen. The author notes that the massive inflow of investment into the Southern China area was promoted by a number of factors. On the part of the PRC, these include the "open door" policy and the subsequent liberalization of economic policies, the limited linkages with Taipei,China, and the improvement of infrastructure. For Hong Kong and Taipei,China, investment has been motivated by major differentials in costs of production and labor costs in particular. In the case of Taipei,China, a rapid and major appreciation of the currency was another reason for investment abroad. Cultural and linguistic affinities and geographical proximity added to the attraction of South China as a production base.

The Southern China Growth Triangle has provided major net benefits to all participants. For the PRC, it has provided exports, foreign exchange and employment as well as access to the larger global economy. For Hong Kong and Taipei,China the triangle has provided a means of implementing structural changes in manufacturing and export patterns at minimal cost. The author, however, stresses that the triangle should be seen as being part of a larger global relationship which includes the technology of Japan and the markets of the United States and other industrial countries. Barriers to trade and the transfer of technology are hence inimical to the development of growth triangles.

Without the "open door" policy and other fundamental policy changes, the Southern China Growth Triangle could not have come into existence. Chen Dezhao, in his paper, investigates the role of public policy in the creation of the triangle. The author found that a number of preferential policies has played an important role in the success of the Southern China Growth Triangle. These policies include reductions in income and industrial and commercial taxes to lighten the burden for both domestic and foreign investors. Policies for land use, finance, and trade were also designed to reduce transaction costs and to provide the enterprises operating in the triangle greater access to the domestic as well as world market. There are, however, major policy variations among the different regions in the triangle. In general, policies applied in the Special Economic Zones (SEZs) are much more liberal than those in other parts of the triangle, although the policy differentials have narrowed over time.

Policy changes were implemented through a process of consultations among the major institutions concerned. Furthermore, there is a fairly clear delineation of responsibilities for instituting policy changes. The central government is responsible for issues such as overall direction and planning of SEZs; while the provincial government is responsible for addressing problems arising between SEZs and other areas under its jurisdiction. Some policies, including regulations on foreign investment, are formulated by the SEZs themselves.

The provision of adequate infrastructure is a major prerequisite of growth triangles, an issue which Yue-man Yeung explores in his paper. The author describes how massive investment infrastructure development has enabled members of the Southern China Growth Triangle to take advantage of new opportunities as the world economy moves toward greater integration. The author further shows that the massive investment in infrastructure was possible due to the effective partnership between the government and the private sector, as well as the ability of the central government to decentralize the decision-making process.

Despite the immense progress that has been made, there is a need to address serious problems. Priorities need to be established within the PRC regarding the development needs of South China in relation to those of other provinces. Furthermore, infrastructure projects must also be weighed against projects in other sectors. Individual cities and local authorities need to be dissuaded from their present practice of planning within narrow territorial perspectives, with decisions driven by concerns about prestige rather than the economic viability of projects. The authorities will also have to plan for the expansion of the triangle. The main goal in the 1990s will be the systematic development of large-scale projects to take infrastructure development to a higher level, with wider networks, more modern facilities, and increased scope for international trade and cooperation.

Growth triangles are dynamic institutions in the sense that both the intensity of cooperation as well as the areas included in the triangle are subject to change. Wang Jun analyzes in his paper the process of expansion of the Southern China Growth Triangle in the past and possible developments in the future. He concludes that cooperation has expanded according to relative changes in labor and land costs. The impetus given by the changing comparative advantages was reinforced by the common cultural heritage of the people of Hong Kong and the Pearl River Delta as well as the "special policy, flexible measures" granted to Guangdong and Fujian provinces by the central government. Expansion of existing areas of the triangle to the inland areas of Guangdong and the neighboring provinces of Guangxi and Hunan is already under way. The speed and efficiency with which this expansion will take place depends critically on effective policy and administrative coordination.

The volume contains two papers on the Johor-Singapore-Riau (JSR) Growth Triangle. A comprehensive overview of this growth triangle is given by Sree Kumar who shows how dynamic central governments, state relationships, and recognition of changing comparative advantages have led to the rapid creation of the JSR. The author, however, concludes that despite substantial progress, the JSR Growth Triangle faces substantial challenges. In his view, the most pressing external issue is competition from other developing countries in Asia with low-cost production bases. These include the SEZs in the People's Republic of China, the export processing zones in Viet Nam, and, possibly in the near future, the free trade zones in the Philippines. The critical factors that will determine the competitiveness of the JSR as well as other triangles will continue to be low wages, rents, and land costs, and the provision of good infrastructure.

Within the JSR Growth Triangle itself, the author identifies four outstanding policy issues which need to be addressed: (i) financing of infrastructure development; (ii) establishment of an appropriate property rights regime; (iii) provision of basic services and manpower development; and (iv) support for small and medium enterprises. The author also emphasizes that in order to avoid deceleration in the development of the JSR, there is a need to ensure harmonization of labor, social, and legal restrictions at high rather than low levels of public sector responsibility.

The progress and prospects of the JSR Growth Triangle are viewed from a different perspective by G. Naidu. The author discusses the rationale for the triangle, public policy initiatives which significantly contributed to its development, and the impact on subregional development. Naidu notes that there is uneven support for JSR among its members. Support is strongest in Singapore and weakest in Malaysia. A perception among many Indonesians and Malaysians is that Singapore is likely to derive the largest benefits from the subregional economic grouping. Part of the explanation for the Malaysian and Indonesian perception has to do with complex intranational distributional issues emanating from the participation of Johor and Riau in the growth triangle.

The weakest link in the triangle is the Johor-Riau islands segment. There are no investments from Johor in Riau, and except for an Indonesian proposal to develop tourist facilities in Johor, planned and actual investment flows from Indonesia to Johor are minimal. The same situation holds for trade linkages, as both Johor and Riau are capital-importing members of the triangle. Moreover, entrepreneurs in Johor and Malaysia, unlike their counterparts in Singapore, are not as ready for the regionalization of their activities. It is unlikely that investment and trade linkages between Johor and Riau will develop in the near future because they lack complementarity and are physically distant from each other. Johor's limited ability to play an active role in the JSR Growth Triangle is also due to its status as a state in a federal structure and its inability to act unilaterally on key important issues.

Two papers discuss the prospects for regional economic cooperation in the Northeast Asia region. Hiroshi Kakazu gives a comprehensive overview of the rationale for cooperation and the progress that has been made since the late 1980s. The author also discusses the origin and concept of the Tumen River Area Development Programme, and the strategies for, and constraints to, actual implementation. The author concludes that despite the potential and even without major political problems such as the territorial dispute between Russia and Japan, there is a large number of institutional and economic issues that need to be resolved before the project can proceed. No comprehensive development strategy and objectives has yet been formulated. Furthermore, not all the countries have given the same amount of support to the project. Economic and institutional conditions in Mongolia, the Democratic People's Republic of Korea, and Russia are in a state of flux but a substantial degree of stability will be needed if multi-regional cooperation is to be viable and plans are to be formulated. The lack of consensus on ends and means of developing the triangle is also reflected among donor countries and agencies. There is little support from the European Community and the United States for using public funds for Tumen Delta projects. Support from Japan is higher but the central government has never officially made any major commitments to the project.

Hirokazu Shiode examines the North Korean perspective on the Tumen River Area Development Programme. The author reviews the economic progress, various policy initiatives and liberalization measures adopted by the Democratic People's Republic of Korea since the late 1980s. As the author notes, the establishment of a free economic and trade zone in December 1992 was the culmination of the process of policy reforms which had begun in 1984. However, there remain a number of impediments to the realization of effective multilateral cooperation in the Tumen River area. Political problems are a major, if not the main, impediment given the complexity of bilateral relations and diversity of political systems. Furthermore, genuine regional cooperation may be limited by the insistence on national sovereignty by each of the three countries over the land leased to the Tumen River Economic Zone. Economic nationalism is also an impediment to investment in infrastructure as each country intends to establish a large-scale infrastructure project. Further confidence-building measures in foreign relations and a more detailed picture of both potentials and problems may be needed before the Programme can be substantially implemented.

Overall, the papers in this volume strengthen the perception that growth triangles are a new and potentially powerful tool of economic development. As the studies on the Southern China and JSR Growth Triangles show, the benefits from this particular form of regional cooperation can be substantial. Potential benefits, however, should not be confused with actual benefits; neither should difficulties in creating and sustaining a growth triangle be underestimated. Political stability, common vision and objectives, and the ability and willingness on the part of the governments to modify internal policies for the sake of regional cooperation are critical ingredients for success. Incentives for cooperation will be stronger where differentials in factor endowment are sharp and economic complementarities exist. Sustained development of a growth triangle will depend on the extent to which the public and private sectors can cooperate harmoniously.

April 1994

Abbreviations and Acronyms

ADB	Asian Development Bank
AFTA	ASEAN Free Trade Area
APEC	Asia-Pacific Economic Cooperation
ASEAN	Association of Southeast Asian Nations
BAPPEDA	Riau Regional Development Planning Agency (in dialect)
BIDA	Batam Industrial Development Authority
BKPMD	Riau Investment Coordinating Board (in dialect)
CEPT	Common Effective Preferential Tariff
CPC	Coastal Port Cities
COMECON	Council for Mutual Economic Assistance
DAC	Development Assistance Committee
DPRK	Democratic People's Republic of Korea
dwt	dead-weight ton
EAEC	East Asian Economic Caucus
EC	European Community
EOI	export-oriented industrialization
EPZ	Export Processing Zone
ESCAP	Economic and Social Commission for Asia and the Pacific
ETDA	Economic and Technological Development Areas
FDI	foreign direct investment
FETZ	Free Economic and Trade Zone
GATT	General Agreement on Tariffs and Trade
GDP	gross domestic product
GLC	government-linked company
GNP	gross national product
GVFEZ	Greater Vladivostok Free Economic Zone
ha	hectare
IMF	International Monetary Fund
IUJ	International University of Japan
JSR	Johor-Singapore-Riau
KW	kilowatt

MFN	most favored nation
MIDA	Malaysian Industrial Development Authority
MIER	Malaysian Institute of Economic Research
MNC	multinational company
MW	megawatt
NAFTA	North America Free Trade Agreement
NT dollar	New Taiwan dollar
NEA	Northeast Asia
NIE	newly industrializing economy
NPT	Nuclear Non-Proliferation Treaty
ODA	Official Development Assistance
OECD	Organization for Economic Co-operation and Development
PRC	People's Republic of China
PRDA	Pearl River Delta Area
PMC	Programme Management Committee
ROK	Republic of Korea
SCEZ	Southern China Economic Zone
SEZO	Special Economic Zones Office
SEZ	Special Economic Zone
SREZ	Subregional Economic Zone
sq km	square kilometer
TEDA	Tumen Economic Development Area
TEU	twenty-foot equivalent unit
TRADP	Tumen River Area Development Programme
TREZ	Tumen River Economic Zone
UN	United Nations
UNDP	United Nations Development Programme
UNIDO	United Nations Industrial Development Organization
USSR	Union of Soviet Socialist Republics

Notes

The symbol "..." in tables means rounded to zero.
The symbol "– " or "--" in tables means not available.

Growth Triangles: Conceptual and Operational Considerations

■ Min Tang and Myo Thant[1]

INTRODUCTION

One of the most important developments in the world trade system in the 1990s has been the emergence and strengthening of regional trading blocs. A number of proposals have been made in the Asia-Pacific region for increased economic cooperation and trade liberalization, but concrete achievements have been limited. Recently, however, several localized economic cooperation zones — known as "growth triangles" — have emerged in Asia. In their most basic form, growth triangles exploit complementarities between geographically contiguous areas of different countries to gain a competitive edge in export promotion. To be effective, they require close cooperation between the private and public sectors of each of the countries involved. In general, the private sector provides the capital for investment, and the public sector provides infrastructure development, fiscal incentives, and a favorable administrative framework.[2]

Interest in growth triangles has been heightened by the success of the southern part of the People's Republic of China (PRC) in achieving high rates of growth through economic cooperation with neighboring economies. Singapore has recently moved to formalize its ties with the southern Malaysian state of Johor and the islands of the Riau archipelago in Indonesia. Discussions to create growth triangles in other parts of Asia are also underway, with plans for the Tumen River Area Development Programme in North-east Asia being the most advanced.

This paper analyzes some of the major conceptual issues underlying the growth triangle phenomenon. It is organized into six parts. The first section provides a definition of growth triangles and discusses the ways in which they differ from other forms of regional economic cooperation. The second section describes the general need for growth triangles, while the third section discusses the conditions necessary for their successful operation. The fourth section outlines the major costs and benefits that need to be assessed in evaluating the welfare implications of growth triangles. The fifth section discusses prospects for the development and extension of the growth triangle concept in Asia, and the final section presents the main conclusions.

ETYMOLOGY OF GROWTH TRIANGLES

Growth triangles are also known as subregional economic zones (Chia and Lee, 1992), natural economic territories (Scalapino, 1992) or extended metropolitan regions (McGee and Macleod, 1992). They are transnational economic zones spread over well-defined, geographically proximate areas covering three or more countries where differences in factor endowments are exploited to promote external trade and investment.

The term "growth triangle" came into common use after the then Deputy Prime Minister of Singapore, Goh Chok Tong, used it in December 1989 to describe the subregional economic coopera-tion involving Singapore, southern Johor, and Batam Island in Indonesia. The economic cooperation between Hong Kong, Taipei,China, and the southern PRC (mainly parts of Guangdong and Fujian provinces) has been referred to as the Southern China Growth Triangle. The Tumen River Area Development Programme, which includes parts of Jilin province in the PRC, Siberia in Russia, and the Democratic People's Republic of Korea, has also been described as a growth triangle.[3] Other growth triangle initiatives include the Northern ASEAN Growth Triangle, consisting of the northern states of Malaysia, northern Sumatra in Indonesia, and southern Thailand; the Eastern ASEAN Growth Triangle, consisting of Mindanao in the Philippines, North Sulawesi in Indonesia, and Sandakan in Malaysia. The Yellow Sea Economic Zone, which includes a portion of the coast of Bohai in the PRC and the western and northern parts of Kyushu and Yamaguchi in Japan, has occasionally been called a growth triangle as well.

Growth triangles emerge as a result of two forces, both of which have existed separately for some time: regional economic cooperation and large flows of foreign direct investment (FDI).

The traditional rationale provided for regional cooperation in Asia is that it leads to an increase in economies of scale, exploits complementarities in production, and enlarges the size of markets. This rationale has been widely accepted for many years, yet until recently most regional cooperation efforts were thwarted by go-it-alone development strategies followed by countries seeking political and economic autonomy after their emergence from colonial rule. Interest in regional cooperation has been rekindled, however, by the reduction of political tensions between countries in the region, as well as by the globalization of production processes, which has in turn led to the regional distribution of production and increased vertical integration. Asian countries have also felt the need to react to perceived protectionist trends in developed countries, the difficulties in concluding the Uruguay round of General Agreement on Tariffs and Trade (GATT) talks, and the emergence of the European Community (EC) and the North American Free Trade Agreement (NAFTA) as trade blocs. Regional cooperation is now seen as a means of both enhancing development and providing some measure of insurance against adverse changes in the external economic climate.

Foreign direct investment is a well-established feature of development in Asia (see Figure 1). Early investment in Asia primarily supported extraction of natural resources for use elsewhere. Starting around the early 1960s, however, investment flows became more oriented toward the export of manufactured goods. Investment decisions were based on such factors as the availability of low-wage labor and the existence of favorable business and investment policies. Meanwhile, the relative importance of investment from outside Asia gradually diminished, first as a result of Japanese investment in Northeast and Southeast Asia and later as a result of the rapid growth in investment from the region's newly

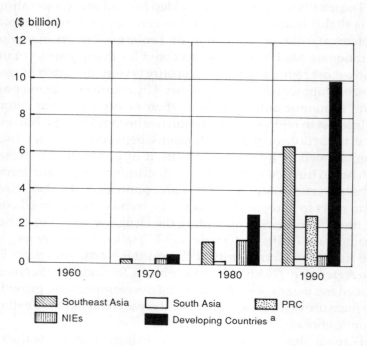

Figure 1
FOREIGN DIRECT INVESTMENT TO DEVELOPING COUNTRIES IN ASIA IN SELECTED YEARS

($ billion)

Legend:
- Southeast Asia
- South Asia
- PRC
- NIEs
- Developing Countries [a]

[a] Developing countries include the People's Republic of China, countries in Southeast Asia, South Asia and the NIEs.

Source: IMF, *International Financial Statistics*, various issues.

industrializing economies (NIEs). Investment to relocate labor-intensive manufacturing in low-wage economies grew sharply after the currency realignments following the Plaza Accord of 1985. Japanese investment in other Asian economies grew again in the late 1980s, when the rising yen reduced the cost competitiveness of Japanese exporters and forced them to move to new offshore production bases (see Table 1).

Investment in a few countries in Southeast Asia and parts of the PRC has accounted for much of the phenomenal growth in overall investment in the last few years.[4] Rapid exchange rate appreciation (about 40 per cent in two years) has led to an outflow of investment from Taipei,China to the PRC and Southeast Asia. Since 1987, more than 4,000 companies have set up operations in Southeast Asia, pouring an estimated $12 billion into the region. Despite longstanding political problems and worries about US trade policy, about 7,000 companies have set up operations in the PRC alone, with total investments of at least $6 billion (*International Economic Newsletter*, March 1993).

Table 1. Japanese Overseas Direct Investment, 1986-1990
($ million)

	1986	1987	1988	1989	1990	Cumulative Total 1951-1990
ASEAN	856	1,524	2,713	4,684	4,082	27,437
Indonesia	250	545	586	631	1,105	11,540
Malaysia	158	163	387	673	725	3,231
Philippines	21	72	134	202	258	1,580
Singapore	302	494	747	1,902	840	6,555
Thailand	124	250	859	1,276	1,154	4,422
Brunei	1	0	0	0	-	109
People's Republic of China	226	1,226	296	438	349	2,823

Source: Government of Japan, Ministry of Finance.

These high investment growth rates have been accompanied by rapid increases in wages, which have eroded much of the initial cost advantage that host countries possessed. Growth triangles are therefore a sensible solution for countries which still rely on massive inflows of foreign investment but which face rising labor costs. By removing barriers to flows of inputs and capital, and by cooperating with one another in other ways, geographically contiguous countries are able to maintain their export competitiveness.

Each triangle has a group of investing countries and a group of receiving countries. The countries in the investing group provide capital, technology, and management skills to the receiving group. Hong Kong, Republic of Korea, Japan, Singapore, and Taipei,China are all investors in growth triangles. Their motives for investment range from high domestic labor costs to a desire to obtain reliable sources of strategic raw materials.[5] In contrast, members of the receiving group provide skilled and non-skilled labor, land, and other natural resources. Countries in the receiving group are usually at an earlier stage of economic development than those in the investing group. Some countries are both investors and recipients of investment. For example, the PRC has large investments in Hong Kong, whose own investments have supported the emergence of the Southern China Growth Triangle. Similarly, Malaysia receives investment as a participant in the Johor-Singapore-Riau (JSR) growth triangle, but is likely to be an investor in the Northern ASEAN Growth Triangle.

THE NEED FOR GROWTH TRIANGLES

The developing countries of Asia, whose economies are among the most dynamic in the world today, are taking steps to create more liberal and open economic environments with greater reliance on market forces for pricing and investment decisions. As a result, despite a slowdown in world trade growth and sluggish demand in the industrial world, these countries have maintained high levels of economic growth and a respectable export performance. This success has been supported by a steady inflow of foreign investment, which has helped raise productive capacity and improve labor productivity.

Asia's developing countries, which have become more connected with prevailing circumstances in the rest of the world, have been increasingly concerned about the impact of emerging trading blocs (e.g., EC and NAFTA) on exports and capital inflows. It is not surprising, then, that various Asia-Pacific economic and trade groups have been proposed in recent years for the purposes of promoting trade and defending the region against actions taken elsewhere.

There are, however, fundamental problems in forming an EC or NAFTA-type trading bloc in Asia:

(i) Trading blocs require large volumes of internal trade. Although intraregional trade in Asia has increased in absolute terms in recent years, the US and EC are still the major markets for Asian exports and sources of imports. The share of trade with the EC and North America in total Asian trade was as high as 40 per cent in 1991;[6]

(ii) Trading blocs require member countries to have similar laws and regulations governing trade and investment flows. The developing countries of Asia, however, have a diverse range of economic systems, making it difficult to harmonize trade and investment practices;

(iii) Per capita income levels of member countries should be close enough so that adjustments in trade flows do not cause massive changes in the distribution of income and employment (Schott, 1991). Income disparities in Asia are wide, however. For example, the per capita income of Japan is about 40 times that of the Philippines and 100 times that of Viet Nam. These differences are much larger than those among EC and North American countries;

(iv) Geographical proximity is often the central element of a trading bloc because of the importance of transportation and communications. However, Asian developing countries are widely dispersed, and their transportation and communication networks are frequently poorly developed, making transaction costs high; and

   (v) Political commitment and policy coordination among
        the member countries are fundamental prerequisites for
        a trading bloc. Yet Asian developing countries have
        very different political interests, historical backgrounds,
        and social and economic systems, making such coordi-
        nation difficult.

   Growth triangles are not necessarily affected by these problems. Unlike trading blocs, which require national changes in
institutional and administrative arrangements, growth triangles
usually involve only portions of countries. This reduces political
and economic risks. Should a triangle succeed, its benefits can be
easily extended to other parts of its member countries. This has
happened in South China, where development began in four Special Economic Zones (SEZs) and extended gradually to the Pearl
River Delta area of Guangdong and Fujian provinces. On the other
hand, adverse consequences can be restricted mainly to the area
concerned. This is particularly attractive for countries in transition
from centrally planned economies to market economies.
   Growth triangles can be established at a lower cost and in less
time than formal trading blocs, which typically involve many years
of discussion and preparation. One country can also form several
growth triangles to test various approaches to regional cooperation. The PRC, Malaysia, and Indonesia are all establishing several
triangles at the same time.
   While trading blocs focus largely on supplying the markets of
member countries, growth triangles are export-oriented structures
for which the size of the regional market is relatively unimportant.
This makes growth triangles particularly appropriate for Asia,
whose internal markets are far smaller than those of North America
and Europe. Growth triangles are also capable of conferring economic benefits to non-member countries, both by offering market
access and by allowing foreign investment.
   Growth triangles are different from export processing zones
(EPZs). EPZs are well-demarcated enclaves outside a nation's normal customs barriers, where foreign firms enjoy favored treatment
with respect to the importation of intermediate goods, taxation, and
access to infrastructure. In exchange, most of the output of EPZs is
exported. For a host country, the major benefits are foreign

exchange earnings and employment, while for investors the attraction is the availability of a low-cost export platform.

Like EPZs, growth triangles exploit the international mobility of capital and the comparative advantage of low-cost labor. A significant difference, however, is the involvement of more than one country. By exploiting economies of scale and integrating the resource endowments of their members, growth triangles can be far more competitive. Moreover, growth triangle activities are not limited to manufacturing, and may include service sector activities such as tourism and labor exports. On the other hand, the policy coordination required, especially for distribution of benefits, is much more complex in growth triangles than in EPZs.

KEY FACTORS FOR SUCCESS

What makes a growth triangle appropriate in a given area, and what makes it successful once it is operational? Answers to these questions are important not only for understanding existing growth triangles, but also for establishing new ones.

Based on the experiences in Southern China and in the Johor-Singapore-Riau triangle, the most important factors for the success of growth triangles are economic complementarity, geographical proximity, political commitment, policy coordination, and infrastructure development.

Economic Complementarity

Economic complementarity derives from the parties' different stages of economic development or from differences in factor endowments. Both the Southern China and Johor-Singapore-Riau triangles contain fairly well-developed urbanized areas and less developed, low-income areas (see Table 2). Southeast Asia's leading urban centers — Hong Kong, Singapore, and Taipei — have strong industry sectors, well-developed financial markets, fairly advanced infrastructure facilities and well-trained labor forces. Their limited supply of unskilled labor and the scarcity of land have, however, pushed up labor costs and property prices, reducing the competitiveness of their economies in the world market.

Table 2. Basic Indicators for Southern China and Johor-Singapore-Riau Growth Triangles

	Southern China					Johor-Singapore-Riau			
	Hong Kong	Taipei, China	Guangdong	Fujian	TOTAL	Singapore	Johor	Batam	TOTAL
Area (sq km)	1,075	36,000	18,000	12,000	67,075	639	18,914	--	˙19,553
Population (million)	5.7	20.4	62.8	30.0	118.9	2.8	2.2	0.1	5.1
Per capita GNP ($, 1991)	13,200	3,070	535	350	--	12,890	3,594	500	--
Total GDP ($ billion)	59.7	180.3	33.6	10.5	284.1	34.6	4.3	...[a]	38.9
GDP Growth Rate (1991)	3.9	7.3	17.3	15.4	--	6.7	9.0	--	--
Unskilled Labor Cost ($ per month)	708	--	103	--	--	350	150	90	--
Land Cost ($/sq m/month)	24.7	--	1.9	--	--	4.25	4.08	2.3	--

-- = not available.

... = rounded to zero.

[a] $0.045 billion.

Sources: Chia Siow Yue & Lee Tsao-Yuan (1992).

In contrast, neighboring areas which lack capital and managerial skills have an ample supply of both labor and land. Thus, a redistribution of labor-intensive industries from the well-developed areas to relatively less developed areas would be mutually beneficial.

Economic complementarity within a triangle is also characterized by differences in levels of technology and the quality and experience of personnel. The abundance of "soft technology" (Chen, 1993) — i.e., expertise — in Hong Kong's service sector has been one of the main reasons for its development into an international financial center and a conduit for capital flowing into the region.

Taipei,China, is particularly rich in "hard" and "soft" technology in the industry sector. A restructuring of its industry sector toward technology-intensive and capital-intensive manufacturing began in the mid-1980s. As a result, industries such as textiles, apparel, and leather have declined in importance or have been gradually phased out. At the same time, there is a shortage of opportunities for domestic investment of financial capital, which has become abundant after an extended period of huge trade surpluses.

In Singapore, both the manufacturing and service sectors are capable of serving a wider economic and geographic base, and neighboring areas can benefit from Singapore's managerial, operational, and logistical networks.

An even broader basis for economic complementarity can be found in the Tumen Delta area, which allows for the integration of the capital and technology of Japan and the Republic of Korea, the natural resources of Russia and North Korea, and the abundant labor and agricultural resources of the PRC.

Complementary contributions need not come only from the parties that are physically in the triangle. In Shenzhen, only half the FDI came from Hong Kong and Taipei,China in 1990. A similar situation can also be found in Batam (see Table 3). Economic complementarity among the parties within the Tumen Delta itself is rather weak, and capital is expected to come largely from Japan and the Republic of Korea. Furthermore, since a growth triangle usually has an export-oriented production structure, its outputs depend largely on external markets rather than internal markets, thus reducing the importance of economic complementarity within the triangle, on the final demand side at least.

Table 3. Foreign Direct Investment in Shenzhen and Batam, 1990

	Shenzhen		Batam	
	Value ($ million)	Share (Per Cent)	Value ($ million)	Share (Per Cent)
Hong Kong	215	51.4	39	5.4
Taipei,China	3.7	1	--	--
Singapore	8.9	2.1	347	48
Japan	127	30.4	54	7.5
USA	17	4.1	172	24
Others	14.1	3.7	113	16

Sources: Chen (1993); Kumar (1993).

Geographical Proximity

Empirical studies have shown that countries tend to trade with their neighbors if transportation and communication costs can be minimized (Summers, 1991). Hence, it is not surprising that geographical proximity is one of the most compelling factors for capital to move from Hong Kong to Guangdong, for investment to flow from Taipei,China to Xiamen, or for Singaporean companies to relocate in Johor and Batam. Moreover, similarities in language and cultural background, which often prevail between geographically proximate areas, are conducive to better understanding and closer business relationships. A good example is the Southern China triangle, where interpersonal bonding and business trust have been fostered by linguistic affinity. Cantonese is spoken in Hong Kong and Guangdong while Fujianese is spoken in Taipei,China and Fujian province.

Political Commitment and Policy Coordination

The political commitment of the governments involved and policy coordination among the parties are the other key factors for the success of a growth triangle. At the national level, there is a need to implement appropriate policies relating to tariffs, employment regulation, real estate, finance, foreign investment, and foreign exchange. All such policy directives and initiatives must be strongly supported and implemented by both central and local governments. For example, high-level government commitment was critical in the relaxation of Indonesian regulations on foreign direct investment in Batam, allowing 100 per cent foreign equity ownership, local processing of investment applications, and the private sector establishment of industrial estates (Chia and Lee, 1992).

In the Tumen Delta triangle, political commitment has been assured by the countries involved from the very start of the development program. The Tumen Delta triangle has also demonstrated that with high-level political support, multilateral development organizations — in this case the United Nations Development Programme—can play a catalytic role by providing initial financing for project study and design while maintaining a nonpartisan role.

Compared with the Johor-Singapore-Riau and Tumen Delta triangles, formal policy coordination among the members of the Southern China triangle is relatively weak, with the development of the triangle having been spurred largely by market forces and private sector initiatives. However, government policies are still crucial in determining whether and to what extent economic linkages actually take place. The PRC's economic reforms and "open door" policy initiated in 1978 laid the foundation for economic success in Guangdong and Fujian provinces. In 1979, the Chinese government abandoned its long-held policy of self-reliance to set up four SEZs, featuring tax concessions, expanded land use rights, and simplified procedures for foreign investment projects. The Hong Kong government has also played a major role in encouraging the private sector to relocate its production bases to South China. In Taipei,China, government controls on imports of products from the mainland, as well as on indirect export and investment, have been gradually liberalized since 1985.

Infrastructure Development

Infrastructure development is the single most important factor in the creation of an economic environment conducive to the development of a growth triangle. In the Southern China triangle, for example, the preparation of the four SEZs involved large-scale land development and capital construction. In the first stage of development, infrastructure construction took place under the concept of "Five Opens" and "One Leveling." Water supply, power supply, roads, navigation lines, and telecommunications were opened, and land was leveled to allow for building. An infrastructure development program on an even larger scale was initiated in 1986, focused on expressway and railway links between the SEZs and the rest of Guangdong and Fujian provinces, as well as on air links to the rest of the country and the world. Massive investment was also directed to the development of electrical power and telecommunications projects (see Table 4).

A similar trend can also be found in the Johor-Singapore-Riau Growth Triangle. While infrastructure is relatively well-developed in the Johor area, large infrastructure projects are still required in the Batam Industrial Park and in the Bintan Integrated Development Project area. This kind of development is likely to play an even more important role in the Tumen Delta growth triangle, where infrastructure is almost non-existent.

EVALUATING THE COSTS AND BENEFITS OF GROWTH TRIANGLES

Most studies on growth triangles have been descriptive, and have not assessed in detail their potential benefits. Data for measuring costs and benefits accurately are not available for most triangles. Furthermore, cost-benefit analyses are likely to differ from country to country, and spillover effects, which are important benefits, are inherently difficult to measure. Yet without a proper assessment of actual and potential costs and benefits, resource use cannot be optimized. Perhaps more importantly, a clear understanding of the balance and distribution of costs and benefits is critical to productive and sustainable relations among member countries. Finally, knowledge of the costs and benefits is needed not only for the efficient expansion of existing triangles and the creation of new ones, but also for a realistic assessment of the possibilities and limitations of growth triangles in general.

Table 4. Infrastructure in Special Economic Zones in South PRC

Zhuhai	Shenzhen	Shantou	Xiamen
Seaports			
Jinzhou deepwater port opened 1987.	78 berths in four ports.	Seven berths at end of 1988.	Four deepwater berths, one designed for container ships.
	Two 350 TEU container terminals.		
Xiangzhou port for fishing and trading (11 berths).			
Airports			
Zhuhai heliport completed 1983.	Huangtian Airport opened 1991.	Airport expansion.	Xiamen International Airport opened 1983.
New airport planned for Sanzo Island, Western Zhuhai.	Heliport at Nantou for oilexploration in South China Sea.	Eight route services (one international) by 1988.	
Railways			
	Second Beijing-Kowloon railroad being constructed.	Guangzhou-Meizhou-Shantou railway being constructed.	Electrification of Yingtan-Xiamen under construction.
	Shekou container terminal linked to Guangzhou-Kowloon Railway completed 1993.		
	Guangzhou-Shenzhen construction 1991-1994.		
Roads			
By 1988, 373.5 km of roads and 105 bridges.	302 km Zhuhai-Guangzhou-Shenzhen superhighway to be completed mid-1990s.	50 km of roads by 1988; Shenzhen-Shantou highway being constructed.	New causeway (or bridge or tunnel) planned between Xiamen Island and mainland.
Communication			
151 telephone lines in 1988 to Hong Kong and Macau; IDD lines to 150 countries.	3,526 long distance telephone lines in 1990; mobile telephones increased by 3,000 in 1990.	153,000 telephones in urban area in 1992.	Digitized telephone exchange introduced and microwave telecommunication system installed.

(continued on next page)

Zhuhai	Shenzhen	Shantou	Xiamen
Electricity			
New supply station began operation in 1985.	Power plants constructed and electricity bought from China Light and Power Ltd. of Hong Kong.	In 1981 10 KW power line linking urban district with SEZ; in 1985 new 110 KW power station completed; new thermal power plant approved for construction in 1988.	New thermal power plant approved for construction in 1990.
Water Supply			
	Seven reservoirs with holding capacity over 1 million cubic meters in city; new reservoir completed with holding capacity 952,000 cu m	2 km pipeline constructed in 1982; 25.8 km water pipeline in SEZ for 2,070 consuming units by 1988.	

Source: Yue-man Yeung (1993).

Benefits

At the core of each triangle is the idea that diverse factor endowments among contiguous areas enhance the individual members' competitiveness in export promotion. In theory, growth triangles exploit the international mobility of capital and combine it with existing labor resources to produce traded goods which are then exported elsewhere. Although all the benefits and costs of a growth triangle stem from this single feature, the individual objectives of member countries are likely to differ. Capital-abundant countries would generally hope to realize a high rate of return on the export of their capital, while labor-abundant or land-abundant countries might opt for capital importation to realize high returns on manufactured exports. For a capital-exporting member, the abundance of low-cost labor in a nearby area allows economic restructuring, and the relocation of "sunset" industries and rationalization of the use of resources for production and distribution through vertical integration.

Labor cost differentials within a triangle can be substantial. For example, in 1989 the average monthly wage rate for labor in the Hong Kong manufacturing sector was HK$5,520, while rates for equivalent jobs in nearby Guangzhou and the Shenzhen SEZ were only HK$800. Similarly, the monthly wage rate that same year was $350 in Singapore for unskilled labor, $150 in Johor and $90 in Batam (Chen and Ho, 1993; Kumar, 1993). Economic restructuring in response to such differentials allows the capital exporter to move into high value-added service activities required by the region in general and the triangle in particular. Other benefits to the capital exporter may include access to leisure and entertainment activities which have a high labor content, an assured supply of raw materials, and the creation of new markets for its products and services.

For the capital-importing members of a triangle, the static benefits are similar to those associated with EPZs: foreign investment, exports, and foreign exchange earnings. Foreign investment and receipts in foreign exchange for exported items are particularly beneficial. Exports have increased at tremendous rates in both the Southern China and Johor-Singapore-Riau triangles. The PRC's exports to Hong Kong increased from $5.7 billion in 1981 to over $26.7 billion in 1991. Over the same period, Hong Kong exports to the PRC increased from $1.9 billion to close to $17.5 billion (Chen and Ho, 1993). Similarly, total exports from Batam increased from only $20.9 million in 1986 to $210 million in 1991. However, it should be noted that net foreign exchange earnings from exports may be considerably less than gross earnings, due to leakage abroad for factor payments and particularly for imported inputs. When environmental considerations, which are generally not accounted for, are also included, the net foreign exchange receipts may decline even further.

Employment generation can be another substantial benefit, as the experience of Batam shows. In 1985, the entire population was only 58,000. This surged to 107,600 by 1991. The number of workers on the island increased from slightly over 6,000 to nearly 23,000 over the same period (Kumar, 1993). However, as in the case of export earnings, not all employment generation can be regarded as an unalloyed benefit. Appropriate labor may not always be available within the triangle. In cases where it must be imported from other regions, transaction costs should be included in the cost-benefit calculation. In other cases, the reverse situation may prevail, with costs being incurred to prevent migrant labor from moving to the growth triangle in response to perceived or real income differentials. In such cases, the barriers erected to prevent movement are in themselves both a cost and a distortion of the labor market, as well as a cause of inefficient labor use. The movement of labor is one of the more contentious issues in both the Southern China and JSR triangles.

Other things being equal, the generation of formal employment opportunities should lead to an improvement in the real income of labor within the growth triangle. However, the benefits of higher incomes must be balanced against the costs of possible social disruption in both labor-sending and labor-receiving areas. Higher incomes may also be temporary, particularly for laborers returning to localities where the skills they acquired while working in a triangle are either poorly remunerated or unneeded.[7]

The benefits discussed thus far can be viewed as short-term. In contrast, there are long-term spillover effects, such as technology transfer and skills development. Extensive foreign ownership of firms, a predominance of assembly processes, the use of proprietary technology, and the absence of local research and development capabilities are likely to limit the transfer of technology, however, even over longer periods. A more likely benefit is the upgrading of the labor force. On-the-job training allows workers to learn important values and practices, such as discipline, managerial techniques, and quality control. These skills can be retained and transferred.

Another potential long-term benefit is linkage with other segments of a national economy. Increased incomes and an expanding labor force will promote service industries within the triangle and generate other employment opportunities outside. If it is successful, a growth triangle may also serve as a catalytic agent for the development of other sectors, by providing an example to potential investors and encouraging governments to institute or hasten policy reform. The extent and importance of this kind of linkage may be limited by the export-oriented nature of production, the type of technology attracted, the high dependence on imported inputs, and limitations on quality control over domestically procured inputs. Yet for the capital-importing members of a triangle, at least some of the foreign investment inflows will lead to the upgrading of managerial skills and provide access to new, more demanding overseas markets.

A growth triangle can also provide in a physically limited area the type of unregulated policy environment that is conducive to export promotion. Potential adverse political and economic effects of policy decisions are limited by the small size of the area; if policies within a triangle are effective, however, they can be extended to the economy as a whole. Growth triangles may therefore be appropriate for countries having difficulty overcoming economic, political, or environmental limitations. The growth triangle concept may be particularly attractive at the incipient stages of an economic reform process, both as a transitional instrument and as a way to cement and support ongoing reforms.[8] Valuation of such benefits is almost impossible, but insofar as triangles promote the removal of distortions elsewhere in the economy, they undoubtedly can have a large positive impact.

Costs

When assessing the costs of a growth triangle, one must look both at the total costs and the way in which those costs are shared by the participants. Although it is difficult to apportion costs precisely, some division between direct and indirect costs is required. Direct costs include those associated with the development and maintenance of the triangle. Key development costs include site preparation, installation of roads, provision of power and water supplies, and construction of residential facilities for laborers. The total costs incurred for these activities are likely to be substantial even in areas that are not physically remote. Where port facilities already exist within a triangle area, development costs may be considerably reduced.

Maintenance is necessary if a growth triangle is to retain its advantage over outside areas. Maintenance costs are likely to be high where public administration and management skills are in short supply. Such deficiencies may spur rent-seeking behavior, which may, in turn, reduce the overall attractiveness of a triangle to private investors. To combat this, an independent agency can be created to manage a triangle, minimize distortions to entry and access, and ensure that the provision of infrastructure keeps up with evolving needs. The need for an independent agency may be especially strong if planning and administrative capabilities, including resource mobilization and financial planning, are weak. This is most likely to be the case in areas that are far from a country's political center.[9]

Indirect costs include subsidies, concessions and incentives, tariff and customs duty exemptions, and other allowances given to attract developers and investors. This category of costs also includes subsidies on the cost of land, buildings, and utilities, as well as subsidies to encourage the use of domestic raw materials. Significant policy changes may be necessary to induce investment inflows, or at least to harmonize policies with other members of the triangle, and this may entail additional costs. Repatriation guarantees, arbitration procedures, incentives to encourage pioneer industries, and R & D tax exemptions may also involve costs for member countries or for interest groups within those countries.

Tariffs are more likely to be considered costs than benefits, particularly during the incipient stages of a growth triangle's development. Tax revenues may increase as a result of increased incomes, output, and exports, but given the tax structure, collection problems, and tax-related incentives that prevail in many developing countries, the net increase is not likely to be substantial.

The costs of a growth triangle also include negative externalities, or undesirable outcomes. Reference has already been made to the resources needed to stem potential labor and population inflows and the costs of environmental degradation. The diversion of investment and capital from other parts of a member country also carries a cost. There may be costs associated with institutional efforts to resolve domestic or external problems relating to growth triangles, in particular the allocation of benefits across regions. Potential problems include widening regional income disparities, social and ethnic problems, and transaction difficulties between the central and lower levels of government in cases where substantial autonomy has been previously given to the latter (*Asian Development Outlook*, 1992).

Not all members of the population within a growth triangle will have access to the new economic opportunities, yet all will face higher costs of goods and services due to the gradual process of factor price equalization. Income differentials between those within the triangle and external groups may likewise increase due to differential access to employment and investment opportunities and public goods.

Intracountry relations within a triangle present another set of costs. Harmonization of policies to minimize differences in industrial standards, customs classifications, labor regulations, and tariff and non-tariff barriers is frequently necessary. Costs associated with harmonization occur both at the development stage and during a triangle's operations. It is necessary to find ways to minimize the absolute level of these costs, and to spread them equitably among members. Harmonization becomes necessary as the industrial structure within a triangle changes in response to external realities. For more developed countries, this is likely to involve a "hollowing-out" of industrial capacity, while for less developed countries it should involve the acquisition and improvement of technology.

The distribution of costs and benefits represents a major challenge for participants in a growth triangle. Dissatisfaction with the distribution of benefits may be particularly acute where there has been massive use of public funds for infrastructure development. Explicit policies must ensure that the benefits of a growth triangle are spread to other parts of member countries and that regional income inequality is not heightened. Manufacturing tends to concentrate near large markets. This can be circumvented if policies ensure that transportation costs are low and economies of scale make other areas attractive to manufacturing firms (Krugman, 1991).

THE FUTURE OF GROWTH TRIANGLES

Partly as a result of the high growth rates witnessed in the southern PRC, and partly because of the fanfare with which the Johor-Singapore-Riau triangle was unveiled, growth triangles are being envisaged for other parts of Asia. Two prominent initiatives are the North ASEAN Growth Triangle in Southeast Asia and the Tumen River Area Development Programme in Northeast Asia. The latter has received substantial financial assistance from the United Nations Development Programme for feasibility studies. Whether growth triangles will become lasting features of the Asian landscape or just another term in the development lexicon will depend on a number of factors.

The future of growth triangles in Asia will be determined by the continued flow of foreign direct investment to the region and the willingness of neighboring countries to cooperate economically. Although these two conditions may seem rather uncomplicated, the limited progress of other forms of regional economic cooperation, and some of the problems experienced in existing triangles, suggest that the challenges and constraints are not trivial.

Regional cooperation requires strong political will and a sustained commitment from the public sector, if only to reduce risk and uncertainty (Pangestu et al, 1992). Continued flows of foreign investment require the maintenance of a reasonably open global trading system. Policy-induced reductions in demand in the industrialized countries could curtail the effectiveness of the export-led growth strategy which underpins the growth triangle concept. On balance, however, domestic, regional and global trends suggest that growth triangles do have a future.

There are domestic forces which favor the expansion of growth triangles in countries that have pursued outward-oriented, export-led growth strategies, as well as in countries that have only recently discarded serious biases against exports. Countries in the former group have benefited from the adoption of export promotion policies, but are now confronted with populations that expect high growth rates and increasing standards of living. At the same time, however, foreign investment, which is critical for high export growth, is deterred by rapidly rising wages and by shortages of skilled labor and infrastructure. Growth triangles provide a way for countries that are becoming less attractive to investment to maintain some competitiveness while they take steps to broaden their export base and improve industrial efficiency.[10]

For countries that have only recently adopted export-led economic strategies, growth triangles provide a good way of demonstrating the potential of those strategies to accelerate economic development. Increases in foreign investment, employment, and exports are also needed to offset losses suffered in the transition to a new economic system. For these countries, growth triangles will be particularly attractive as ways to gain entry into world markets during a time of difficult economic reform and restructuring.

Intra-Asian investment is both a condition and a desired result of the development of growth triangles. Japan must restructure its economy to improve the quality of life of its citizens and reduce external imbalances. The newly industrializing economies of Asia must also restructure in response to changes in relative factor endowments. Intra-Asian investment should increase as a result of this restructuring, and growth triangles would be logical beneficiaries.

The emergence of regional economic alliances and trading blocs could also promote the development of growth triangles. The difficulties surrounding the Uruguay round of GATT negotiations, along with the strengthening of the European Community and the emergence of the North American Free Trade Agreement, are likely to encourage many Asian countries to rethink the costs and benefits of regional cooperation. They could see growth triangles as ways to increase their competitiveness and protect themselves against adverse changes in the external economic climate, while not requiring great sacrifices in economic sovereignty. Growth triangles may also be seen as a way of restoring balance in negotiations with external trading blocs.

CONCLUSIONS

Although the lack of data and the novelty of the topic preclude definitive conclusions, some fairly robust observations may be made. The first is simply that the growth triangle is an appropriate form of regional cooperation for many Asian countries. Growth triangles are more export-oriented than trading blocs, and less likely to provoke retaliatory action from outside interests. They can also be established at relatively low cost within a short period of time. Should conditions warrant, they can be expanded incrementally.

Despite the potential of growth triangles, several conditions need to be met to ensure their success. A prime requirement is the existence of economic complementarity between the different members of the triangle. Differentials in factor endowments should be of such a magnitude that cooperation between different countries or parts of countries is mutually beneficial. Geographical proximity is necessary to reduce transaction and transport costs, and to take advantage of cultural and linguistic affinities. Members must be politically committed and willing to forego some measure of sovereignty, and physical infrastructure, particularly ports and harbors, must be sufficiently well developed to keep operating costs low. Finally, benefits must be distributed as equitably as possible among the constituent members of the triangle.

This paper examined the major costs and benefits associated with growth triangles. It is possible to conclude that members must minimize start-up costs, ideally by taking advantage of existing infrastructure facilities. In terms of benefits, long-term considerations such as regional development and human capital development may be more important than traditional concerns such as foreign exchange earnings and employment generation. Growth triangles may also be useful in demonstrating the importance of overall economic reforms that reduce distortions.

While the potential benefits are substantial, so too are the costs. Major direct costs relate to capital development expenditure and physical maintenance. Other significant costs include those involved in stemming large-scale population movements. Substantial hidden costs may result from environmental degradation and increased income disparities.

On the whole, however, the future of the growth triangle seems assured. For many countries, growth triangles are a means of increasing exports despite rising labor costs. The willingness to enter into regional cooperative ventures is also facilitated by continuing economic restructuring within Asia, which will likely lead to an increased flow of investment funds. Finally, with trade blocs and protectionist trends emerging in other parts of the world, the growth triangle may well be seen as a means for Asian countries to protect themselves against harsh global realities while promoting cost competitiveness in exports.

Endnotes:

1.   Economists, Economics and Development Resource Center, Asian Development Bank.
2.   The authors wish to thank Meera Kumar who read an early draft and Naved Hamid for his advice and comments, particularly in the early stages of preparation of this paper. The views expressed in this paper are those of the authors solely and do not necessarily reflect the views and policies of the Asian Development Bank.
3.   Mongolia, Republic of Korea, and Japan are also participants in this triangle through the provision of capital and natural resources.
4.   Responses by Japanese manufacturers include accelerating the transfer of production overseas, greater efforts to procure components locally in overseas production bases, increases in imports, and greater investment in technology (Thomson, 1993).
5.   Not all activities within a triangle have a manufacturing basis and not all are export-oriented. The inclusion of service sector industries such as tourism, however, does not seriously diminish a triangle's major reason for being, which is its function as an extended manufacturing and export platform.
6.   Underscoring the difficulties faced by a trading bloc composed of developing nations is the fact that ASEAN has been the only significant attempt at regional trade liberalization. Despite a recent spate of activity and the ASEAN Free Trade Area (AFTA), rapid progress is not likely. AFTA is saddled by its vagueness, extensive exemptions, and the differential rates at which members are required to cut their tariffs. Furthermore, non-tariff barriers have yet to be addressed (Vatikiotis, 1993).
7.   See Warr (1989) for a good discussion on the proper valuation of these traditional benefits in the context of export processing zones.
8.   This is true for formerly centrally planned economies such as Viet Nam, as well as for economies that are not centrally planned but have traditionally had a strong bias toward inward-looking development strategies.
9.   The JSR triangle has relied on an informal agreement for which there is political endorsement at the highest levels. However, in view of the complaints about shortages of power, water, telephone services, slow labor recruitment, and cumbersome customs and immigration procedures, some re-evaluation of the present policy may be in order. For a description of problems in

the JSR triangle, see *Far Eastern Economic Review* (7 January 1993); *Asiaweek* (31 July 1992), and *Bangkok Post* (13 October 1992).

10.   Over the longer term, cost competitiveness because of large labor endowments may diminish as new technologies substantially reduce the share of labor in value-added, thereby reducing one of the strongest rationales for growth triangles.

Bibliography

Asian Development Bank, "Growth Triangles in Asia," in *Asian Development Outlook 1992*. Manila and Hong Kong: ADB and Oxford University Press, 1992.

_____. *Asian Development Outlook 1993*. Manila and Hong Kong: ADB and Oxford University Press, 1993.

Chen, Edward K. Y. and Anna Ho, "Southern China Growth Triangle: An Overview," paper presented at the Workshop on Growth Triangles in Asia, Asian Development Bank, Manila, 24-26 February 1993.

Chia, Siow Yue and Lee Tsao-Yuan, "Subregional Economic Zones: A New Motive Force in Asia-Pacific Development," paper presented at the 20th Pacific Trade and Development Conference, Washington, D. C., September 1992.

Economic and Social Commission for Asia and the Pacific (ESCAP), "Challenges and Opportunities, Restructuring the Developing ESCAP Economies in the 1990s with Special Reference to Regional Economic Cooperation," in *ESCAP Bulletin*, No. 41 (1990).

Government of Malaysia. *Economic Report 1992/93*. Kuala Lumpur: Ministry of Finance, 1992.

International Economic Newsletter, "Taiwan Seeks New Pastures," No. 9 (1993).

Kraar, Louis, "Asia's Hot New Growth Triangle," in *Fortune*, 5 October 1992, pp. 54-63.

Krugman, Paul, "Increasing Returns and Economic Geography," in *Journal of Political Economy*, No. 99 (1991), pp. 483-99.

Kumar, Sree, "Overview Paper on the Johor-Singapore-Riau Growth Triangle," paper presented at the Workshop on Growth Triangles in Asia, Asian Development Bank, Manila, 24-26 February 1993.

Levin, Michael, "Back on Familiar Ground," in *Asian Business*, October 1992.

McGee, T.G., and Scott Macleod, "Emerging Extended Metropolitan Regions in Asia-Pacific Urban System: A Case Study of the Singapore-Johor-Riau Growth Triangle," paper presented at the Workshop on Asia-Pacific Urban Systems: Towards the 21st Century, The Chinese University of Hong Kong, February 1992.

Pangestu, Mari et al, "A New Look at Intra-ASEAN Economic Cooperation," in *Asean Economic Bulletin*, No. 8 (1992), pp. 333-52.

People's Republic of China. *Statistical Yearbook of China 1992*. Beijing: State Statistical Bureau, 1992.

Riedel, James, "Intra-Asian Trade and Foreign Direct Investment," in *Asian Development Review*, No. 9 (1991), pp. 111-46.

Scalapino, Robert A., "The United States and Asia: Future Prospects," in *Foreign Affairs*, Winter 91/92 (1992), pp. 19-40.

Schott, Jeffrey J., "Trading Blocs and the World Trading System," in *The World Economy*, Vol. 14, No. 1 (1991).

Selywyn, Michael, "Asian Chinese Head for Home," in *Asian Business*, April 1993.

Summers, Lawrence H., "Regionalism and the World Trade System," paper presented at the Federal Reserve Bank of Kansas City, August 1991.

Thomson, Robert, "Rising Yen Adds Urgency to 'Post Bubble' Restructuring," in *Financial Times*, 7 April 1993.

Vatikos, Michael, "Markets or Mirage," in *Far Eastern Economic Review*, 15 April 1993.

Warr, Peter G., "Export Processing Zones, The Economics of Enclave Manufacturing," in *World Bank Research Observer*, No. 4 (1989).

Worthy, Ford S., "Where Capitalism Thrives in China," in *Fortune*, 9 March 1992.

Yeung, Yue-man, "Infrastructure Development - The Southern China Experience," paper presented at the Workshop on Growth Triangles in Asia, Asian Development Bank, Manila, 24-26 February 1993.

Southern China Growth Triangle: An Overview

■ Edward K.Y. Chen[1] and Anna Ho[2]

INTRODUCTION

The Southern China Growth Triangle currently consists of Hong Kong, Taipei,China, and the four special economic zones (SEZs) in South China (Shenzhen, Zhuhai, and Shantou in Guangdong, and Xiamen in Fujian). The members operate under different political and economic frameworks, with their cooperation and integration being driven solely by mutual needs and private sector initiatives.

This paper is divided into six parts. The first section provides background information about each member economy. The second section investigates the key factors leading to the emergence of the growth triangle, while the third describes the ways in which cooperation and integration have been carried out. The next section examines the benefits which each member economy has derived from the formation of the growth triangle, and the fifth section discusses the triangle's problems and prospects. In the final section, an attempt is made to sum up the practical and conceptual implications of the growth triangle for other developing economies.

Hong Kong

Hong Kong gained its title as one of Asia's "little dragons" in the 1970s. It registered an average growth rate of 8.7 per cent between 1971-1984 and 6.3 per cent between 1985-1991 as a result of its export-oriented industrialization. The unique economic and geo-graphical environment of Hong Kong later made it an international financial center. Some of the features of this environment are:

(i)   A well-established British legal framework, with a fully independent judiciary;

(ii) A large number of nationals who speak both English and Chinese;

(iii) A laissez-faire economic policy adopted by the colonial government, which fostered adventurous and innovative entrepreneurs and a vigorous business environment; and

(iv) A central location in the Asia-Pacific region, with an excellent harbor and a long coastline, all of which contributed to its development as an entrepot in the 1950s and 1960s and as the world's leading container port in the 1980s and 1990s.

There are, however, limitations to Hong Kong's industrial development, as reflected in the economic restructuring undertaken during the 1980s. While the share of the service sector in GDP increased from 55.7 per cent in 1980 to 66.1 per cent in 1990, that of the manufacturing sector declined from 23.8 per cent to 16.7 per cent in the same period. The share in employment of the manufacturing sector fell from 46 per cent in 1980 to 29.54 per cent in 1990 while that of the service sector rose from 42.14 per cent to 59.45 per cent. Hong Kong has meanwhile developed into a multidimensional commercial center whose activities range from finance to telecommunications, entrepot trade, and technology transfer. This has made Hong Kong attractive as a regional headquarters for multinational companies (MNCs).

Hong Kong is undergoing a transformation from the first stage of export-led development, which relies on the export of labor-intensive products, to a stage in which capital-intensive, technology-intensive, and knowledge-intensive products are exported (Chen, 1988). This transformation is decidedly market-driven, as the labor cost of manufacturing in Hong Kong has risen abruptly over the last decade.

The limited land area has also restricted the development of Hong Kong's manufacturing sector. Large-scale production, which is land-intensive, has not been feasible. It has also been difficult for Hong Kong to move into high-tech manufacturing areas because of the longstanding noninterventionist policy in industry, which has resulted in a relatively low technological capability (Chen and Li, 1991).

Based on 1989 data, the manufacturing sector had the highest labor cost content in its products (see Table 1). Value-added as a percentage of gross output was lowest in the sector, as was value-added per person, which is an indicator of productivity.

As a consequence of its low profit margins, the manufacturing sector is expected to adopt a new strategy. Manufacturing enterprises are already providing support services such as the packaging, promotion, and design of products manufactured elsewhere. Vertical integration of production processes has also been developing rapidly between Hong Kong and its foreign production bases, particularly in the People's Republic of China (PRC).

Table 1. Key Indicators of Hong Kong's Major Economic Sectors, 1989

	Value-Added/ Gross Output (per cent)	Labor Cost/ Value-Added (per cent)	Value-Added/ Person (HK$ 000)
Manufacturing	27.6	59.0	108
Wholesale, Retail and Trade, Restaurants and Hotels	51.4	48.6	150
Financing, Real Estate, and Business Service	71.8	36.4	379
Transport, Storage, and Communications	49.6	46.0	212

Source: Government of Hong Kong.

On the whole, Hong Kong has established an effective infrastructure, an advanced international and local telecommunications
system, and an efficient local transportation network. One significant constraint, however, has been its inadequate airport, which has
curtailed further growth of the tourist industry, trade, and finance.

Taipei,China

Taipei,China is also one of the four "little dragons." Its economy
developed vigorously in the 1960s, when it achieved an average
annual GNP growth of 10.2 per cent with an inflation rate of only
3.3 per cent. In the 1970s, Taipei,China underwent an industrial
restructuring, which can be seen in the rapid change in the composition of exports. The export share of relatively high-tech manufactured goods (e.g., chemicals and pharmaceuticals) and capital
goods rose dramatically, while that of labor-intensive
semimanufactured products fell by over 30 per cent. In the 1980s,
Taipei,China's economy benefited from a boom in its stock and
property markets, and registered a significant trade surplus.

By the end of the 1980s, Taipei,China's rapid growth seemed
to have come to a halt (see Table 2). The movement of major
economic indicators showed that economic performance weakened
around 1988, and that the economy was suffering from several
problems:

(i)   Overheating, with a large proportion of capital sunk in
      unproductive speculative activities in the property and
      stock markets. The resulting high property prices raised
      the cost of production and cut returns on investment.
      The annual rate of change in private sector investment
      in terms of fixed capital formation dropped from dou-
      ble-digit growth during the 1970s to 3.9 per cent in 1981,
      and became negative in 1983 and 1985;

(ii) A general labor shortage caused by the diversion of
      labor from secondary to tertiary industries;

(iii) Rapidly growing trade surpluses, which from 1985 to
      1987 stood at over $45 billion, a large portion of which

Table 2. Taipei,China: Key Growth Indicators, 1985-1991
(per cent)

	GDP Growth	Growth of Gross Capital Formation	Share of Private Gross Capital Formation	Growth of Domestic Demand
1985	5.0	-5.8	58	2.5
1986	11.6	10.1	61	6.3
1987	12.3	18.5	63	15.0
1988	7.3	14.6	67	14.6
1989	7.6	15.3	61	10.6
1990	4.9	7.7	51	7.3
1991	7.3	9.3	51	8.1

Note: All figures are based on 1986 constant prices.

Source: Taiwan Statistical Data Book (1992).

was with the United States. Under US pressure, Taipei, China had to appreciate its currency. Thus, from the mid-1980s to the present, the New Taiwan (NT) dollar appreciated by over 35 per cent, thereby eroding the competitive edge of Taipei,China's manufacturing industries. The huge trade surplus also exerted inflationary pressures;

(iv) Political uncertainty caused by independent activists, which undermined investor confidence; and

(v) An overcrowded industrial environment and a high level of pollution, which created strong antagonism toward heavy industries from domestic environmentalists. Demonstrations against heavy industries have become commonplace in certain industrial regions, and industrial diversification has been checked.

The government launched the Six-Year Development Plan to revive the economy. The plan is to spend as much as $300 billion on infrastructure in order to boost domestic demand. It remains to be seen whether such an enormous government outlay will crowd out private investment and/or revitalize the economy.

Unfortunately, with all these obstacles facing the industry sector, it has not been possible for Taipei,China to undergo a structural change similar to that which is taking place in Hong Kong. Several essential ingredients are lacking for the development of a service-based economy. English is not widely spoken, and the legal system is not internationally recognized. Taipei,China's political status is awkward. In traditional industries, Taipei,China has lost its competitive edge to other low-wage countries in the region, especially the PRC. In high-tech industries, its technological capability is considerably behind that of South Korea and Japan.

People's Republic of China

Since 1979, the PRC's economic reforms and open door policies have attracted worldwide attention. Extensive promotion of the household responsibility system in the rural areas and the establishment of the four SEZs to experiment with flexible economic policies marked the beginning of a new era in the PRC's development. The tasks assigned to the SEZs by the central government were well-summarized in a speech delivered by Xue Muquio, then advisor to the State Planning Commission, when he visited Hong Kong for a seminar organized by the *Economic Reporter* in 1980: "In three or five years from now, we [PRC] shall import mainly items which require less investment and generate quicker profit and those that will help to increase China's foreign exchange earnings."

To this end, the SEZs were located in Guangdong and Fujian, the two southern provinces from which most Chinese expatriates originate, and also the areas nearest to the capital-abundant economies of Hong Kong and Taipei,China.

To create an attractive environment for foreign investment, the central government invested billions of yuan over the past decade to turn the SEZs into modern cities. The SEZs were granted a higher retention rate for foreign currency earned so as to afford local governments a higher degree of economic freedom. Further, they were given the authority to grant permits for foreign investment up to a specified amount and were allowed to operate under a reformed labor employment system, which saw the introduction of contract employment for workers. As labor supply was abundant, wage levels could be kept low compared with those in Hong Kong and Taipei,China.

Aside from offering cheap land and labor, the SEZs exempt foreign-owned enterprises from paying corporate tax for the first three profit-making years, after which they are required to pay a preferential rate of 15 per cent per annum. This compares favorably with the rate elsewhere in the country (33 per cent), in Hong Kong (17.5 per cent), and in Taipei,China (25 per cent).

In recognition of the SEZs' success in attracting foreign capital, the central government opened 14 coastal cities, in which investors receive similar preferential treatment. The SEZs have thus spearheaded the PRC's economic revolution.

EMERGENCE OF THE SOUTHERN CHINA GROWTH TRIANGLE

Changing comparative advantages and economic restructuring in Hong Kong and Taipei,China resulted in the relocation of some of their traditional production processes to lower-cost bases. The opening up of the PRC and the establishment of the SEZs came at an opportune time, providing investors from Hong Kong and Taipei,China with the most convenient and logical places for the diversification and rationalization of their production. The emergence of the triangle was driven mainly by private sector initiatives, although government policies played a supportive role. The member economies have interacted and cooperated with one another, encouraging each to specialize in the realm in which it has a comparative advantage.

Economic Complementarity

Hong Kong

Of the factors essential for economic development, Hong Kong is particularly rich in entrepreneurs. The British colonial government had long ago provided a stable political environment and a set of consistent and prudent economic policies that encouraged flexibility and enabled entrepreneurs to flourish. The adaptive-ness of Hong Kong's industries to the changing international trading environment became evident during the 1960s, when it was still in the first stage of export-oriented industrialization (Chen, 1988).

Hong Kong has excellent infrastructure, with particularly impressive communication, road, and electricity supply systems. Its airport surpasses Tokyo International Airport (Narita) in the number of passengers handled, and its container terminals com-pete with those of Singapore for first place in the world in terms of volume handled. With these advantages, Hong Kong is host to more than 150 offices and 160 representative offices for foreign banks, and therefore holds and attracts an enormous pool of finan-cial and business experts such as financial specialists, accountants, and lawyers. The abundance in "soft technology" in the service sector has been one of the major reasons for Hong Kong's develop-ment into an international financial center from the 1970s. The finance sector's share in GDP rose from 14 per cent to over 20 per cent between 1970 and 1990, while its employment share rose from less than 2 per cent in 1971 to 11 per cent in 1991. Other supporting factors for the rapid development of Hong Kong's finance sector include: (i) national treatment for all foreign investors, with no differentiation between domestic and offshore markets (London is the only other such market in the world); (ii) a highly unregulated market, with government control kept to a minimum; (iii) low taxation; and (iv) an exchange rate linked to the US dollar.

Factors (i), (ii), and (iii) enabled Hong Kong to be one of the world's money management centers. It embraces the largest number of fund management companies in Asia. These same factors also contributed to Hong Kong's stature as a center for the formation of concerted international loans; 70 to 80 per cent of syndicated loans for Southeast Asia and the PRC are arranged in Hong Kong. Factor (iv) has had the effect of stabilizing the Hong Kong dollar and therefore minimizing the foreign exchange risks of overseas inves-tors through an "arbitrage and competition" mechanism.[3]

As an international financial center, Hong Kong can generate huge amounts of capital for domestic investment. In 1990, it had a net export of financial services of over HK$2 billion from insurance, banking services, and the buying and selling of financial assets.

Hong Kong severely lacks labor and land, however. The shortage of labor stems from changes in demographic characteristics (birth rate, labor participation rate, etc.) and also to some extent from emigration. Hong Kong relied on massive labor inflows from the PRC at various times, but tight controls on legal and illegal immigrants adopted since the early 1980s have reduced the labor supply from migration. The relatively inadequate institutional and practical training provided by both the private and public sectors has also hampered Hong Kong's ability to upgrade its industries. A shortage of quality labor will be the single most serious obstacle to the development of Hong Kong's industry sector once the first stage of export-oriented industrialization has been completed. Despite the structural change in manufacturing signalled by a noticeable decline in labor-intensive and land-intensive industries and a rise in technology-intensive and knowledge-intensive industries over the last two decades, manufacturing's share of GNP has shrunk (Wong, 1992). In 1992, only 600,000 Hong Kong workers were still engaged in manufacturing, compared to over 1 million in the peak years of the 1980s. In the past few years, manufacturing industries have lost about 10 per cent of their employment to the service industries each year (Lin and Ho, 1991). The relocation of Hong Kong manufacturing industries overseas began in the early 1970s as a way for companies to minimize production costs and circumvent import quotas imposed by the developed-country markets. More recently, the opening up of the PRC has attracted Hong Kong industries to South China. Table 3 presents the factor cost differentials between Hong Kong and Guangdong.

Taipei,China

Unlike Hong Kong, Taipei,China's strength still lies mainly in its industry sector. This is borne out by manufacturing's share in GDP, which stood at over 34 per cent in 1990.[4] This compares with only a 17 per cent share in GDP for Hong Kong's manufacturing sector for the same year. The industrial restructuring in Taipei,China is largely concentrated in technology-intensive and capital-intensive manufacturing. In the early 1990s, the fastest growing industries were in heavy chemical products and light petroleum and coal products, with annual growth rates of 23 per cent and 19 per cent, respectively. Industries such as textiles, wearing apparel, and leather started to decline in the mid-1980s because their labor-intensive and land-intensive nature made them vulnerable to the high wages and property prices brought on by the boom of the 1980s. Nevertheless, compared to Hong Kong and South China, Taipei,China is richer in both "hard" and "soft" technology in the industry sector.

Financial capital is also abundant in Taipei,China. This capital, which is domestically based, was created by the huge trade surplus realized from export expansion in the last decade. The relative lack of investment opportunities on the island means that the huge capital stock is available for opportunities abroad. Taipei,China's per capita income grew at an annual rate of over 5 per cent from 1980 to 1990, mainly as a result of the production of indigenous firms led by ingenious entrepreneurs. Like Hong Kong, Taipei,China faces a shortage of land and labor, and is under pressure to develop more capital-intensive and technology-intensive industries and to relocate traditional industries overseas.

The export boom has also meant higher energy consumption. Imports of consumer goods (mainly household electrical appliances) rose at an annual average rate of 34 per cent. Demand for services, data on which are unavailable, is believed to be more income-elastic than demand for consumer products, making Taipei,China an attractive market for tertiary industries (Kuznets, 1966).

South China's SEZs

The SEZs' biggest advantage lies in their abundance of land and labor. Based on 1989 figures, the monthly rental for factory space in the Shenzhen SEZ was only HK$15-29 per square meter, while in Hong Kong it was HK$193 per square meter. About 75 per cent of the SEZs' total labor force was engaged in agricultural activities, and this huge labor pool could be readily tapped for the manufacturing sector. The manufacturing wage rate in Hong Kong averaged HK$5,520 per month in 1990 while the average wage in the SEZ was less than 7 per cent of that (see Table 3).

The SEZs are, however, poorly endowed with other factors for development, particularly entrepreneurship, soft and hard technology, capital, professional skills, and infrastructure. Technology and capital can be transferred from abroad on demand, and foreign

**Table 3. Factor Cost Comparison Between Hong Kong
and Guangdong, 1989**
(HK$)

	Monthly Wages in Manufacturing	Flatted Factory Rental Per Month	Space (sq m) Selling Price
Guangzhou	1,000-12,000	27	1,856-2,145
Shenzhen SEZ	800	15-29	1,475
Dongguan	740	10	n.a.
Hong Kong	5,520	193	12,000

Source: Ng, C.Y. and P.K. Wong (1991).

entrepreneurs can be attracted if the environment is favorable. On the other hand, the mobility of professional personnel is curtailed by the unfavorable working environment in the PRC.

Effects of Complementarity

The comparative advantages of the three members of the growth triangle are distinctive. Hong Kong has expertise in financial and commercial services, and has an abundance of capital and industrial entrepreneurs. Taipei,China has considerable capital resources, and its technology is superior to that of Hong Kong and the PRC in new and heavier industries. South China has plenty of land and a large pool of trainable labor. With these characteristics, it is not difficult to predict the ways in which they are likely to integrate. With cost differentials in production factors, trading in production inputs and manufactured products is bound to occur among the members.

Hong Kong has become an exporter of capital, tertiary services, and entrepreneurship, with investments in the SEZs and the Pearl River Delta region amounting to $916 million in 1991. Of this amount, a large proportion was in manufacturing. Taipei,China also exploited land and labor opportunities in the PRC and invested

$3.7 billion by 1991. The relocation of land-intensive and labor-intensive manufacturing processes in South China, along with the maintenance of technology-intensive and knowledge-intensive processes in Hong Kong and Taipei,China, is a good example of vertical integration among the members of the growth triangle.

Hong Kong's multidimensional and flourishing service sector has now reached the PRC as well as Taipei,China. In particular, Hong Kong's banks and brokerage firms have been actively seeking investment opportunities in the other two territories, where demand for financial services is rising rapidly. Hong Kong's involvement in Taipei,China's retailing business (department stores and supermarkets) and tourism industry has also become significant.

Geographical Proximity and Cultural Affinity

The member economies in the triangle share several favorable geographical and cultural factors. For instance, it takes only 45 minutes to reach Hong Kong from Shenzhen by train, and Taipei,China faces Fujian province across the Taiwan Strait. Most of the Chinese people in Hong Kong and Taipei,China can trace their roots to Guangdong and Fujian provinces, respectively. The ties of the mainlanders with the nationals from Hong Kong and Taipei,China are rooted mainly in language and culture. With this common background, Hong Kong and Taipei,China can engage in business with the SEZs much more easily than can other countries.

One should not attach too much importance to cultural affinity, however. Its role is subsidiary to that of economic complementarity and favorable policies. In a survey of Hong Kong investors in the PRC in the early 1980s (Chen, 1983), it was found that cultural affinity was regarded by them as only moderately important as a motivation for investing. Many of the top-level government officials in the SEZs are actually not Guangdong and Fujian natives. Today, many Hong Kong entrepreneurs with origins in Guangdong are very active investors in Shanghai and Northeast China despite their lack of cultural affinity with these regions. There may be a difference between large and small investors, however. Larger investors have more bargaining power and are less dependent on personal relationships, while these relationships are important for small investors.

Nonetheless, enterprises from Hong Kong and Taipei,China seem to find the distinctive bureaucratic organization of the SEZs tolerable, and can bear problems such as the long time needed to negotiate a contract and difficulties with meeting production deadlines and quality control requirements. Over 90 per cent of the foreign direct investment in the SEZs was from Hong Kong in the early 1980s, when political tensions across the Taiwan Strait were at their height. In the late 1980s, Taipei,China's share of FDI in the SEZs, especially in Xiamen, grew dramatically. In 1990, over 50 per cent of Xiamen's FDI was from Taipei,China.

Government Support

The success of the economic cooperation between the member economies of the Southern China Growth Triangle can also be attributed to the strong support from the Beijing and Taipei governments. The significant policies laid down by the government of the PRC are as follows:

(i)   The "Four Modernizations" (in agriculture, industry, national defense, and science and technology) became the guiding development strategy in 1979. The implication was that the PRC was to abandon its long-held policy of self-reliance and isolation from the world economy. Instead of veering away from the capitalist world market, it harnessed its own productive powers through controlled imports of technology and the promotion of its exports;

(ii) The "Three Contacts Policy" (direct mail, direct air and sea links, and direct trade) with Taipei,China was proposed in 1979. In addition, a variety of preferential treatment was given to businessmen from Taipei,China when making investments and carrying out other economic activities in the PRC. From this point on, Beijing's Taipei,China policy was governed by the principle of "Peaceful Unification;"

(iii) Four special economic zones were set up in 1980 with a series of preferential measures, including tax concessions (affecting corporate tax, customs duty, and industrial and commercial taxes); reductions in land use fees, land exploitation fees, and road tolls; and lower charges for water, electricity, telephone service, etc. Furthermore, the procedures and formalities required for local authorities to apply for use of foreign funds were significantly simplified;

(iv) Import taxes on goods from Taipei,China were reduced in 1981 to below the prevailing import tariffs;

(v) Fourteen coastal port cities and Hainan Island opened in 1984 and began offering preferential treatments similar to those in the SEZs. This confirmed the government's commitment to economic reform and an open door policy; and

(vi) Land use rights were granted to the Shenzhen Special Economic Zone in 1987. This marked the first step in the reform of the land use system in the PRC. Similar reforms were quickly adopted by other SEZs and by the newly opened coastal cities. Land users can now apply to the bureau concerned and acquire land use rights through negotiation or bidding. The longest term for land use is 70 years for residential use, 40 years for commercial, tourist, and recreational use, and 50 years for industrial purposes.

Taipei,China had long prohibited any contacts with the mainland. The situation improved after 1985, when import controls on Chinese products were gradually liberalized. From then on, a series of bans on contacts were lifted and other measures were enacted:

(i) Indirect export to the mainland was allowed in 1985;

(ii) The indirect import of a narrow range of goods from the mainland was permitted in 1987;

(iii) Also in 1987, foreign exchange controls were lifted, thus giving domestic entrepreneurs freedom to invest not only in the mainland but also abroad;

(iv) In the same year, Taipei,China allowed its people to visit the PRC. Millions of Chinese from Taipei,China visited the mainland every year thereafter;

(v) In 1991, the Ministry of Economic Affairs in Taipei officially legalized indirect investment in the mainland and requested investors to register with the ministry. Some 2,750 firms have thus far registered, but the actual number is probably greater;

(vi) The Statute for Relations across the Taiwan Strait was passed in 1992. This lifted the decades-old ban on a wide range of contacts with the mainland, including direct air and shipping links. The law also allowed Taipei,China to import Chinese workers to ease its severe labor shortage. Nationals from Taipei,China were allowed to visit the mainland for up to four years; and

(vii) The Mainland Affairs Council lifted the 40-year-old ban on banks investing in the mainland in 1992.

The PRC formulated its open door, united front policy toward Taipei,China as early as 1981, and has adhered to it ever since. Taipei,China has been playing a relatively passive role, taking a cautious attitude toward reviving contacts, commercial or otherwise, with the mainland. But in reality, it is difficult if not impossible for Taipei to stop such contacts, especially if carried out via third parties such as Hong Kong, Singapore, or Japan. There is little that the government can do to stop market forces at work.

Hong Kong has always been a free port and has maintained a close economic relationship with both Taipei,China and the People's Republic of China. Indeed, the PRC had to depend more heavily on trading with Hong Kong when it closed its doors to much of the world during the Cultural Revolution. There was therefore no need for the Hong Kong government to adopt any new policies to facilitate its triangular economic relationship with the PRC and Taipei,China.

INTEGRATION BETWEEN MEMBER ECONOMIES

Integration between the member economies can be analyzed in terms of intraregional trade, cross-border investments, and the transfer of labor, technology, and management skills.

Intraregional Trade

Intraregional trade among Hong Kong, Taipei,China, and the People's Republic of China (not only the SEZs) has been beneficial to the three parties. Tables 4 and 5 show Hong Kong's importance as a major trading partner of the PRC. If present trends continue, it is expected that the PRC will soon replace the US as Hong Kong's biggest export market by the end of 1993. Much of the recorded trade volume is due to the production of Hong Kong manufacturers in South China's SEZs. As Table 6 shows, Hong Kong is also important as a conduit for indirect trade between the PRC and Taipei,China.

Cross-Border Financial Flows

Cross-border investments require a higher degree of cooperation between member economies than is required in regular trade. Investments require long-term commitments or contract terms, while trading can be a one-time-only activity. For the purposes of this paper, joint ventures, cooperation schemes, and wholly foreign-owned corporations are all classified as foreign direct investment (FDI). These usually result in close cooperation and facilitate technology transfer among the participants. Compensation trade,[5] export processing production, and leasing are classified as non-FDI foreign investment because these tend to be simple operations with short recoupment periods which are more sensitive to international market conditions than to conditions prevalent in the SEZs.

Much of Hong Kong's investment in Guangdong is in export processing operations. In most of these operations, raw materials

Table 4. Hong Kong's Imports from PRC in Selected Years

	Value ($ million)	Annual Growth (per cent)	Share of PRC Exports (per cent)	Share of HK Imports (per cent)
Imports				
1960	207	-	11.2	20.2
1966	487	-	20.5	27.4
1970	470	-	20.8	16.1
1975	1,383	-	19.0	20.3
1977	1,741	-	22.9	16.6
1979	3,038	-	22.2	17.7
1981	5,276	-	24.0	21.5
1983	5,888	-	26.5	24.4
1984	7,131	21.1	27.5	25.5
1985	7,568	6.1	27.7	25.5
1986	10,462	38.2	33.8	29.5
1987	14,776	41.2	37.4	30.5
1988	19,406	31.3	40.8	30.4
1989	25,215	29.9	48.0	34.9
1990	30,274	20.1	48.8	36.8
1991	37,610	24.2	52.4	37.7
Imports for Re-Export				
1960	-	-	-	-
1966	94	-	5.3	29.1
1970	97	-	3.3	20.2
1975	300	-	4.4	21.3
1977	455	-	4.3	21.6
1979	962	-	5.6	24.1
1981	1,951	-	8.0	26.2
1983	2,300	-	9.5	29.8
1984	3,778	23.6	12.7	28.0
1985	3,778	23.6	12.7	28.0
1986	5,620	48.8	15.8	35.8
1987	9,185	63.4	19.0	39.2
1988	14,322	55.9	22.4	40.6
1989	20,517	43.3	28.4	54.3
1990	30,822	50.2	37.4	58.1
1991	40,473	31.3	40.5	59.0

Sources: Government of Hong Kong; State Statistical Bureau (PRC).

Table 5. Hong Kong's Exports to the PRC in Selected Years

	Value ($ million)	Annual Growth (per cent)	Share of PRC Total Imports (per cent)	Share of HK Total Exports (per cent)
Exports				
1960	21	-	1.1	3.1
1966	13	-	0.6	1.1
1970	11	-	0.5	0.4
1975	33	-	0.5	0.6
1977	44	-	0.6	0.5
1979	383	-	2.5	2.5
1981	1,961	-	8.9	9.0
1983	2,531	-	11.8	11.5
1984	5,033	98.9	18.4	17.8
1985	7,857	56.1	18.6	26.0
1986	7,550	-3.9	17.6	21.3
1987	11,290	49.5	26.1	23.3
1988	17,030	50.8	30.8	27.0
1989	18,816	10.5	31.8	25.7
1990	20,305	7.9	34.3	24.8
1991	26,631	31.2	49.9	27.1
Re-Exports				
1960	19	-	2.8	10.0
1966	10	-	0.8	3.6
1970	6	-	0.2	1.2
1975	28	-	0.5	2.0
1977	38	-	0.4	1.8
1979	263	-	1.7	6.6
1981	1,438	-	6.6	19.3
1983	1,675	-	7.6	21.6
1984	3,590	114.3	12.7	33.6
1985	5,907	64.5	19.5	43.7
1986	5,241	-11.3	14.8	33.4
1987	7,716	47.2	15.9	32.9
1988	12,157	57.6	19.3	34.5
1989	13,268	9.1	18.1	29.9
1990	14,219	7.2	17.3	26.9
1991	19,656	38.2	20.0	28.7

Sources: Government of Hong Kong; State Statistical Bureau (PRC).

**Table 6. Indirect Trade Between PRC and Taipei,China
via Hong Kong, 1978-1992**

	Value ($ million)	Annual Growth (per cent)	Share of Taipei,China's Total Exports (per cent)
Taipei,China-Hong Kong-PRC			
1978	0.05	-	0.00
1979	21.30	41,459.34	0.13
1980	22.05	1,036.21	1.22
1981	390.39	61.29	1.73
1983	208.23	-46.66	0.94
1984	168.70	-18.98	0.67
1985	425.51	152.21	1.40
1986	985.57	131.61	3.21
1987	812.38	-17.57	2.04
1988	1,232.85	0.59	2.30
1989	2,247.98	82.34	3.71
1990	2,889.08	28.52	4.36
1991	3,282.46	13.62	4.88
1992	4,667.16	42.36	6.13
PRC-Hong Kong-Taipei,China			
1978	46.68	-	0.48
1979	55.83	19.62	0.41
1980	78.42	40.46	0.43
1981	76.31	-2.69	0.35
1983	89.96	17.88	0.40
1984	96.06	6.78	0.43
1985	127.71	32.95	0.49
1986	115.75	-9.36	0.42
1987	144.41	24.76	0.47
1988	290.43	101.11	0.74
1989	479.93	65.25	1.01
1990	585.40	21.98	1.11
1991	766.34	30.91	1.23
1992	1,125.96	47.11	1.57

Sources: Government of Hong Kong; Customs Department (PRC).

and components are imported from or through Hong Kong, and processed products are then exported via Hong Kong. A survey conducted by the Census and Statistics Department of Hong Kong indicated that from January to September 1990, the proportion of trade related to outward processing production by value was estimated to be 61.7 per cent of Hong Kong's total imports from the PRC, 78.6 per cent of domestic exports, and 49.9 per cent of re-exports.[6] These percentage shares have continued to increase annually.

The PRC's contracted and utilized foreign investments by types of foreign venture are shown in Tables 7 and 8, respectively. The sharp rise in contracted investment in joint ventures and cooperation ventures from 1983 to 1985 indicates a higher degree of integration between the cooperating parties. However, at present, commercial credit is still the major type of Hong Kong investment in the PRC.

Xiamen had the biggest amount of contracted FDI among the SEZs at $419 million in 1990, even though this represented a drop of 45.51 per cent from the 1989 level. Taipei,China's FDI contribution in Xiamen is greater than that of Hong Kong. This is due to the closer cultural, linguistic, and geographical ties between these two areas. Foreign investment contributed an output of $3.55 billion during 1990, a rise of 24.8 per cent over that of 1989. Some 69 per cent of exports were produced by foreign enterprises, of which over 90 per cent were in manufacturing.

In 1991, there were 2,064 approved foreign-funded projects in the four SEZs, with utilized foreign investment amounting to $916 million. The volume of economic activity in Shenzhen showed a growth of 20 per cent for that year while the growth rate in Zhuhai was 70.5 per cent, in Shantou 120 per cent, and in Xiamen 82.4 per cent (see Tables 9 to 11 for the major sources of imports and major export markets of Shenzhen, Shantou, and Zhuhai). The impressive growth in the inflow of foreign funds shows that foreign investors have regained the confidence that was shaken by the political disturbances in 1989.

The PRC's investments in Hong Kong have diversified into many sectors since 1979, especially construction, building, shipping, and manufacturing. The PRC's record as a major investor in Hong Kong's manufacturing sector is short, but in 1985 the country became the third largest investor after the US and Japan, and has

Table 7. Contracted Foreign Investment in PRC, 1979-1991

	Foreign Direct Investment					Commercial Credit				Total FDI & Commercial Credit
	Joint Venture	Cooperative Venture	Fully Foreign-Owned Firms	Joint Exploration	Total FDI	Compensation Trade	Processing/ Assembly	Leasing	Total Commercial Credit	
Value ($ million)										
1979-82 (average)	32	682	83	355	1,152	182	49	-	231	1,384
1983	188	503	40	1,000	1,731	192	83	-	175	1,917
1984	1,067	1,484	100	0	2,651	162	63	-	225	2,875
1985	2,030	3,496	46	360	5,932	260	98	44	402	6,333
1986	1,375	1,351	20	81	2,834	313	140	43	496	3,330
1987	1,950	1,283	471	5	3,709	428	165	18	610	4,319
1988	3,134	1,624	481	57	5,295	532	205	156	894	6,189
1989	2,659	1,083	1,654	204	5,600	475	148	72	694	6,294
1990	2,697	1,257	2,445	192	6,617	203	137	50	390	7,007
1991	6,080	2,137	3,667	92	11,977	266	148	30	445	12,422
Share of Total Contracted Foreign Investment (per cent)										
1979-82 (average)	2.3	49.3	6.0	25.7	83.2	13.2	3.5	-	16.7	100.0
1983	9.8	26.2	2.1	52.2	90.3	5.3	4.3	-	9.7	100.0
1984	37.1	51.6	3.5	0.0	92.2	5.6	2.2	-	7.8	100.0
1985	32.1	55.2	0.7	5.7	93.7	4.1	1.5	0.7	6.3	100.0
1986	41.3	40.6	0.6	2.4	85.1	9.4	4.2	1.3	14.9	100.0
1987	45.1	29.7	10.0	0.1	85.9	9.9	3.8	0.4	14.1	100.0
1988	50.6	26.2	7.8	0.9	85.6	8.6	3.3	2.5	14.4	100.0
1989	42.2	17.2	26.3	3.2	89.0	7.5	2.4	1.1	11.0	100.0
1990	38.5	17.9	34.9	2.7	94.4	2.9	2.0	0.7	5.6	100.0
1991	48.9	17.2	29.5	0.7	96.4	2.1	1.2	0.2	3.6	100.0

Note: Processing/assembly and leasing were not disaggregated before 1984.

Source: *Almanac of China's Foreign Relations and Trade*, various issues.

Table 8. Utilized Foreign Investment in PRC, 1979-1991

	Foreign Direct Investment					Commercial Credit			Total Commercial Credit	Total FDI & Commercial Credit
	Joint Venture	Cooperative Venture	Fully Foreign-Owned Firms	Joint Exploration	Total FDI	Compensation Trade	Processing/Assembly	Leasing		
Value ($ million)										
1979-81 (average)	22	118	0	106	246	94	34	-	128	374
1982	34	178	39	179	430	122	97	-	219	649
1983	74	227	43	292	636	186	83	-	280	916
1984	255	465	15	523	1,258	98	63	-	161	1,419
1985	580	585	13	481	1,659	169	98	31	298	1,956
1986	804	794	16	260	1,875	181	140	48	369	2,244
1987	1,486	620	25	183	2,314	222	91	20	333	2,647
1988	1,975	779	226	213	3,194	317	69	161	546	3,740
1989	2,037	752	371	232	3,393	261	56	64	381	3,773
1990	1,258	676	684	243	3,483	159	79	30	268	3,761
1991	2,299	764	1,135	170	4,366	208	85	7	300	4,667
Share of Total Contracted Foreign Investment (per cent)										
1979-81 (average)	5.9	31.6	0.1	28.3	65.9	25.1	9.1	-	34.2	100.0
1982	5.2	27.4	6.0	27.6	66.3	18.3	14.9	-	33.7	100.0
1983	8.1	24.8	4.7	31.9	69.4	21.5	9.1	-	30.6	100.0
1984	18.0	32.8	1.1	36.9	88.7	6.9	4.4	-	11.3	100.0
1985	29.7	29.9	0.7	24.6	84.8	8.6	5.0	1.6	15.2	100.0
1986	35.8	35.4	0.7	11.6	83.6	8.1	6.2	2.1	16.4	100.0
1987	56.1	23.4	0.9	6.9	87.4	8.4	3.4	0.8	12.6	100.0
1988	52.8	20.8	6.0	5.7	85.4	8.5	1.8	4.3	14.6	100.0
1989	54.0	19.9	9.8	6.1	89.9	6.9	1.5	1.7	10.1	100.0
1990	33.4	18.0	18.2	6.5	92.9	4.2	2.1	0.8	7.1	100.0
1991	49.3	16.4	24.3	3.6	93.6	4.5	1.8	0.1	6.4	100.0

Note: Processing/assembly and leasing were not disaggregated before 1984.

Source: *Almanac of China's Foreign Relations and Trade*, various issues.

Table 9. Major Export Markets of Shenzhen and Shantou, 1990

	Shenzhen		Shantou	
	Value ($'000)	Share (per cent)	Value ($'000)	Share (per cent)
Hong Kong	2,548,470	85.0	169,710	57.5
US	95,040	3.1	21,490	7.3
Singapore	41,540	1.4	19,120	6.5
Japan	39,520	1.3	15,690	5.3
Germany	14,270	0.5	10,660	3.6
Thailand	5,190	0.2	-	-
Malaysia	-	-	5,200	1.8
Others	251,970	8.4	53,170	18.0
Total Exports	2,996,000	100.0	295,040	100.0

Source: *Almanac of China's Foreign Relations and Trade* (1991-1992).

Table 10. Major Sources of Imports of Shenzhen and Shantou, 1990

	Shenzhen		Shantou	
	Value ($'000)	Share (per cent)	Value ($'000)	Share (per cent)
Hong Kong	1,613,870	65.2	819,920	90.9
Japan	79,630	3.2	32,200	3.6
UK	21,830	0.9	-	-
US	16,800	0.7	11,510	1.3
Germany	-	-	10,940	1.2
Taipei,China	-	-	8,070	0.9
Singapore	5,610	0.2	6,960	0.8
Macao	-	-	6,450	0.7
Thailand	-	-	2,670	0.3
France	420	0.2	-	-
Others	736,840	29.8	3,430	0.4
Total Imports	2,475,000	100.0	902,150	100.0

Source: *Almanac of China's Foreign Relations and Trade* (1991-1992).

Table 11. Zhuhai: Origin and Destination of
Imports and Exports, 1990

	Imports		Exports	
	Value ($'000)	Share (per cent)	Value ($'000)	Share (per cent)
Hong Kong	134,634	84.3	359,470	73.6
Macao	18,330	11.5	83,670	17.1
Others	6,706	4.2	45,510	9.3
Total Exports	159,670	100.0	488,650	100.0

Source: Almanac of China's Foreign Relations and Trade (1991-1992).

retained this position to date. Relatively high technology-based industry is the major focus of Chinese investments in Hong Kong. In addition to generating profits, such investments also train Chinese personnel in such fields as information technology and industrial management. According to the statistics released by the New China News Agency, the PRC's FDI in Hong Kong stood at $20 billion in 1992.

Taipei,China's investments in the PRC, which in 1979 totalled only $100 million, increased to $300 million in 1987 (Pei and Xiam, in Lin, 1992). After that, investments grew substantially, reaching $3.7 billion in 1991. In that same year, it was estimated that more than 2,700 firms from Taipei,China were operating in the PRC (Chung-hua Institution for Economic Research, 1991).

The sectoral and geographical distribution of the investments from Taipei,China in the PRC are shown in Tables 12 and 13, respectively. Two notable points may be drawn from these tables. First, there is a concentration of Taipei,China's sunset industries; second, the relocation of electrical engineering and vehicle manufacturing has been significant, suggesting that some transfer of technology and management skills in the more sophisticated industries took place.

Table 12. Taipei,China's Investment in PRC Industry by Subsector as of April 1991

Subsector	Number of Firms	Amount ($ million)
Footwear	306	59.00
Electric Engineering	242	102.00
Vehicles	202	79.00
Plastics	129	45.00
Apparel	106	18.00
Metal Works	85	30.00
Lighting	67	-
Woolen Knitwear	62	-
Services	62	56.00
Sports Items	59	20.00
Leather	58	-

Source: Tzong-Biau Lin (1992).

Table 13. Taipei,China's Investment in PRC by Region as of April 1991

Region	Number of Firms	Amount ($ million)
Guangdong	411	121.1
Shenzhen	378	111.6
Xiamen	275	92.2
Shanghai	78	87.0
Guangzhou	146	55.9
Fuzhou	119	44.9
Fujian	204	42.4
Beijing	30	25.0
Jiangzu	56	24.6
Shandong	46	18.0
Dongguan	188	15.7
Zhejiang	56	14.8
Hainan	49	15.0
Shantou	39	12.0
Zhuhai	42	11.3

Source: Tzong-Biau Lin (1992).

Hong Kong's FDI constituted only 4.6 per cent of the cumulative total FDI received by Taipei,China in 1990. The volume of Hong Kong's investments there actually grew by 66 per cent between 1960 and 1990. Up until the mid-1980s, investments were by and large in manufacturing, particularly basic metal products. The direction of the investments started to change by the end of the 1980s toward the service sector, focusing on retailing, banking, and insurance due to the escalating per capita income enjoyed by Taipei,China in the late 1980s.

From 1959 to 1990, Taipei,China's cumulative FDI in Hong Kong came to only $61 million. This compares with the $199.6 million recorded in 1991 alone. Although there are no detailed statistics on Taipei,China's FDI in Hong Kong, it is obvious that many of these investments are related to the burgeoning indirect trade and investments between the mainland and Taipei,China. About 75 per cent of the investments are in the service sector, which is where Hong Kong's comparative advantage now lies.

Financial Integration

Financial linkages between the PRC and Hong Kong are portrayed in Tables 14 and 15. As Table 14 shows, before 1985 the PRC's borrowing was dominated by soft loans provided by governments and international institutions such as the Asian Development Bank (ADB) and the World Bank. Hong Kong's share in total foreign loans was rather small. However, as the PRC's commercial loan holdings increased after 1985, Hong Kong became a major creditor.

After 1979, the flow of capital between the PRC and Hong Kong grew steadily (see Table 15). From 1979 to 1982, the PRC underwent a rapid expansion, enhanced by heavy imports and borrowing. The net claims of Hong Kong banks on the PRC were mainly on banks, and the claims on non-bank customers were insignificant until 1985. From the beginning of 1982 to mid-1985, Hong Kong banks had net liabilities to the PRC, as this was the period when the latter accumulated sizable foreign exchange reserves. Hong Kong was under a cloud of political uncertainty over its future, and this led to economic and monetary crises in October 1983. Substantial Chinese loans to Hong Kong banks, however, stabilized Hong Kong's monetary system during this critical period.

Table 14. Hong Kong's Loans to PRC, 1979-1989

	As Lender	As Syndication Center	Total	Increase in Claims of HK Banks on Non-Bank Customers in China
Value ($ million)				
1979-82 (average)	19.0	75.0	94.0	26.0
1983	9.0	104.0	113.0	5.0
1984	51.0	250.0	301.0	123.0
1985	73.0	513.0	586.0	570.0
1986	244.0	1,538.0	1,782.0	1,280.0
1987	401.0	2,400.0	2,801.0	590.0
1988	580.0	1,945.0	2,525.0	2,186.0
1989	488.0	718.0	1,206.0	1,179.0
Share of Total Foreign Loans to PRC (per cent)				
1979-82 (average)	1.5	6.0	7.6	2.1
1983	0.6	6.9	7.5	0.3
1984	2.7	13.0	15.7	6.4
1985	2.1	14.5	16.6	16.1
1986	2.9	18.3	21.2	15.2
1987	5.1	30.7	35.8	7.5
1988	5.9	19.8	25.7	22.3
1989	9.4	13.8	23.2	22.7
Share of Total Commercial Loans to PRC (per cent)				
1979-82 (average)	7.5	30.0	37.3	10.3
1983	5.2	60.1	65.3	2.9
1984	11.5	56.6	68.1	27.8
1985	5.3	37.1	42.4	41.2
1986	4.7	29.9	34.7	24.9
1987	9.1	54.5	63.7	13.4
1988	12.2	41.0	53.3	46.1
1989	17.1	25.1	42.2	41.3

Source: Government of Hong Kong.

**Table 15. Liabilities to PRC and Claims on PRC
by Hong Kong Banks, 1979-1992**
($ million at year end)

	Liabilities to PRC Banks	Claims on PRC Banks	Claims on Non-Bank Customers	Net Liabilities or Claims
1979	43	1,177	22	1,156
1980	191	1,389	98	1,297
1981	950	1,166	130	346
1982	1,779	936	105	(838)
1983	2,374	1,089	110	(1,175)
1984	2,962	1,366	233	(1,363)
1985	2,821	3,116	803	1,098
1986	3,482	3,926	2,083	2,527
1987	5,978	5,428	2,673	2,123
1988	7,574	7,760	5,052	5,238
1989	7,366	7,826	5,432	5,892
1990	14,830	8,920	6,184	274
1991	17,873	13,262	5,910	1,299
1992	19,132	14,391	6,774	(2,033)

Source: Government of Hong Kong.

From mid-1985 onwards, the loans of Hong Kong banks to Chinese non-bank customers increased rapidly, and net claims on Chinese banks shrunk. This was a period of trade deficits and foreign exchange shortages in the PRC. In contrast, Hong Kong's economy boomed after the signing in September 1984 of the Sino-British agreement over the future of Hong Kong.

Of late, Hong Kong banks have been holding net liabilities to the PRC's non-bank customers because Chinese investments are increasingly being financed by the equity market rather than by the Hong Kong banking sector. In the early 1990s, an increasing number of Hong Kong's public companies with Chinese interests expanded their shares in Hong Kong. It is believed that this trend will continue, as a consequence of which loan financing of investments in the PRC will become less important.

The PRC has a strong influence on Hong Kong's finance sector. The Bank of China Group consists of nine banks from the PRC, four banks from Hong Kong, and one bank from Macau incorporated under the leadership of the Bank of China, Hong Kong, and the Macau Regional Office. The important role played by the Bank of China Group in Hong Kong's banking sector was demonstrated to the public when it joined the Hong Kong and Shanghai Banking Corporation to resolve the Ka Wah Bank Crisis in 1987, and also when it provided a HK$100 million stand-by credit for the Hong Kong Commodity Futures Exchange to prevent the further collapse of the market in October 1987. The Group thus showed its capability to carry out central banking activities on behalf of the Hong Kong government. In January 1993, the Hong Kong government announced that the Bank of China would become the territory's third note-issuing bank beginning in May 1994.

To some extent, Hong Kong and South China have entered a de facto monetary union, in that the Hong Kong dollar has become the principal unit of account, medium of exchange, and store of wealth in South China. It was recently estimated by the Hong Kong Bank that 30 per cent of Hong Kong's currency issue was circulating in the PRC, mainly in South China.

BENEFITS OF ECONOMIC INTEGRATION

Hong Kong

Hong Kong has reaped many economic benefits from its close integration with the PRC and Taipei,China. One is the income generated from trade and cross-border investment. In 1985, the PRC replaced the US as Hong Kong's largest trading partner. According to official Hong Kong trade statistics, re-exports of Chinese and foreign products to the PRC accounted for 62 per cent and 28 per cent of Hong Kong's total re-exports in 1991, respectively. Most of this trade involved outward processing production, which constituted nearly 70 per cent of Hong Kong's total imports from the PRC, over 76 per cent of domestic exports, 48 per cent of re-exports, and 55 per cent of total exports to the PRC. The profits generated from this trade, including outward processing production, are estimated to be over 10 per cent of Hong Kong's GDP (Hsueh and Woo, 1992).

As the PRC continues to post high rates of growth, Hong Kong's role as an entrepot will increase. It was estimated by the Hong Kong Trade Development Council that the value-added of Hong Kong's entrepot trade was as much as 25 per cent compared with the average of 10-15 per cent for other entrepots. This is because Hong Kong's role as an entrepot between the PRC and the rest of the world goes beyond the handling of goods to include a great deal of professional service. If other activities involving the PRC are included, especially the Bank of China Group's substantial role in financing Hong Kong businesses, it can be expected that up to 25 per cent of Hong Kong's national income is from the "China trade" (Hsueh and Woo, 1992).

Owing to the political problems that remain between the mainland and Taipei,China, Hong Kong is a stepping stone for investments from Taipei,China to the PRC. Taipei,China's investments in Hong Kong in 1991 amounted to $199.6 million, a jump of 200 per cent from the year before. Part of this must be for reinvestment in the PRC.

Another benefit that Hong Kong has derived from the growth triangle is the relocation of manufacturing processes to the PRC, which has facilitated Hong Kong's industrial and economic restructuring. The moving out of sunset industries has released resources, mainly land and labor, for newly developing industries. The relocation of industries has not given rise to any notable problems of "hollowing-out." Nonmanufacturing processes such as design, testing, storage, and sales have, however, remained in Hong Kong because of its better transportation and communication systems and its more advanced service sector. At the same time, the tertiary sector there has expanded and diversified at a rapid rate.

Taipei,China

The economic benefits that Taipei,China has derived from the growth triangle are less immediately apparent than those of the other two members. Even though there was a rapid rise in the volume of trade in the triangle from the mid-1980s, this represented an insignificant proportion of Taipei,China's total trade. In 1991, only 6 per cent of total exports and 1.6 per cent of total imports were traded in the triangle. The direct income generated from this aspect of economic cooperation was therefore small (Lin and Huang, 1992).

However, Taipei,China probably enjoyed some indirect and intangible benefits from the formation of the growth triangle. This can be gleaned from the following:

(i) The PRC served as an outlet for Taipei,China's surplus capital. In 1987, Taipei,China invested a total of $100 million in 80 different projects in the PRC. This increased to over $2 billion in 2,800 projects by the end of 1990. Such outflow of capital helped to reduce the domestic pressure on inflation. It also reduced unproductive speculation in the stock and property markets;

(ii) As in the case of Hong Kong, the relocation of Taipei,China's manufacturing bases to the PRC facilitated industrial and economic restructuring. Taipei, China's investments in the mainland were mainly in sunset industries such as footwear, plastics (especially toys), and apparel. The relocation of some manufacturing processes helped maintain the cost competitiveness of the products. With the PRC's increasing demand for Taipei,China's capital and intermediate products, a new market with a huge potential is emerging for Taipei, China's growing industries;

(iii) The PRC has relatively abundant land and is less conscious of environmental issues. Taipei,China's investors are seeking opportunities to establish heavy industries there rather than face strong domestic opposition. The opening up of such investment opportunities in the PRC enables Taipei,China to export "dirty" industries, in addition to gaining access to lower costs of production; and

(iv) To exploit the high income market, many investors from Hong Kong have taken active part in developing the

Watson's, Giordano, Welcome, and Park and Shop have set up branches on the island. Hong Kong's investment in Taipei,China's finance sector has also been noticeable. Since Taipei,China's service sector lags far behind that of Hong Kong, the inflow of FDI from Hong Kong will create positive linkages and demonstration effects.

South China

The most obvious and direct benefit for the PRC, other than the enormous trade surplus (HK$240 billion in 1991) it enjoys, is the huge income generated by the influx of FDI. Statistics for the SEZs themselves are not available, but statistics for Guangdong and Fujian provinces are instructive. In 1990, Guangdong's growth rates of 9.4 per cent for income and 16.4 per cent for industrial output were much higher than the national rates of 4.8 per cent and 7.6 per cent, respectively.[7] In the Pearl River Delta area, real income has increased by an estimated 20 per cent in the past few years.

Another notable benefit has been the expansion in investment in capital construction, including infrastructure. In 1990, capital construction expenditure grew in Guangdong at 16.2 per cent while the national growth rate was only 9.8 per cent. Increasingly, these investments are being financed by interests from Hong Kong and Taipei,China. For example, the Shenzhen-Pingnan Railway, which was opened in the summer of 1993, is solely financed by Hong Kong investors.

The inflow of investments from Hong Kong and Taipei,China into South China also creates a series of "linkages" or indirect benefits for the host economy.[8] In the case of the Southern China Growth Triangle, the linkages created by investments from Hong Kong and Taipei,China include the following:

(i)   Millions of jobs have been generated in a place which until recently was made up of farming villages. Unofficial sources place employment created for Chinese workers by Hong Kong firms operating in the Pearl River Delta in 1991 at 3 million;

(ii)   Workers trained by companies from Hong Kong or Taipei,China have moved to local enterprises, thus generating some managerial and technological transfer to the local economy (Thoburn et al, 1990); and

(iii) There has been some technology transfer, mainly of the intermediate type, from firms from Hong Kong and Taipei,China to South China through FDI. The technology being transferred to South China's economy is probably more appropriate than advanced western technology. Hong Kong also acts as an intermediary in screening and transferring technology for many Chinese enterprises in Guangdong.

PROBLEMS AND PROSPECTS

Potential for Further Growth

In assessing the growth triangle's potential for further development, several factors should be taken into consideration.

Unexploited Complementarities

There exist complementarities between the members which have not yet been exploited. The integration between the three economies still leaves much to be desired. Trading, a great proportion of which is induced by export-processing operations, and export processing activities are the major forms of cooperation between the members. Only the comparative advantage of cheap labor and land in South China has been exploited by these activities. There are other possibilities for development in South China which have been neglected. For example, there is an abundance of high quality scholars and research experts available throughout the mainland.[9] Expanded industrial and commercial research activities could, therefore, be carried out in the SEZs at a low cost. Equipment and parts could be imported from the outside world. Expenditures on research and development by Hong Kong industries are relatively low by international standards. This is partly due to the high cost of retaining research personnel. This is also because Hong Kong's industries are oriented towards low value-added products and look for quick returns.

Untapped Natural Resources

South China has a rich supply of raw materials. Guangdong province is one of the chief tungsten ore producing regions. An extensive pyrite deposit is located in Yunfu, Guangdong. The PRC's tungsten, antimony, vanadium, titanium, zinc, lithium, pyrites, rare-earths, magnetite, fluoride, barite, graphite, and gypsum reserves are the largest in the world. Tin, molybdenum, tantalum, niobium, mercury, coal, asbestos, and talcstard are in second and third places, and iron, nickel, lead, and manganese come in fourth according to data from the Chinese Academy of Social Science in 1989. If further improvements in the extraction, processing, and transportation of these resources could be achieved with foreign investment in the near future, industrial development in the Pearl River Delta region will proceed rapidly;

Unexploited Service Potential

The potential of the services market in the Pearl River Delta region is great. Considering the flourishing consumption of sophisticated consumer products in South China, and assuming that per capita incomes will continue to rise, demand for services such as tourism, restaurants, department stores, and financial services should grow. The realization of such potential will bring benefits to all the economies taking part in the triangle; and

Scope for Geographical Expansion

The potential for geographical expansion is high because land and other inputs are readily available from other parts of the mainland. The cost of production can be reduced and the market expanded as economic integration and cooperation spread into the central and northern parts of the PRC, provided that developments in transportation and communication can keep up.

Problems to Overcome

Political Instability

Despite the increasing economic links between the member economies, the existing political tensions between them cannot be concealed. There are worries that Taipei,China's economy will become overdependent on the PRC's resources and markets. There is also the fear that the Chinese government may exert pressure on the government of Taipei,China through its influence over the latter's investors in the PRC. Also, with an ever-growing threat from the Democratic Progressive Party, the ruling Nationalist Party may find it difficult to position itself on policies toward the PRC.

The political uncertainty in Hong Kong after 1997 has long been a threat to businesses there. Even though there are strong economic links between Hong Kong and the mainland, and the Basic Law which guarantees "one country, two systems" has been promulgated, the changeover of sovereignty to the PRC, a country with a completely different legal and administrative system, might dampen the confidence of domestic and foreign investors. Public disagreements between the British and Chinese governments over political reforms in Hong Kong seem to indicate that the PRC is putting political principles above economic consequences.

Trade Friction

The PRC and Hong Kong together had a massive trade surplus in 1990 of $8.71 billion with the US, of which 16.8 per cent or $1.45 billion was accounted for by outward processing production by Hong Kong companies. Moreover, there was an increase of 33.3 per cent in the PRC's export of machinery and electrical products to the US in 1990, of which $2.99 billion stemmed from such outward processing production. Hong Kong is possibly the biggest beneficiary of the trade between the PRC and the US, as it re-exports its own outward processing products from the PRC to the US and also re-exports US products to the PRC, making profits in the process but creating friction between the US and the PRC, both of which claim to be running a deficit. To a certain extent, Taipei,China plays the same role of Hong Kong, in that it has set up outward processing production bases in the PRC as well. The overdependence of the growth triangle on the US market is making all the economies vulnerable to the revocation of the most favored nation (MFN) status granted by the US to the PRC.

Evasion of Controls

Evasion of controls in the PRC takes on many forms, including bribery in licensing, fake invoicing, and smuggling. Many evasions occur through Hong Kong because of its proximity to the PRC and its flexible and versatile market system. False invoicing is reported to be serious among Hong Kong investors in the PRC (Ta Kung Pao, 7 January 1989). It is inevitable and perhaps understandable when evasions occur at the beginning of a country's economic development. However, when such illegal activities compromise the fair conduct of business, they will, in the long run, have adverse effects on the future development of the economy. Efforts to tackle this problem could be of vital importance to the future of the growth triangle.

Lack of Planning in Infrastructure

Whether or not economic cooperation among the members develops further, the communication and transportation systems that link them must be improved. At present, road transportation within the region is subject to severe problems. Overloading and congestion are common, with trucks and vans causing many of the tie-ups. The lack of planning in road construction has left many new roads unused because of uncompleted sections. There is no congestion yet in rail transport, but new railways have not been built in years. As the Kowloon-Canton railway approaches saturation, many enterprises will need to transport their goods by road.

There is, in general, a severe lack of planning and coordination in the construction of infrastructure in the PRC. For example, each city or district develops its own electricity and water supply on a small scale to meet its own needs. This has prevented economies of scale from being realized. The same is true of the port facilities in South China. Too many small ports with low capacity in cargo handling again prevent the realization of economies of scale. Airports have the same problem. The SEZs and the surrounding cities all want to build airports of their own regardless of whether they will be of adequate standard or not.

Inadequate Technology Transfer

A large proportion of Hong Kong's direct investment in the PRC consists of wholly-owned outward processing factories, which make up 43.2 per cent of the former's enterprises in the latter. This kind of investment involves lower risk and shorter terms of contract, but as it produces low value-added and labor-intensive manufacturing goods, technology transfer is largely limited to intermediate technology which may not be adequate for further development of the Southern China region.

Prospects for the Triangle

Despite the problems, the prospects for the growth triangle are on the whole encouraging. The growth triangle will expand northward into the mainland owing to fast-rising land prices and wages in Guangdong. South China itself will undergo economic transformation and expansion. Hong Kong and the Pearl River Delta will be the center of coordination for the enlarged growth triangle. The possibility of geographical expansion will widen the scope of economic cooperation and integration, with more resources being made available. The relocation of some industries from Guangdong to the neighboring provinces is a case in point. Meanwhile, the development of more sophisticated industries and of the service sector has prevented the economy of South China from hollowing out.

Prospects for the triangle will of course depend on the prospects for economic development of the member economies. For the PRC, there is little doubt that its open door policy and economic reforms will continue. The extensive integration of its economy with the global economic system has made it virtually impossible for the PRC to turn back the clock. In the course of further liberalization, and in the absence of effective macroeconomic regulatory tools, the Chinese economy will inevitably continue to be subject to cyclical fluctuations. Yet the long-term prognosis is definitely favorable. Hong Kong also has to face the challenge of both political and economic transformation.

Hong Kong still has an important role to play in the economic development of the PRC, especially in the coastal region. Inasmuch as foreign investors have confidence in doing business in the PRC, there is no reason why they should not come to Hong Kong after 1997 when it shall have reverted to Chinese sovereignty. This assumption is supported by the fact that despite the row over Hong Kong's political reform, there has been no reduction, thus far, in the flow of foreign direct investment into Hong Kong. Similarly, Taipei,China has to face the challenge of political and economic transformation. However, with a relatively sophisticated technology infrastructure already built in, it should not be too difficult for Taipei,China to successfully upgrade and diversify its industries.

An important factor affecting the further development of cooperation among Taipei,China, Hong Kong, and the People's Republic of China may be the policy (or, more precisely, the lack of policy) of Taipei,China toward Hong Kong and the mainland after 1997. It seems that the government of Taipei,China has not yet made up its mind on what tack to take. For the Southern China Growth Triangle to continue to develop, Taipei,China must further liberalize its policy toward the mainland and maintain or deepen its existing economic relationship with Hong Kong. In view of the tremendous economic benefits that Taipei,China can derive from participating in the activities of the growth triangle, it is anticipated that, in the end, its government will make an effort to at least maintain its existing level of economic interaction with Hong Kong and the People's Republic of China.

CONCLUSIONS

The emergence of the triangle has been driven mainly by private sector agents seeking to exploit the existence of factor price differentials. Complementarities in the comparative advantages of the member economies have also been a strong driving force. Moreover, government support, geographical proximity, and cultural affinities have facilitated the cooperation in this closely interacting economic zone.

The most intriguing aspect of the Southern China Growth Triangle may be its structural division of labor. Hong Kong, as the nucleus, plays the role of a trading partner, a middleman, a facilitator, and a financier for the other two parties. The PRC as a hinterland is relatively underdeveloped economically but rich in all factor endowments except capital. Taipei,China has plenty of capital and technology but cannot or would rather not establish direct links with the hinterland for political and economic reasons.

Hong Kong has the most advanced tertiary sector and social and physical infrastructure. Thus, its involvement as an intermediary serves to reduce transaction costs. From a trading perspective, Townsend (1978) constructed a model to explain the need for intermediation between agents. He assumed that establishing a bilateral trade link between economic agents involves a fixed transaction cost. Thus, an exchange structure in which everyone is linked to everyone else as in the Walrasian model is generally inefficient; an efficient structure minimizes the number of bilateral trade links and necessarily involves intermediation. To a large extent, Townsend's model applies to all kinds of economic integration within growth triangles.

The Southern China Growth Triangle differs in many ways from many highly organized economic groupings such as the European Community (EC) and the Organization of Petroleum Exporting Countries (OPEC). First, the formation of the triangle was not formal, as no official negotiations took place between the member economies. Second, integration within the triangle is largely vertical. There has so far been little intraregional trade on final goods produced by the member economies themselves, but a huge amount of intra-industrial and commodity trade occurred. Such an economic grouping can be called an "outward-dependent" growth triangle because the demand and supply are both generated externally. Therefore, the growth triangle is, at present, quite vulnerable to market conditions in the outside world, in particular the US and Europe.

One can expect an expansion in size owing to market forces in the exploitation of factor price differentials and complementary comparative advantages. This will probably take the form of more and more export processing zones being established around the original triangle. The expansion of the Johor-Singapore-Riau Growth Triangle to include Bintan, Bulan, Galang, Karimum, Rempang, and Singkep is an example of such development. One policy change that could facilitate this kind of expansion in the Southern China triangle would be to make it easier for visitors to Hong Kong from the mainland and Taipei,China to obtain entry visas. Meanwhile, infrastructure development and administrative reform will have to be undertaken to solve the problems associated with the rapidly growing traffic of people and vehicles across the border.

Faced with the emergence of other zones (e.g., Shanghai-Pudong), the Southern China Growth Triangle will increasingly have to compete for capital. Yet, under a free market system, healthy competition should lead to benefits for everyone. It is expected that each zone will further specialize and establish links with other zones to generate mutual benefits.

The emergence of growth triangles should not be interpreted as a revival of protectionism, but rather as a new source of economic dynamism in the Asia-Pacific region. After all, the Southern China Growth Triangle has demonstrated to the world that a market-driven subregional zone can provide an economic environment and institutional framework for rapid economic growth and development despite differences in economic and political systems among its members.

Endnotes:

1.   Director, Centre of Asian Studies, The University of Hong Kong.
2.   Assistant Research Officer, Centre of Asian Studies, The University of Hong Kong.
3.   See Jao (1992) for an explanation of this mechanism. "Arbitrage" means that if the market rate rises over the officially fixed rate by more than the transactions cost, banks will have the incentive to buy US dollars with Hong Kong banknotes from the Exchange Fund at the fixed rate, for resale in the open market; and conversely, if the market rate falls below the fixed rate by more than the transactions cost, banks will have the incentive to buy US dollars in the open market for resale to the Exchange Fund at the fixed rate. "Competition" means that a financial institution

cannot quote a US dollar rate that deviates too much from the official rate without losing business to its competitors. Thus, "arbitrage" in tandem with "competition" can generate market forces that make for convergence towards the official rate.

4.   All data on Taipei,China in this section were obtained from the *Taiwan Statistical Data Book* (1992).

5.   To quote Sung (1992): "The foreign partner provides China with equipment and receives products in return. The Chinese distinguish between direct compensation, where the products are produced by the equipment supplied, and indirect compensation (also known as 'counter trade'), where the foreign partner is compensated with other products. The foreign partner does not participate in the management of the Chinese enterprise though he is often involved in quality control, as he usually markets the product."

6.   To quote Sung (1992) again: "This is also known as contractual manufacturing-processing. The foreign partners subcontract their manufacturing-processing operations to their Chinese partners, and pay a processing fee. The foreign partners provide the necessary materials or components and design specifications, and sell the finished product."

7.   Sources of data for these are the State Statistical Bureau and Guangdong Statistical Bureau's public announcements on economic and social developments in 1990; *Renmin Ribao (People's Daily)*, 23 February 1991; and *Nanfang Ribao (Southern Daily)*, 7 March 1991.

8.   Thoburn et al (1990) define "linkages" as foreign investment projects that raise the return on investments of domestic firms as they purchase domestic inputs or as they supply domestic users.

9.   In 1991, 4.88 million senior scientists and engineers were listed and classified by the Academic Society of China Science and Technology Association System.

Bibliography

Chen, E.K.Y., "Multinationals from Hong Kong," in Sanjaya Lall et al, eds., *The New Multinationals*. New York: John Wiley and Sons, 1983.

_____, "The Economics and Non-Economics of Asia's Four Little Dragons," University of Hong Kong Supplement to *The Gazette*, 21 March 1988.

Chen, E.K.Y., and K.W. Li, "Industrial Development and Industrial Policy in Hong Kong," in E.K.Y. Chen et al, eds., *Industry and Trade Development in Hong Kong*. Hong Kong: Centre of Asian Studies, The University of Hong Kong, 1991.

Chia, S.Y., and T.Y. Lee, "Sub-Regional Economic Zones: A New Motive Force in Asia-Pacific Development," paper presented at the 20th Pacific Trade and Development Conference, Washington, D.C., 10-12 September 1992.

Hong Kong Bank, "Monetary Integration Between Hong Kong and China," in *Economic Report*, February 1993.

Hsueh, T.T., and T.O. Woo, "The Development of Hong Kong-China Economic Relationship," paper presented at conference on Twenty-Five Years of Social and Economic Development in Hong Kong, The University of Hong Kong, 16-19 December 1992.

Jao, Y.C., "The Development of Hong Kong's Financial Sector, 1967-92," paper presented at conference on Twenty-Five Years of Social and Economic Development in Hong Kong, The University of Hong Kong, 16-19 December 1992.

Kao, C., "A Greater China Economic Sphere: Reality and Prospects," in *Issues & Studies*, Vol. 28, No. 11 (November 1992).

_____, "An Analysis of Economic Relations Between Taiwan and Mainland China," paper presented at a workshop on China's Economy, Centre of Asian Studies, The University of Hong Kong, 15 January 1993.

Kimuram, Y., S. Suda, and Y. Sone, "Hong Kong: Entering a New Phase," in *Asian Perspectives*, Vol. 8, No. 5 (December 1991).

Kuznets, Simon. *Modern Economic Growth: Rate, Structure, and Spread*. New Haven: Yale University Press, 1966.

Lee, T.Y., "Sub-Regional Economic Zones in the Asia-Pacific: An Overview," paper presented at the International Symposium on Regional Cooperation and Growth Triangles in ASEAN, Singapore, 23-24 April 1992.

Lin, T.B., "Economic Nexus Between the Two Sides of the Taiwan Straits — With Special Emphasis on Hong Kong's Role," paper presented at the conference on Economic Development of ROC and the Pacific Rim in the 1990s and Beyond, Taipei, 25-29 May 1992.

Lin, Y.J., and C.S. Huang, "Development of Trade and Investment Between Two Sides of the Taiwan Straits," paper presented at the Conference on Global Interdependence and Asia-Pacific Cooperation, Hong Kong, 8-10 June 1992.

Liu, P.W., Y.S. Wong, Y.W. Sung, and P.K. Lau, "A Symposium of Perspectives on China's Reform and Opening Policy as Seen from the Achievements of the Pearl River Delta-Economic Development and Investment Outlook," research report for the Nanyang Commercial Bank Ltd., Hong Kong, 1992.

Ohashi, H., "Economic Relations Between China and Hong Kong," in *Jetro China Newsletter*, No. 95 (November-December 1991).

Smart, J., and A. Smart, "Personal Relations and Divergent Economies: A Case Study of Hong Kong Investment in South China," in *International Journal of Urban and Regional Research*, Vol. 15 (November 1991).

Sung, Y.W., "The Economic Integration of Hong Kong with China in the 1990s: The Impact on Hong Kong," Canada and Hong Kong Project, Research Paper No. 1, University of Toronto-York University Joint Centre for Asia Pacific Studies, 1992a.

_____. *The China-Hong Kong Connection, the Key to China's Open-Door Policy*. Cambridge: Cambridge University Press, 1992b.

Tan, C.H., "Growth Triangles from Several Angles: A NIE Perspective Based Upon Hong Kong Guangdong Industrialization," Discussion Paper No. 130, School of Economics, The University of Hong Kong, 1992.

Thoburn, J.T., H.M. Leung, E. Chau, and S.H. Tang. *Foreign Investment in China Under the Open Policy*. Hong Kong: Averbury, 1990.

Townsend, R.M., "Intermediation with Costly Bilateral Exchange," in *Review of Economic Studies*, 45 (1987), pp. 417-25.

Wong, Teresa Y.C., "Hong Kong's Manufacturing Industries: Transformations and Prospects," paper presented at conference on Twenty-Five Years of Social and Economic Development in Hong Kong, The University of Hong Kong, 16-19 December 1992.

Woo, K.C., "The China-Hong Kong Economic Partnership," paper presented at the Asia 2010 Conference, Melbourne, 20 July 1992.

Yasukuni, K., "Complementary Economic Relations Between Guangdong Province and Hong Kong," in *Pacific Business and Industries*, Vol. III, No. 13 (1991).

Foreign Investment in the Southern China Growth Triangle

■ Pochih Chen[1]

INTRODUCTION

Of the economic groupings in the Asia-Pacific region, the growth triangle composed of Hong Kong, Taipei,China, and South China (Guangdong and Fujian provinces) is particularly noteworthy because of its large size and rapid growth. The success of this triangle may be attributed to the dynamic economic growth of the participants, and to the involvement of the private sectors in all three areas. The purpose of this paper is to analyze some of the conditions necessary for success in economic cooperation, particularly with respect to foreign investment.

The paper is divided into five sections. The first presents the major reasons for the investment flows from Taipei,China and Hong Kong to South China. The next section discusses the amount and distribution of this investment. The economic consequences of these investments in South China and the contribution they have made to economic development in Taipei,China and Hong Kong are discussed in the next two sections. The final section presents the conclusions.[2]

RATIONALE FOR INVESTMENT

Theoretical Background

In conventional theories, the primary motives for foreign direct investment (FDI) include expanding the market, avoiding trade barriers, utilizing the host country's resources, taking advantage of differences in government regulations and tax systems, enhancing or realizing monopoly power, and obtaining a higher rate of return on capital. Within a growth triangle an additional benefit of foreign investment comes from possible vertical "complementarity in production" among the regions concerned. Another form of vertical complementarity, "complementarity in development," involves the continuous movement of comparative advantage in products or production processes from one region to another, accompanied by a movement of capital, technical expertise, and other factors of production. In the Southern China Growth Triangle, these two kinds of complementarity are important and interrelated.

Setting aside transportation and transaction costs and other barriers to trade, the cheapest way to produce a commodity is to select a location where it can be manufactured at the lowest possible cost. A perfect division of labor along these lines is usually impossible, however, because of transportation costs and other expenses involved in allocating different production processes to different locations. If two regions have different comparative advantages in two successive processes for a particular commodity, cooperation between them might suffer, especially if transportation costs are high and trade barriers exist. Similarly, if firms in different regions are not on friendly terms, transaction costs between them would rise.

Consequently, regions that have varying international comparative advantages, and that are close to each other both geographically and culturally, tend to cooperate vertically in production. Foreign direct investment can strengthen the relationships between firms, further reducing transaction costs and enhancing cooperation. Since vertical complementarity in production can increase the international competitiveness of the products being produced, areas cooperating in this way may develop faster than other areas provided there is sufficient demand for their products. Thus, vertical complementarity in production, bolstered by foreign direct investment, is an important factor for a growth triangle.

Complementarity in development is as important as, if not more important than, complementarity in production. Due to the changes in international comparative advantage over time, industries tend to be phased out as a country becomes more developed. Operations in these industries are often shifted to less developed countries, and then to even less developed countries. This process has been referred to as the "flying geese" phenomenon.

Often there are important location-specific production factors (e.g., specialized machines, technology and know-how, market information and channels, trademarks and goodwill). When industries move away, the domestic demand for and value of these factors is likely to decline. If these factors can be exported to less developed countries, however, they are likely to obtain much higher prices. Consequently, the reutilization of specific factors of production can be an important reason for international investment. Such investment can generate higher returns for these factors than if they were to be kept in the original country. At the same time, it allows the receiving country to obtain these factors at a lower cost than if it were to develop its own supply. International investment of this type can thus speed up the industrial development of both countries (Chen, 1991).

The efficient transfer of many production factors (e.g., design, management, and marketing ability) often involves the international movement of skilled people. This, as well as international investment by related industries, is most easily done if the host country's culture, customs, and language are similar to those of the investing country. Moreover, if the two countries are geographically close to each other, industries in the home country are better situated to support host country industries through complementarities in production.

Rationale for the Southern China Growth Triangle

The Southern China Growth Triangle is the first successful triangle in East Asia. Its rapid development has shown how, by exploiting geographical proximity and cultural affinity, neighboring territories can grow together without sacrificing cooperation with other countries and regions.

The open door policy of the People's Republic of China (PRC), announced in 1978, was the first important step in stimulating rapid economic cooperation in the southern China region. With the new policy, the PRC decentralized its international trade, partly liberalized the prices of traded goods, and relaxed foreign exchange controls (Lardy, 1991). Moreover, Shenzhen, Zhuhai, Shantou, and Xiamen were designated special economic zones (SEZs), designed to attract foreign direct investment including that from overseas Chinese. A number of incentives were also offered by the national and local governments to prospective investors (Chang and Shih, 1989). The local governments of Guangdong and Fujian allowed foreign investments valued below $100 million, while other local governments allowed foreign investments not exceeding either $30 million, $10 million, or $5 million. Foreign investors enjoyed preferential treatments, such as income tax holidays and reductions and/or exemption from local income tax. A multiple foreign exchange rate system, foreign exchange control, and rent reduction also became effective measures for subsidizing exports and attracting foreign investors.

The PRC adopted a number of strategies to promote investment and trade specifically from Taipei,China. In January 1979, the government announced plans to establish the "three links " (mail, travel, and trade) and "four exchanges" (science, culture, sports, and arts) with Taipei,China. In the "Temporary Regulations about Expanded Trade with Taiwan" published by the Ministry of Foreign Economic Affairs and Trade, PRC's trade with Taipei,China was defined as "a specific form of trade which should be aimed at increasing the economic ties between Taiwan and Mainland China so as to unify and to attract Taiwanese businessmen and to create the conditions for the unification of the mother country." Guided by this purpose, and possibly by the economic goals of local governments, investors from Taipei,China enjoyed privileges that were not accorded to other investors. For example, products made in Taipei,China were exempted from tariffs in 1980 and 1981. Smuggling by fishermen in the Taiwan Strait was encouraged and even regarded by the government as valid small-scale trade. Taipei,China's investors in the SEZs were allowed to sell 30 per cent of their products on the local market, and its residents were given equal rights as Chinese citizens in economic and judicial affairs.

Infrastructure also improved beginning in 1979, especially in South China and its SEZs. In the 1980s, Shenzhen city alone constructed roads totalling 300 km, installed 100,000 telephone lines, and started the construction of its international airport. It also began building new railways and railway stations, seaports, power plants, and other infrastructure. Zuhai spent more than $1 billion for infrastructure in the 1980s, and is now building an international airport, freeways, and a railroad to Guangzhou. Deep seaports will be constructed to compete with those in Hong Kong, Shantou, and Xiamen. Other areas in South China are undertaking similar projects on a smaller scale.

With these incentives and development efforts, South China succeeded in attracting investments from Hong Kong, Taipei,China, and other countries. In the process, it attained an impressive rate of economic growth. The growth rate of industrial production alone in the Pearl River Delta achieved more than 20 per cent per year in the 1980s. Thus, South China's booming economy and its increasing and changing consumption patterns themselves became incentives for new foreign investment.

As Hong Kong has been a gateway or window between the PRC and the outside world, the latter's economic development (especially in South China) has been beneficial for the former. Because of the rising land and labor costs in Hong Kong, manufacturers with capital, technology, and technical know-how have set up operations in the SEZs. Other NIEs have also discovered the advantages offered by the PRC's export processing zones.

In addition to the "push" factors for outward investment (e.g., labor shortages, rising wages, high land costs), the ample supply of land and labor, low transportation costs, the absence of a language barrier, and the large potential domestic market in the PRC were major attractions for investors from Hong Kong (Border, 1993). In Guangdong, for example, monthly wages in the more developed areas in 1990 were at most only one-fifth of those in Hong Kong. Rent for land in Shenzhen and Donggoan is also from seven to nearly 20 times less expensive than in Hong Kong (Hwang, 1992).

Investments from Hong Kong to South China have not been limited to the transfer of declining labor-intensive industries. Expanding offshore assembly operations and other kinds of vertical cooperation are also major sources of investment. Traditionally, the manufacturing sector in Hong Kong has been relatively less important than in other NIEs. Yet Hong Kong has joined forces with South China in the last 15 years to form a much more self-sufficient "national" economy, which may be called "Greater Hong Kong" (Kimura, 1991).

In the case of Taipei,China, Yen et al. (1992) have indicated that low wages, a sufficient supply of labor, the absence of a language barrier, cultural similarities, and low rent for land are the most important reasons for Taipei,China investors to invest in the PRC. There was a large trade surplus in Taipei,China in the 1980s, with the trade surplus' share of GDP reaching nearly 20 per cent in 1986. Since 1985, international pressure to reduce this surplus has been so intense that the New Taiwan (NT) dollar had to be rapidly appreciated against the US dollar. Thus, the exchange rate moved from about NT$40 to NT$26 per US dollar between 1985 and 1989. This appreciation was higher than that of most currencies in the world. Since 1980, the NT dollar appreciated against all the major currencies except the Japanese yen. Wages in Taipei, China also rose rapidly in the second half of the 1980s due to the booming economy. This was particularly true in the service sector, but unit labor costs in the manufacturing sector also increased much faster than those of major competitors. The international competitiveness of Taipei, China's traditional labor-intensive exports thus declined sharply during this period. In order to maintain the same market position as before, firms from Taipei,China have had to diversify their exports away from labor-intensive products.

The pressure for structural change in exports after 1985 was further reinforced by two factors. These were the decline in domestic investment since 1980, and the deteriorating share of the manufacturing sector in GDP. Insufficient domestic investments also played a significant role in Taipei,China's trade surplus before 1985 (Chen, 1989). The policy of reducing the trade surplus almost solely by exchange rate appreciation exerted great pressure on the tradeable goods sector.

The share of the manufacturing sector in Taipei,China's GDP had been quite high in the early 1980s compared to that of most developed countries. The experiences of many developed countries indicate that the share of manufacturing increases early in development, then decreases in the later stages. The highest recorded share of the manufacturing sector in the major western countries was about 40 per cent (Chen and Lee, 1988). Taipei,China reached a comparable level in 1987 before declining to 34 per cent in 1991, indicating that the manufacturing sector grew much more slowly in this period than the economy as a whole. Some manufacturing industries also experienced difficulties and had to undergo change. Thus, investments abroad, especially in less developed countries, became an attractive option.

The increase in land costs by more than three times in the latter half of the 1980s also prompted Taipei,China to invest abroad, while rising real estate values at home enabled old firms and other landlords to acquire more funds for foreign investment by selling their land at high prices. The costs of adhering to strict environmental regulations, an increase in competition, and government incentives in the less developed countries have also been mentioned by investors as other reasons for investing abroad.

Foreign investments from Taipei,China increased tremendously after 1986. Table 1 shows the approved foreign investments from Taipei,China to countries other than the PRC. Taipei,China's investments in developing countries increased faster than its investments in developed countries. Moreover, Taipei,China's investments in developing countries seem to have been underestimated by the data that have been approved for release by the government. This is suggested by data on approved investments in host countries. Financial flow data also reveal a much larger amount of capital net outflow vis-a-vis the amount of approved foreign investments.

In addition to the economic transformation, political and economic policies also changed in important ways. Starting from 1985, indirect export to the PRC was allowed. The range of raw materials and semiprocessed goods that were permitted to be imported indirectly from the PRC increased beginning in 1987. Residents from Taipei,China were allowed legal entry in 1987; since then more than 4.5 million have visited the mainland. Liberaliza-

Table 1. **Approved Foreign Investment from Taipei,China**
by Destination
($'000)

	Asia-Pacific	Americas	Europe	Africa	Total
1980	5,951	35,130	1,000	25	42,105
1981	6,738	1,795	2,231	-	10,764
1982	9,132	2,500	-	-	11,632
1983	6,705	2,858	-	1,000	10,563
1984	6,685	32,178	-	400	39,263
1985	4,213	35,830	891	400	41,334
1986	9,129	46,738	194	850	56,911
1987	21,302	70,250	10,199	1,000	102,751
1988	75,433	125,335	17,005	963	218,736
1989	296,372	553,439	73,325	7,850	930,986
1990	604,281	669,011	265,903	13,012	1,552,207
1991	932,089	369,186	350,232	4,523	1,656,030
1992	375,355	202,222	292,807	16,875	887,259
1959-79	44,069	14,637	142	411	59,260
1959-92	2,397,452	2,161,109	1,013,929	47,309	5,619,801

Source: Ministry of Economic Affairs, Taipei,China.

tion of the international flow of capital also progressed after 1987. Consequently, trade with and investment in the PRC became easier for businesses. Although it was facilitated by policy changes, the rapid development in trade and investment across the Taiwan Strait was mainly a result of market mechanisms.

FORMS OF INVESTMENT

Hong Kong has long been the top investor in the PRC, providing more than half the FDI in the country (Sung, 1991). Because of noneconomic barriers and the greater distance from the PRC, Taipei,China's investments there are much smaller. Since Taipei,China and Hong Kong are at different stages of development than the PRC, and since South China is the developing region

closest to these economies, geographically and culturally, the potential for utilizing complementarity in production and development to form a Southern China growth triangle is very high. The
potential for complementarity in production can be shown by the
significant differences in wage rates, land prices and rent. Differences in export commodity structure may reveal the differences in
the comparative advantage more directly.

The share of highly labor-intensive products in Taipei,China's
exports to the US in 1991 was 46 per cent, while the share of such
products in exports to the PRC stood at 58 per cent. Sixty-eight per
cent of the PRC's exports to the US are accounted for by low human-
capital-intensive products, while the share in Taipei,China is only
38 per cent (see Table 2). In general, Taipei,China's comparative
advantage is greater in products utilizing less labor and more

**Table 2. Factor Intensities of US Imports from PRC, Hong Kong, and
Taipei,China, 1991**
(per cent)

Factor Intensity	PRC	Hong Kong	Taipei,China
Labor Intensity			
High	57.7	57.9	46.3
Medium	34.3	38.4	47.2
Low	8.0	3.7	6.5
Capital Intensity			
High	11.9	6.6	12.2
Medium	43.5	73.6	66.1
Low	44.6	19.8	21.7
Human Capital Intensity			
High	10.8	18.7	28.6
Medium	21.0	26.1	33.8
Low	68.2	55.2	37.6
Energy Intensity			
High	3.5	3.3	3.3
Medium	46.3	55.1	42.9
Low	50.2	41.6	53.8

Source: Author's computations.

capital, including human capital[3]. These products include intermediate goods, machinery, heavy chemical products, and high-technology products. The same pattern is found in the exports of these countries to the European Community.

Given these significant differences in comparative advantage, both Taiwanese and Hong Kong investors are strongly attracted to labor-intensive industries in the PRC. It was only recently, however, that such direct investments were permitted from Taipei,China. After indirect investment in the PRC was allowed by Taipei,China, investors did not accurately report their investments to both governments. In early 1991, Taipei,China required firms established prior to 1991 to register their investments in the PRC, and a total of 2,503 firms with an aggregate investment of $754 million did so. This is much lower than the approximately 2 billion approved by the PRC from 1987 to 1990 (Chung Chin, 1993). In 1991 and 1992, the amount of investment from Taipei,China to the PRC recorded by the investors stood at $421 million, while the amount recorded by the PRC was $4.8 billion. Because of this wide discrepancy, the government of Taipei,China asked its firms to report their investments again in 1993. Data released in June 1993 indicate that 9,090 investments in the PRC have either been approved by or reported to the Chinese government. These investments total $2.96 billion (see Table 3). Since $5.1 billion of these were approved in the first month of 1993, the figure for investment before 1992 is still much less than the amount approved by the PRC.

Cumulative investments in the PRC from Hong Kong are about nine times as large as those from Taipei,China, and account for 59 per cent of all contracted foreign investment in 1991. Although some of this may in fact be Taiwanese investment channeled through Hong Kong, and although Taipei,China's investment has been increasing rapidly, investment from Hong Kong is still much more important.

Hong Kong's investments are expected to be even higher in South China, and especially in Guangdong. In 1990, 78 per cent of the approved FDI in Guangdong was from Hong Kong. In the SEZs in the province, Hong Kong investment accounted for 70 per cent of the total, while in Fujian the level was 53 per cent. Since these figures include indirect investment from Taipei,China through

**Table 3. Taipei,China Investment in PRC by Industry
(as of 6 June 1993)**

Industry	$'000	Number
Electrical and Electronic Machinery	364,118	1,208
Tobacco and Beverages	261,641	694
Plastic Products	255,272	776
Rubber Products	253,727	496
Basic Metals	231,852	771
Precision Instruments	216,601	891
Wearing Apparel & Accessories	192,657	487
Building Materials	168,723	223
Nonmetallic Mineral Products	144,866	454
Textiles	137,379	318
Others	737,768	2,780
Total	2,964,604	9,098

Source: Ministry of Economic Affairs, Taipei,China.

Hong Kong, it is difficult to determine how much Hong Kong invested in South China, let alone in the whole of the country. In fact, of Hong Kong's contracted investment in the PRC in 1990, 57 per cent and 17 per cent were in Guangdong and Fujian, respectively.

Taipei,China's investments in the PRC are also concentrated in South China, with 67 per cent of those reported to Taipei,China's government in 1991 located in Guangdong and Fujian. Similarly, 67 per cent of the investments approved by the PRC as of 31 January 1993 were in South China. As expected, the bulk of investments was in traditional labor-intensive industries. Ninety per cent of Taipei,China's investments in the PRC were through Hong Kong. It is clear from the available data that the role of Hong Kong as an intermediator between Taipei,China and the PRC is still quite important.

IMPACT OF INVESTMENT ON HONG KONG AND TAIPEI,CHINA

Taipei,China

A study by Yen et al (1992) simulated the effect of the 2,503 cases of investment registered as of 1991. The study estimated the direct output effects of losing these investments and estimated the direct output effects of exports from Taipei,China to the PRC induced by these investments. Linkage effects were also estimated. Based on the estimated output effects of the manufacturing sector, the impact on employment was also calculated. The estimated reduction in employment in Taipei,China's manufacturing sector was about 50,000 jobs or about 2.5 per cent of the total employment in the manufacturing sector. The total amount of investment in the 2,503 cases was only $754 million — far less than the $6.8 billion approved by the PRC to the end of 1992 — so presumably the actual effect on Taipei,China was much greater. However, the simulation may in fact overestimate the impact, as it neglects the general equilibrating effect that normally accompanies shifts in investment.

The dampening effect on labor demand caused by Taipei, China's investment abroad has actually been a benefit rather than a loss to the economy. Along with outward investment and changes in other factors of production, it has created more room for domestic investment in new industries. Table 4 shows a breakdown of Taipei,China's exports by product type. The shares of primary products, consumer goods, and processed food declined between 1989 and 1991, while the share of intermediate products and capital goods increased. This was part of a general trend that began several years earlier. The share of heavy chemical exports increased from 36 per cent in 1986 to 47 per cent in 1991, while the share of high-technology products increased from 28 per cent to 36 per cent. It is clear from all indicators that Taipei,China's export structure has changed significantly.

Table 5 provides more information about this structural change. The share of highly labor-intensive commodities declined from 47 per cent in 1986 to 40 per cent in 1991, while the share of commodities with low labor intensity increased from 15 per cent in 1987 to 21 per cent in 1991. Products with high capital intensity

Table 4. Taipei,China Exports by Product, 1989 and 1991
(per cent)

	To All Countries		To Hong Kong		To ASEAN[a]	
	1989	1991	1989	1991	1989	1991
Agriculture, Forestry, & Livestock	0.96	0.91	0.58	0.39	0.23	0.29
Processed Food	3.57	3.63	0.96	0.80	3.72	2.13
Beverages & Tobacco	0.03	0.05	0.02	0.09	0.03	0.01
Energy & Minerals	0.06	0.04	0.02	0.02	0.29	0.14
Construction Materials	0.29	0.23	0.39	0.22	0.10	0.18
Intermediate Products	40.00	46.41	70.36	76.41	64.87	67.60
Nondurable Consumer Goods	27.42	22.00	7.77	7.61	6.90	6.41
Durable Consumer Goods	10.30	8.51	4.25	3.05	3.26	2.27
Machinery	15.47	16.10	13.42	10.68	20.41	20.16
Transportation Equipment	1.89	2.12	2.24	0.69	0.19	0.81

[a] Excludes Brunei and Singapore.

Source: Statistical Yearbook of the Republic of China 1992.

increased from 22 per cent in 1987 to 30 per cent in 1991, and those with low capital intensity dropped from 28 per cent in 1986 to 19 per cent in 1991.

When commodities were reclassified according to the degree of human capital intensity, the speed of adjustment seemed to be even faster than in the previous two cases. The proportion of products with a high degree of human capital intensity in Taipei,China's exports increased from 18 per cent in 1986 to 27 per cent in 1991, while the proportion of products with low human capital products declined from 48 per cent in 1986 to 34 per cent in 1991.

Since Taipei,China is an open economy, changes in international comparative advantage and trade structure always have a significant impact on the structure of production, although the changes in production may not be as significant as those in trade. Actually, the growth rate of highly capital-intensive industries has been only slightly higher than that of other industries. However,

Table 5. Taipei,China Exports by Factor Intensity, 1989 and 1991
(per cent)

Factor Intensity	To All Countries		To Hong Kong		To ASEAN[a]	
	1989	1991	1989	1991	1989	1991
Labor Intensity						
High	43.4	40.1	27.5	25.2	29.6	29.1
Medium	37.8	38.7	27.8	32.7	35.8	38.5
Low	18.8	21.2	44.7	42.1	34.6	32.4
Capital Intensity						
High	26.6	29.8	51.6	49.5	47.8	45.6
Medium	50.7	51.0	35.2	33.5	39.5	42.1
Low	22.7	19.2	13.2	17.0	12.7	12.3
Human Capital Intensity						
High	24.3	27.2	25.7	24.3	37.2	39.5
Medium	38.1	38.5	42.8	40.5	35.9	36.0
Low	37.7	34.3	31.5	35.2	26.9	24.5
Energy Intensity						
High	13.1	13.9	34.1	32.9	28.1	23.2
Medium	45.3	45.7	37.2	43.0	47.3	53.0
Low	41.6	40.4	28.7	24.1	24.6	23.8

[a] Excludes Brunei and Singapore.

Source: Author's computations.

the growth rate of highly human capital-intensive industries has been much higher than that of other industries in recent years, as industries with low human capital intensity ceased to grow after 1987. When industries in the manufacturing sector were cross-classified by capital intensity and human capital intensity, the growth rates of different groups of industries were quite different from each other. In general, highly human-capital-intensive industries tended to have higher growth rates. The industry group with high human capital intensity and low capital intensity grew by 86 per cent in the past five years. In contrast, the industry group with low human capital intensity and low capital intensity declined by 18 per cent.

Although these changes are not solely attributable to Taipei,China's investment in the PRC or in other countries, the relative growth of intermediate products and machinery suggests that these investments may be playing a significant role. Table 4 also shows the exports of Taipei,China to Hong Kong and the ASEAN countries (Thailand, Malaysia, Indonesia, and the Philippines but excluding Brunei and Singapore). The exports to Hong Kong actually include the bulk of Taipei,China's exports to the PRC. The higher shares of intermediate products in Taipei,China's exports to these two regions compared to other countries may have something to do with Taipei,China's investments in ASEAN and the PRC. Since Taipei,China's exports to these two regions approximate the export structure of advanced countries, expanding trade and maintaining investment relations with these regions has not only been an important factor for improving Taipei,China's exports in recent years, but should also be a valuable guide for development in the future.

Hong Kong

The economic consequences of Hong Kong's investments in South China are comparable to those on the other side of the Taiwan Strait. There were 900,000 factory workers in Hong Kong in the early 1980s; in 1991 there were only 650,000. Meanwhile, it was reported that the number of workers in Hong Kong's manufacturing concerns in Guangdong had reached three million. The development of the Pearl River Delta has given Hong Kong an offshore manufacturing sector, helping Hong Kong to create a more complete national economy with enhanced competitiveness in the world market (Suda, 1992).

As a result of the transfer of manufacturing enterprises to Guangdong, the share of manufacturing in Hong Kong declined from 42 per cent in 1980 to 36 per cent in 1985, and further to 28 per cent in 1990. This decline was not only caused by outward investment, but also by the rapid development of South China, which raised the demand for services.

The PRC absorbed only 2 per cent of Hong Kong's exports in 1978, but its share jumped to 27 per cent in 1990. The value of re-exports in 1988 exceeded the value of local exports for the first time (Hwang, 1992). Part of the growth in exports may be attributed to the indirect trade between Taipei,China and the PRC. Still, the economic cooperation between Hong Kong and South China has dramatically reduced the importance of the labor-intensive manufacturing sector in the former while encouraging the growth of trade and other service sectors. This has made Hong Kong's industrial structure similar to that of the advanced countries.

However, the export commodity structure of Hong Kong did not change as significantly as that of Taipei,China. Compared to the exports of Taipei,China to the US, the exports of Hong Kong to the US were highly labor-intensive and low human-capital-intensive. While Hong Kong's exports to the US have not changed in the past few years, the exports of Taipei,China significantly shifted to advanced products. This difference may be partly explained by the fact that in trade statistics some Chinese products are counted as Hong Kong's exports. However, the opportunity for developing labor-intensive industries, as well as the rising demand for Hong Kong's service sector from the PRC, may have also dampened the effort to upgrade Hong Kong's manufacturing sector.

IMPACT OF INVESTMENT ON SOUTH CHINA

The contribution of Taipei,China's investments to South China and other parts of the country is difficult to quantify. The effects of Taipei,China's investment on the PRC's exports are estimated by Yen et al (1992). Although the effect on total exports is quite low, the effect on the exports of some products (e.g., as rubber and plastic products, electrical and electronic machinery and equipment, and transportation equipment) is more than 10 per cent of the PRC's exports of these items. This estimate is based on the data for the 2,503 firms registered in Taipei,China in early 1991. Since this grossly underestimates the actual level of investment, the impact can be assumed to be much larger. If only half of the investments approved by the PRC before the end of 1992 were realized, the effect would have been five times larger.

It is of course not enough to analyze the effects of Taipei,China's investments using the economic indicators of the whole economy, because such investments account for at most 10 per cent of the

PRC's total foreign investment. However, if the direction of foreign investment from one country were consistent with the trend of economic development of the host country, changes in the indicators of the host country should reveal the effect of the foreign investment from a single country. Some industries in Taipei,China that are losing their international comparative advantage seem to be gaining that advantage in the PRC. Consequently, there have been several opportunities for complementarity in development between Taipei,China and the PRC in the past few years, and investors from Taipei,China and Hong Kong are certain to have utilized these opportunities, and thus contributed to the structural change in the PRC.

The shares of Guangdong and Fujian provinces in the total foreign trade of the PRC were only 6.6 per cent and 0.93 per cent, respectively, in 1979. These shares grew to 23 per cent and 3 per cent in 1991. The value of exports from Guangdong increased from $2,194 million to $13,687 million, while the value of exports from Fujian increased from $190 million to $2,238 million.

Before the open door policy, per capita income in Guangdong was only slightly higher than that for the whole of the country. In 1980, the per capita income in Guangdong was 11.4 per cent higher than the national average, while that in Fujian was 22.6 per cent lower. By 1990, the per capita income of Guangdong was 1.45 times that of the rest of the country, while that of Fujian was 1.04 times higher. That year the per capita incomes of Shenzhen, Zhuhai, and Xiamen were much larger than the national per capita income (10.8, 4.3, and 3 times higher, respectively). The contribution of economic reform is quite apparent in those figures, as is foreign investment, especially from Hong Kong and Taipei,China.

The qualitative changes caused by foreign investment are usually no less important than the quantitative changes. One significant characteristic of the investments of Taipei,China and Hong Kong in the PRC is that the size of each investment tends to be small. Although the average size of a single investment from Taipei,China in 1992 is about three times the average before 1990, it is still less than one-third of the average size of Taipei,China's investment in other countries. This is mainly due to the importance of small and medium-sized firms in Taipei,China's traditional industries. Given their size, and given the similarities in culture and language among the three areas, investments from Taipei,China and Hong Kong can be spread more easily to other parts of the PRC (especially within South China) than investments from other countries. This facilitates the rapid transfer and diffusion of technology. The mobility of investment may have a favorable effect on income distribution and regional development in the PRC, particularly South China.

CONCLUSIONS

Although Taipei,China and Hong Kong are at different stages of economic development and have different international comparative advantages, they both share a similar culture and language with the PRC. Thus, opportunities for complementarity in production, as well as in development, are quite evident among the three economies.

The open door policy and economic reforms in the PRC, along with rising labor and land costs in Hong Kong and Taipei,China, have caused a rapid increase in investment from Taipei,China and Hong Kong in South China, and a corresponding increase in trade among the three areas. Economic cooperation has brought each economy significant benefits, including rapid economic growth and higher income in South China, the development of an offshore manufacturing sector and an advanced service sector in Hong Kong, and the upgrading of the export and manufacturing sectors in Taipei,China.

The massive inflow of investment into South China area has been promoted by a number of factors. On the part of the PRC, these include the open door policy and subsequent liberalization of economic policies, limited linkages with Taipei,China, and the improvement of infrastructure. For both Hong Kong and Taipei, China, investment has been motivated by major differentials in costs of production (labor in particular). In the case of Taipei,China, a rapid and major appreciation of the currency was an added reason for investment elsewhere. Cultural and linguistic affinities and geographical proximity added to the attraction of South China as a production base.

The actual amount of investment in South China is difficult to determine but the available data suggests that Hong Kong investment is by far the most important component of total investment. Further, investment flows from Hong Kong and Taipei,China appear to be qualitatively different.

The Southern China Growth Triangle has provided major net benefits to all participants. For the PRC, it has provided exports, foreign exchange, and employment, as well as access to the larger global economy. For Hong Kong and Taipei,China the triangle has provided a means of implementing needed changes in manufacturing and export patterns at minimal cost.

Hong Kong has served as an intermediator between Taipei,China and South China, but in general the relationships among the three areas have been bilateral in nature, with the relationship between Taipei,China and Hong Kong tending towards competition rather than cooperation. Moreover, both Taipei,China and Hong Kong are still dependent on Japan as a source of technology and high-technology inputs. Japan and the other industrial countries are also increasing their direct investment in the PRC and South China. Therefore, the Southern China Growth Triangle is most accurately seen as a part of a larger growth relationship in the world economy. The technology of Japan and the markets in the US and other industrial countries are still vital components of this larger, global triangle.

The experience of the Southern China Growth Triangle shows that the market mechanism is strong enough to overcome many barriers. While the open door policy in the PRC seems to have been essential, direct cooperation between governments in a potential growth triangle may not be necessary. However, barriers to technology transfer from advanced countries and barriers to international trade faced by developing countries must be reduced. Without this, a growth triangle will quickly lose its energy once the less developed members begin achieving a level of development comparable to that of their more advanced partners.

Endnotes:

1. Professor, Department and Institute of Economics, National Taiwan University.
2. The author is indebted to Yu-chun Lee, Lu-yen Yeh, Wen-jui Yang, and Hui-yi Lo for their advice and assistance.
3. The index of human capital intensity used here is the ratio of workers with college or higher educational level in the direct and indirect employment of each industry. The commodity producing industries are divided into three groups according to the index. Commodities from the industries in the group with the highest index value are called human capital intensive products.

Bibliography

Border, "South China Economic Development Outlines: A Translated and Summarized Report" (in Chinese), in *Mainland Economic Researches*, Vol. 15, No. 2 (1993), pp. 35-51.

Chang, Rong Fong, and Huei Tze Shih. *A Research on the Current State and Competitiveness of the Joint Venture Enterprise in the Coastal Area of Mainland China* (in Chinese). Taipei: Chung Hwa Institute of Economic Research, 1989.

Chen, Pochih, "Policies and Structure Adjustment in Taiwan in the 1980s," in *Proceedings of the Conference on Adjustment and Coordination in Asia-Pacific Region: Structural Changes in 1980s*. Fukuoka: Foundation for Advanced Information and Research, 1989.

_____, "The Role of Taiwanese Capital and Technology in the Economic Development of South East Asia," in Kuang-sheng Liao, ed., *Economic Development of Taiwan and China and Regional Interactions in Asia Pacific*. Hong Kong: The Chinese University of Hong Kong, 1991.

_____, and Hwei-chin Lee. *Report on the Development and Strategies for the Manufacturing Sector* (in Chinese). Taipei: Taiwan Institute of Economic Research, 1988.

Hwang, Chou Hau, "On the Economic Integration of Hong Kong and

Guangdong" (in Chinese), in *Mainland Economic Researches,* Vol. 14, No. 3 (1992), pp. 53-64.

Kimura, Yuki, "A New Phase of Development for the Hong Kong Economy — the Greater Hong Kong Era," in *Asian Perspectives,* Vol. 5 (1991), pp. 29-39.

Lardy, Nicholas R., "China and Open Door Strategies: Outside Perspective," paper presented at the 19th Pacific Trade and Development Conference, Chinese Academy of Social Sciences, Beijing, 1991.

Lee, Shou Cheng, "An Analysis on the Economic and Trade Policies of Communist China Toward Taiwan" (in Chinese), in *National Policy Dynamic Analysis,* No. 21 (1991), pp. 5-9.

Li, Chein, "Rethinking the Fast Development of Economic and Trade Relations Across the Taiwan Strait" (in Chinese), in *Mainland Economic Researches,* Vol. 14, No. 2 (1992), pp. 23-27.

Suda, Shigeto, "Hong Kong's Role as the Capital of the Greater Hong Kong Economic Region," paper presented at the ASEAN-China Hong Kong Forum, Centre for Asian Pacific Studies, Lingnan College, Hong Kong, 1992.

Sung, Yun-wing, "The Economic Integration of Hong Kong, Taiwan and South Korea with Mainland China," paper presented at the 19th Pacific Trade and Development Conference, Chinese Academy of Social Sciences, Beijing, 1991.

Tang, Min, and Myo Thant, "Growth Triangles: Conceptual Issues and Operational Problems," paper presented at the Workshop on Growth Triangles in Asia, Asian Development Bank, Manila, 24-26 February 1993.

Yen, Tzung-tai, Yuh-jiun Lin, and Chin Chung. *A Study on the Investment and Trade by Taiwanese Investors in Mainland China* (in Chinese). Taipei: Chung Hwa Institute of Economic Research, 1992.

Chinese Public Policy and the Southern China Growth Triangle

■ Chen Dezhao[1]

INTRODUCTION

The emergence of the Southern China Growth Triangle, consisting of Guangdong and Fujian provinces (hereafter South China), Hong Kong, Macau, and Taipei,China, would not have been possible without the open door policy and other economic reforms in the People's Republic of China (PRC), particularly the preferential treatment given to investors in special economic zones (SEZs). This is borne out by a comparison of conditions before and after the introduction of the new policies in 1979.

In the late 1970s, the economic links between South China and the outside world were weak. In 1979, for instance, Shenzhen exported only $9 million worth of goods and received no more than 200 foreign tourists. Zhuhai fared little better, exporting less than $20 million. But in that year, South China ushered in the open door era with the establishment of four SEZs. This paved the way for the forging of greater economic ties with Hong Kong, Macau, and other parts of the world, and helped in the creation of Asia's first growth triangle. In 1992, the export volume of the four special economic zones amounted to $12 billion. In 1991, approved foreign investments accounted for one-fourth of the total investments in the entire country (Gao and Ye, 1991).

This paper analyzes the roles played by the central and local governments of the PRC in formulating policies related to the Southern China Growth Triangle. The first section looks at the special features of the growth triangle area. The second section describes the policy coordination between central and local governments. The section that follows discusses in detail the specific policies applied in the Southern China Growth Triangle. The preferential treatment of foreign investment and export enterprises is discussed in the fourth section. The final section presents conclusions.

BACKGROUND

Four types of special areas within the PRC served as the foundations for the evolution of the Southern China Growth Triangle: (i) the special economic zones (Shenzhen, Zhuhai, Shantou, and Xiamen); (ii) the open coastal cities (Zhanjiang, Guangzhou, and Fuzhou); (iii) the economic and technological development zones within those cities; and (iv) the "open coastal economic areas" (the Pearl River Delta and the delta area of Xiamen, Zhangzhou, and Quanzhou in southern Fujian province). Of these areas, special economic zones, with their long track record and greater openness, have played the most important role. (See Appendix 1 for a comparison of the open economic areas in South China.)

Special Economic Zones

In August 1980, the 15th session of the Standing Committee of the National People's Congress promulgated "The Regulations Concerning the Guangdong Provincial Special Economic Zones." Altogether, four SEZs were set up in that year: Shenzhen, Zhuhai, Shantou, and Xiamen.

The choice of Guangdong and Fujian as the locations for special economic zones was based on a number of considerations. The two provinces are not only rich in natural resources, but ideally located. Their proximity to Hong Kong, Macau, and Taipei,China would enable the PRC to use them as springboards to those economies and to the world market. The cultural makeup and skills of the work force in the two provinces were also regarded as advantages for economic cooperation.

Today the special economic zones have three defining features:

(i)   *They are windows between the PRC and the outside world.* The zones have assumed a special role in the PRC's development program, as they have evolved in the course of major changes in the national economic management system. From the beginning, the central leadership asked Guangdong and Fujian to make the SEZs test cases for the reform program and open door policy. The SEZs were to be windows on global technology, management, knowledge, and foreign policy. The country could use the SEZs to observe and understand the changes in the international economy, and countries around the world could in turn observe and understand the changes taking place in the PRC;

(ii) *They are nonexclusive, open areas.* The Chinese government decided at the outset to make the SEZs, coastal cities, and development areas open and nonexclusive. All these areas were to keep in close contact with the rest of the country, both relying on and serving the interior provinces.

(iii) *They have become multifunctional economic entities.* Shenzhen is a good example of a comprehensive SEZ, integrating industry, commerce, farming, animal husbandry, housing, tourism, and other trades as envisioned by the central government.

The development of the SEZs in South China may be divided into two stages. The first stage (1980-1985) saw the laying of the policy foundations and the development of land and buildings to create conditions favorable to foreign investment. In all, more than 70 sq km of land in the four SEZs were developed. Most of the roads, water, and electricity supply networks, postal and telecommunications facilities, harbors and airports, commercial buildings and tourist hotels, and residential housing and other basic facilities were constructed during this stage.

After operating for some time, the SEZs entered the second stage of development (1986-present), characterized by expansion. First, the SEZ in Zhuhai, which had grown from 6.81 sq km in 1980 to 14.1 sq km in June 1983, was expanded to 121 sq km in 1987. Similarly, the SEZ in Shantou, which had grown from 1.6 sq km to 52.6 sq km in 1984, was extended to cover the entire city in 1991. The SEZ in Xiamen was also expanded in June 1985 from the original 2.5 sq km, to encompass the entire island on which it was established and the adjacent Gulangyu Island, for a total of 131 sq km.

POLICY COORDINATION BETWEEN THE CENTRAL AND LOCAL GOVERNMENTS

Decisions on the establishment, development, and strategies for the SEZs were reached through consultation between the relevant localities and the central government. The central government's role in policy formulation took three principal forms.

First, local governments were required to submit their policy suggestions to the central government for review and approval. The central government then outlined policy concepts or suggestions and submitted them to the National People's Congress for consideration. Policies were then promulgated in the form of government decrees or regulations.

Second, the central government or relevant ministries convened regular meetings on specific issues with the participation of officials from the local governments and/or the SEZs. Policy-related decisions were made at these meetings. These were generally circulated to implementing bodies in the form of summary records approved by the State Council. For instance, a national work conference on the SEZs was convened in Shenzhen by the central government in December 1985. At this conference, development objectives for the SEZs were formulated in light of economic developments at home and abroad, and in light of the experience gained by the SEZs during the first five years of their operation. Three different opinions on the further development of the SEZs were aired at the conference. Some argued for developing export-oriented economies in the SEZs that mainly stressed industrial production but also permitted other activities. Others advocated the expansion of tertiary industry, thereby transforming the SEZs into trade centers for economic exchanges with countries across the globe. Still others maintained that a two-way economy should be developed in the SEZs in response to the demands of international and domestic markets. The conference finally decided that the SEZs should build export-oriented economies integrating trade and industry and dominated by high-tech projects to be funded mainly by foreign investors. In addition, a shift in emphasis from framework-building and foundation-laying to industrial production, product improvement, and benefit-raising was endorsed during the conference.

Third, a full-time office for the SEZs was set up under the State Council and made responsible for formulating and implementing policies related to the SEZs, and for coordinating policies between the central and local governments.

The central government is responsible for shaping policies on major issues such as the overall direction and planning of the SEZs. A State Council document from 1982 states that some SEZs are entrusted with decision making power equal to that of the provincial level. The SEZs enjoy a much wider latitude in decision making on economic matters than other local governments, and their development plans and economic targets are checked and ratified directly by the central ministries concerned. Economic and technological development areas, on the other hand, are defined as economic areas under the direct jurisdiction and guidance of the open coastal municipal governments. They adopt special policies, characterized by greater openness than other areas in the same cities, and emphasize export industries and high-technology enterprises.

The central government is responsible for unified control over matters within the SEZs related to foreign affairs, public security, border defense, taxation, customs clearing, banking, foreign exchange, postal service, telecommunications, railways, harbors, civil aviation, etc. Specific regulations concerning these matters are formulated by the respective central ministries under the concerned State Council in light of actual conditions prevailing in the

SEZs. These are then submitted to the State Council for checking and ratification before they are enforced. All other matters outside the unified control of the central government are to be handled by the SEZ government (or administrative commission), with some flexibility in accordance with the spirit of the policies promulgated by the central government.

Of the five SEZs in South China, four are subordinate to Guangdong and Fujian provinces. The SEZ in Hainan enjoys a status equivalent to that of a province. In all five, the SEZ government exercises overall guidance over work in the zone. The provincial government is responsible for solving any problems arising between SEZs and other areas under its jurisdiction. The SEZ submits annual reports to the provincial government to help the province determine the allocation of materials to be supplied by other provinces.

Some policies affecting SEZs, including regulations on foreign investment, are formulated by them rather than by the central or provincial government. These policies are enacted and publicized after being endorsed by the provincial People's Congress. Generally, regulations made to suit local conditions should not run counter to the policies set by the central government. Examples of local policies are Zhuhai SEZ's "Regulations for Further Encouraging Foreign Investment" (April 1989), Shenzhen SEZ's "Regulations on Government Foreign Economic Contracts" (1984) and "Provisional Regulations for the Introduction of Technologies" (1984), and Xiamen SEZ's "Regulations with Regard to Labor Management" (1984).

POLICIES FOR ECONOMIC COOPERATION

Land Use Policies

The Constitution of the People's Republic of China stipulates that "urban land is under state ownership" and that "suburban and rural land is generally under collective ownership with the exception of tracts otherwise designated by law as state-owned. Land close to house foundations, plots or hills for personal needs are also under collective ownership." But "in accordance with legal provisions, the state may requisition land to satisfy the demand of public interests." Land policies in the SEZs have been drawn up under the guidance of these constitutional provisions.

Article 5 of Shenzhen SEZ's "Provincial Regulations for Land Management" states that "work units or individuals granted the permission to use land, obtain only the land use right but not the right of ownership in land. Buying and selling of land in fact or in disguised form is strictly forbidden." This is true in the other SEZs as well. Ignorance of the law can prove costly to the unwary. Any investor in a manufacturing or other concern in the SEZs who needs to use land must be able to produce the relevant contracts, written agreements, and approval certificate issued by the local authorities and submit an application for land use to the departments concerned. The work unit responsible for accepting and approving the application varies from one SEZ to another. For instance, in the Shenzhen SEZ, the work unit is the municipal planning department. In Xiamen, the unit concerned is the rural and urban construction commission. Since an application for land use involves a specific fee, all SEZs stipulate that the pertinent land should be put to use within a certain period; otherwise the certificate for land use rights will be revoked. The term "a certain period" used here varies among the SEZs and is subject to determination by the SEZ government based on local conditions. The Shenzhen SEZ government stipulates that a foreign investor should be able to produce a plan for a construction project within six months after the effectivity of the land use rights certificate, and to break ground for the project in accordance with the plan within nine months; otherwise the land use rights certificate will be revoked and the fee will not be refunded. (These limits are nine months and one year, respectively, in Xiamen SEZ.) This stipulation effectively prevents the practice of "sunning the land," as well as land speculation.

If there is only one foreign investor applying for the use of a given tract of land, then negotiations over the fees and the period of land use may transpire between the investor and the department concerned. Variations exist among the SEZs regarding fees and land use periods. Generally speaking, however, land use fees for commerce are higher than those for industry and commercial residential housing. Fees for commercial residential housing are usually higher than those for industrial use. Even so, in the course of negotiations the criteria for determining land use rights may be influenced by many factors, such as market demand and supply. If many foreign investors apply for permission to use the same tract of land, then open bidding is adopted. In all of the above cases, a portion of the land use fees is turned over to the local budget office and the rest to the central budget office.

While land use rights vary from one SEZ to another, two features are shared by all SEZs: (i) only the maximum land use period is mentioned; and (ii) variations exist among different projects. The length of the period for a specific project is influenced not only by the nature of the project concerned (including whether it involves advanced technology), but also by the location of the site and by prevailing or prospective conditions of demand and supply.

Special government stipulations apply to commercial residential buildings or real estate inside the SEZs. The so-called property rights over commercial residential buildings mentioned here refer to housing ownership and the rights to the site of the housing. Houseowners are allowed by the SEZ government to transfer, mortgage, or lease their housing property rights to others through legal actions such as engaging in housing property transactions (including presale, prepurchase, and auction), granting the property as gift, or exchanging, bequeathing, or inheriting it. The SEZ, however, has the right to requisition the house owner in light of the construction needs of the SEZ by offering reasonable compensation or other forms of settlement.

Labor Policies

There are some common features in labor policy among the SEZs, open coastal cities, and development areas. Foreign-funded enterprises may recruit staff members and workers on their own. However, there are usually labor service companies in the SEZs which recommend to the enterprises for employment only those applicants who have been found to be outstanding after an examination. The contract system used for employment generally includes terms on employment, dismissal, resignation, period of employment, labor insurance, protection, discipline, welfare, etc. Labor contracts are submitted to the labor bureau of the SEZs or open coastal cities. In some areas (e.g., Xiamen), labor contracts may be routinely reported to the municipal labor bureau, whereas in other SEZs (e.g., Shenzhen, Shantou, and Zhuhai) and in other open cities in Guangdong, they are reported for examination and approval purposes as well. The form of payment, wage scales, remuneration, allowances, or subsidies are all decided upon by the relevant enterprises without any interference from the SEZ government. Foreign-funded enterprises may discipline or even dismiss employees who violate enterprise rules and regulations as stipulated in the labor contracts.

Enterprises in all the SEZs are subject to the following labor regulations:

   (i)   They cannot employ workers under the age of 16. Article 4 of Xiamen SEZ's "Regulations for Labor Management" stipulates that "enterprises should not employ school pupils," with the exception of those who work as casual workers during holidays or during the summer or winter vacations;

  (ii)   They must obtain approval from the labor bureau before hiring rural labor or employees from other parts of PRC, and they must seek a temporary residence permit for those workers;

 (iii)   The dismissal of employees must be reported to the labor bureau in the SEZ or open city;

 (iv)   Fees are paid when workers from outside the SEZ are recruited, with the proceeds helping to defray the costs of infrastructure facilities; and

  (v)   Enterprises must make clear in the labor contracts the terms and conditions for employment, dismissal, resignation, remuneration, rewards, penalties, welfare, social insurance, etc., when hiring foreign nationals or employees from Hong Kong, Macau, or Taipei,China.

Financial Policies

Unlike in other parts of the PRC, where funds for capital construction come from state revenues, the "development by borrowing"
approach has been adopted in the SEZs. Funds for capital construction are raised through foreign investment, bank loans, and the
accumulation of earnings by the SEZs themselves. The proportion
of funds coming from each of these sources varies from one SEZ to
another. Between 1980 and 1987, foreign capital accounted for
around 20 per cent of the total (see Table 1).

The SEZs are not required to turn over to the central government their earnings during the first five years of their operation.
State-run enterprises located in the SEZs may also retain their
profits, but enterprises in the SEZs run by interior provinces (also
called "enterprises of internal combination") must remit part of
their profits to their parent firms outside the SEZs.

To encourage firms from the interior of the PRC to invest in the
SEZs, the open coastal cities, and the open coastal areas, the central

Table 1. Source of Capital Construction Funds
for Shenzhen SEZ, 1980-1987

Source	Municipality		SEZ	
	Amount (100 million yuan)	*Per Cent* of Total	*Amount* (100 million yuan)	*Per Cent* of Total
Foreign Capital	19.2	18.6	18.8	19.2
Fiscal Appropriation (city or county)	14.5	14.0	14.0	14.2
Self-Raised by Enterprises	21.6	20.9	20.2	20.7
Home Loans	24.3	23.5	22.3	22.8
State Investment	2.0	2.0	2.0	2.0
Self-Raised by Central Ministry or Province	12.5	12.1	12.4	12.6
Enterprises from Interior Provinces	4.4	4.2	4.1	4.2
Others	4.3	4.1	3.7	3.8

Source: Shenzhen City Council, *The General Prospect of Economic Development in Shenzhen SEZ* (1992).

government issued regulations on preferential treatment in taxation for these enterprises. All work units or enterprises that invest in manufacturing concerns in the SEZs enjoy a 15 per cent reduction in enterprise income tax. If they repatriate their after-tax profits to the interior provinces, they are required to pay back taxes by 20 per cent. However, if they retain their after-tax profits in the SEZs for reinvestment, they are exempted from such tax repayments for five years beginning with the first profitable year. Furthermore, these enterprises are entitled to preferential treatment at customs if they export their own products or import production materials or office equipment for their own use.

TAXATION OF INVESTORS

Preferential tax policies have been initiated in the SEZs, open coastal cities, and development areas to attract foreign investors, including companies, enterprises, and individuals from Hong Kong, Macau, and Taipei,China (see Appendix 2).

Enterprise Income Tax

All foreign-funded enterprises (joint ventures, cooperative enterprises, and wholly foreign-owned enterprises) in the SEZs enjoy a preferential 15 per cent income tax rate. Manufacturing enterprises planning to stay in the SEZs for more than ten years may, upon approval by the tax bureau, enjoy income exemption for two years after the first profitable year and a 50 per cent reduction in the tax for the next three to five years. Incentives accorded to the service sector are not as generous. Foreign-funded manufacturing enterprises enjoy preferential treatment regardless of the amount of their investment, whereas foreign-funded trading firms are not entitled to the same treatment unless they invest more than $5 million. Trading activities enjoy income tax exemption for only one year starting from the first profitable year and receive a 50 per cent reduction for two years thereafter. Nevertheless, wholly foreign firms in manufacturing and trading both receive income tax exemption on profit repatriation and exemption from taxes on income derived from dividends, interests, rents, royalties, and the like.

Income from sources not included in this category may be subject to a 10 per cent income tax.

Industrial and Commercial Tax

Imports of foreign-funded enterprises may enjoy exemption from the industrial and commercial consolidated tax with the exception of mineral oil, tobacco, and alcoholic drinks. Exemption from the industrial and commercial consolidated tax is further granted to tobacco, alcoholic drinks, personal luggage, and other personal effects of foreign investors within reasonable limits. Exports of foreign-funded enterprises are also entitled to tax exemption, with the exception of a few items subject to other regulations or for which a ceiling on the allowable amount has been set. Moreover, products of foreign-funded enterprises sold on the local SEZ market are also entitled to tax exemption, with a 50 per cent reduction for mineral oil, tobacco, alcoholic drinks, and the like. However, if foreign-funded firms sell the items listed above on the market in interior provinces of the PRC, they are made to pay the industrial and commercial consolidated tax retroactively. Even so, items brought from the SEZs to the interior provinces for the personal use of a foreign investor may still enjoy tax exemption as long as they are kept within reasonable limits.

As with the income tax, the industrial and commercial consolidated tax is biased in favor of manufacturing. In accordance with the relevant regulations of the State Council, the income of foreign-funded enterprises from investments in commerce, transport, and trade is subject to tax based on the rates set for the industrial and commercial consolidated tax. The tax rate for foreign investors engaged in banking and insurance is set at 3 per cent.

Policy Differences Among Regions and Zones

Foreign-funded enterprises in the SEZs, whether in manufacturing or not, enjoy a 15 per cent tax rate on their income, whereas those in the development areas within open coastal cities must be engaged in manufacturing or high-technology activities if they are to qualify. Imports of most daily necessities used within the boundaries of the SEZs are entitled to reductions in or exemptions from customs duties; no such allowance is made for foreign-funded enterprises in the development areas.

In open coastal cities such as Guangzhou and Fuzhou, and in economic technological development areas, incentives to foreign investors are not as generous as those given in the SEZs. For instance, only a few foreign-funded enterprises may enjoy the preferential 15 per cent income tax rate. These are firms involved in knowledge-intensive and skill-intensive activities, firms engaged in infrastructure development (energy resources, communications, port improvement, etc.), firms with investments exceeding $30 million, or firms requiring a long period for capital redemption. Even for these enterprises, preferential treatment must be approved by the Ministry of Finance. Projects that do not qualify according to the above criteria may get an 80 per cent discount in income tax if they are involved in the following activities: machine building, electronics, metallurgy, chemicals, building materials, light textiles, packing, medical devices, medicine, agriculture, forestry, animal husbandry or fishery and related processing industries, and construction (Liu, 1993).

Foreign-funded manufacturing or research enterprises in the open coastal economic areas, regardless of whether they are joint ventures or wholly foreign-owned enterprises, pay an income tax of 24 per cent, rather than the normal rate of 30 per cent. For enterprises with direct foreign investment in energy, transportation, port construction, or technology-intensive or knowledge-intensive activities, and for enterprises with a foreign investment volume of over $30 million and which require a long time to realize profits, the income tax rate may be kept at 15 per cent. Even here, preferential treatment requires the approval of the Ministry of Finance. If the legitimate profit of the foreign investors is remitted abroad, it is exempt from the remittance tax.

EXPORT INCENTIVES

To encourage foreign-funded enterprises to export their products, enterprises whose export volume reaches 70 per cent of the targeted volume for the year are entitled to a 10 per cent reduction in income tax. Export products (except petroleum, oil products, and other specified items) are exempt from export tariffs and the consolidated industrial and commercial tax. Imports of raw materials for use by enterprises with foreign capital in the SEZs are also exempt from import tariffs and the consolidated industrial and commercial tax. Since the imported raw materials usually go into the manufactured exports, the preferential treatment for these materials encourages exports from the SEZs.

Preferential treatment is also offered to export-oriented enterprises with foreign capital in the coastal cities and the economic and technological development areas within these cities. For instance, export commodities produced in the coastal cities, except those items prohibited for export by the state, are exempt from the consolidated industrial and commercial tax, while commodities for the domestic market are taxed. Enterprises with foreign capital in the cities enjoy tariff-free treatment for their imported raw materials, spare parts, and packing materials, and are exempted from the consolidated industrial and commercial tax. In the economic and technological development areas, enterprises with foreign capital with a contract term of ten years or longer are exempt from income tax, or enjoy a reduction in income tax for a specified number of years. Export products produced in these areas, except petroleum, refined oil, and a limited number of specified products, are exempt from customs tariffs and the consolidated industrial and commercial tax.

As a result of policies that encourage export-oriented enterprises, exports from the open areas have increased rapidly. In Shenzhen SEZ, the average annual growth rate of exports in the 1980s was 87.3 per cent. Presently, Shenzhen exports over 800 types of commodities, making up 60 per cent of the volume of its total industrial production. Shantou's exports constitute 70 per cent of its total volume of industrial and agricultural products.

CONCLUSIONS

The Southern China Growth Triangle has been a boon to the Chinese economy, serving as a window to the world and having a strong demonstration effect on the rest of the economy. The opening up of South China and the expansion of its economic ties with

Hong Kong, Macau, and Taipei,China has yielded significant results. In South China, the government of PRC has made a great effort to create a healthy policy environment for the development of the special economic zones and the Pearl River Delta area. The growth triangle highlights the fact that government policies may be the single most important factor underlying success. The Southern China Growth Triangle could not have been realized without significant changes in public policy. Further, these changes were effected through a process of consultations between the major institutions concerned.

A number of preferential policies have played an important role for the success of the Southern China Growth Triangle. These policies include the policy that reduces income, industrial and commercial tax to lighten the burden for both domestic and foreign investors. Land use policy, labor policy, financial policy, and trade policy are all designed to reduce transaction costs and to give the enterprises operating in the triangle greater access to the world market. Without these policy changes, the Southern China Growth Triangle would not be successful.

There are, however, major policy variations among the different regions in the triangle. In general, the policies applied in the special economic zones are much more liberal than those in the other parts of the triangle, although the policy differentials have narrowed over time. Policy coordination between the central government and local governments is another critical area. The central government is responsible for formulating policies on major issues such as the overall direction and planning of SEZs. The provincial government is responsible for solving any problems arising between SEZs and other areas under its jurisdiction. Some policies, including regulations on foreign investment, are formulated by the SEZs.

Encouraged by the success of South China, five cities along the Yangtze River valley and the capital cities of 18 provinces have been newly opened to foreign investors. More growth triangle activities are also planned in the Tumen River Delta area of Northeast China and the Yellow Sea economic cooperation zone in East China. The policies which were effective in the Southern China Growth Triangle are expected to be extended to those areas as well.

Comparison of the Open Economic Areas in South China

	Special Economic Zones (SEZs)	Coastal Port Cities (CPCs)	Eco. and Tech. Development Areas (ETDAs)	Open Coastal Economic Areas (OCEAs)
NAMES	· Shenzhen (includes Luohu, Nanshan and Fugang districts) · Zhuhai · Shantou (includes Longhu and Guangao Separate Areas) · Xiamen (includes Xiamen and Gulangyu)	· Zhanjiang · Guangzhou · Fuzhou	· Zhanjiang · Guangzhou · Fuzhou	· Pearl River Delta (includes 11 cities and 42 counties) · Delta Area of Xiamen, Zhangzhou, and Quanzhou (includes 3 provincial cities and 28 counties and cities)
LOCATION	Guangdong and Fujian provinces	Guangdong and Fujian provinces	Guangdong and Fujian provinces	Guangdong and southern Fujian provinces
SIZE (sq km)	Shenzhen: 327.5 Zhuhai: 121.0 Shantou: 52.6 Xiamen: 131.0		Zhanjiang: 9.2 Guangzhou: 9.6 Fuzhou: 4.4	
POPULATION (million)	Shenzhen: 1.02 Zhuhai: 0.17 Shantou: 0.05 Xiamen: 0.37		Guangzhou: 0.01 Fuzhou: 0.05	

Comparison of Preferential Treatment for Foreign-Funded Enterprises in the Open Economic Areas of South China

	Special Economic Zones (SEZs)	Coastal Port Cities (CPCs)	Economic and Technical Development Areas (ETDAs)	Open Coastal Economic Areas (OCEAs)
Income Tax	Enterprises engaged in production with cooperation over 10 years: · Reduced rate of 15 per cent; · Exempt from taxes for 2 years after first profitable year; · 50 per cent reduction from years 3 to 5; · 50 per cent reduction for enterprises using advanced technology; and · 10 per cent reduction for enterprises with export volume of 70 per cent.	Enterprises engaged in production that are technical or knowledge-based; and/or with investment over $30 million; and/or engaged in infrastructure development: · Reduced rate of 15 per cent (with approval from Ministry of Finance). Enterprises engaged in machine-building, electronics, metallurgy, chemicals, building materials, light textiles, packing, agriculture, forestry and related activities, and building: · Reduced rate of 20 per cent (with approval from Ministry of Finance).	Enterprises with cooperation over 10 years: · Reduced rate of 15 per cent for income from manufacturing and production in specified forms of technical development; · Exempt from taxes for 2 years after first profitable year; · 50 per cent reduction from years 3 to 5; · 50 per cent reduction for enterprises using advanced technology; and · 10 per cent reduction for enterprises with export volume of 70 per cent.	Enterprises engaged in production or research activities: · Reduced rate of 24 per cent. Enterprises engaged in energy, transportation, port construction, technology-intensive and/or knowledge-intensive production: · Reduced rate of 15 per cent (with approval from Ministry of Finance). Enterprises with foreign investment of $30 million that require several years to realize profit: · Reduced rate of 15 per cent (with approval from Ministry of Finance).

Export Tariffs	· Exempt for petroleum products and other specified products.	· Exempt except for items prohibited for export.	· Exempt for products produced within zone, except petroleum, refined oil, and other specified products.	· Exempt except for petroleum products and other specified products.
Import Tariffs	· Exempt for equipment, raw materials, office equipment for own use.	· Exempt for production equipment, building facilities and materials, vehicles, office equipment for own use.	· Exempt for building materials, production equipment, raw materials, spare parts, vehicles, office equipment for own use; and · Liable for tariffs on above items which are sold domestically (tariffs based on imported content).	All enterprises: · Exempt for production equipment, building materials for use in foreign investment, raw materials, spare parts, packing materials, vehicles for enterprise use, office equipment, personal appliances and vehicles for foreign investors and staff. Enterprises engaged in export-oriented agriculture or animal husbandry: Exempt for seeds, machinery and other production materials, petroleum products, and other specified products.

(continued on next page)

	Special Economic Zones (SEZs)	Coastal Port Cities (CPCs)	Economic and Technical Development Areas (ETDAs)	Open Coastal Economic Areas (OCEAs)
Consolidated Industrial and Com- mercial Tax	· Exempt from taxes for exports except petroleum and other specified products, and for imports of equipment, raw materials, office equipment for own use.	· Exempt from taxes for imported production equipment, building facilities and materials, vehicles, office equipment for own use; and · Exempt from taxes for export commodities, except items prohibited for export.	· Exempt from taxes for imported production equipment, raw materials, building facilities and materials, vehicles, office equipment for own use; and · Liable for taxes on above items which are sold domestically (taxes based on imported content).	· Exempt for exported products except petro- leum, refined oil, and other specified products.

Endnote:

1.   Member, Executive Board, China Center for International Studies, People's Republic of China.

Bibliography

Almanac of China's Foreign Economic Relations and Trade. Beijing: Water Resources and Electric Power Press, 1992.

Gao, Shangquan and Ye Sen. *China Economic Systems: Reform Yearbook 1990.* Beijing: China Reform Publishing House, 1991a.

_____. *China Economic Systems: Reform Yearbook 1991.* Beijing: China Reform Publishing House, 1991b.

Liu, Meixiu, "Foreign Investment in the Pearl River Delta," in *Asia-Pacific Economic Review*, No. 2 (1993).

Special Economic Zones Office. *An Introduction to China's Coastal Open Areas.* Beijing: Shenzhen City Council, 1991.

_____. *The General Prospect of Economic Development in Shenzhen SEZ.* Beijing: Shenzhen City Council, 1992.

Infrastructure Development in the Southern China Growth Triangle

■ Yue-man Yeung[1]

INTRODUCTION

Much of the rapid economic development in the Asia-Pacific region in recent years has taken place across national boundaries, as economic agents have attempted to capitalize on differing endowments of land, capital, and labor. Economic hubs, or growth triangles, have been established to enable countries to maximize the advantages to be derived from the possession of these factors of production, and to produce synergistic conditions conducive to economic growth. The objective of this paper is to examine how economic growth in the Southern China Growth Triangle (consisting of Guangdong and Fujian provinces, Taipei,China, and Hong Kong) has been facilitated by infrastructure development, and how development planning has taken account of the prospect of political integration between the People's Republic of China (PRC) and Hong Kong by 1997.[2]

The paper is divided into five sections. The first section briefly traces the development of infrastructure in the Southern China Growth Triangle. Only cursory attention is devoted to Taipei,China and Hong Kong, since information about these economies is readily available and much has been written about their economic and infrastructure development. The emphasis on Guangdong and Fujian provinces is deliberate, with the four special economic zones (SEZs) within them being given special attention where appropriate. In this section and throughout the chapter, infrastructure is broadly defined to include facilities such as roads, railways, ports, airports, water, electricity, and housing. The second section examines the sequencing of infrastructure developments in the Pearl River Delta area, and looks at prospects for future development. The costs of infrastructure development and financing arrangements are analyzed in the third section. In the fourth section, public policies relating to pricing, crowding-out of investment, and environmental concerns are evaluated. The lessons to be learned from past experiences and prospects for future infrastructure development in the region are spelled out in the fifth section, which also discusses the role that bilateral and multilateral institutions can play.

For the purposes of this paper, South China will refer to Guangdong and Fujian provinces of the PRC, while Southern China will refer to these provinces plus Hong Kong and Taipei,China.

SURVEY OF INFRASTRUCTURE DEVELOPMENT

Rapid economic development in Hong Kong and Taipei,China over the past decades has been based to a large measure on heavy but judicious investment in infrastructure. This has enabled these economies to reach their present preeminent positions, with their export-oriented manufacturing and service industries accounting for much of their growth.

Hong Kong

In Hong Kong investments in infrastructure were gradual but consistent during the years after World War II, with the greatest burst of activity occurring in the 1980s after the adoption of an open door policy by the PRC in 1978. In 1963, the PRC was approached about the possibility of supplying water to Hong Kong from the East River (Dong Jiang). This became the first in a series of agreements governing sales of water by Guangdong to help Hong Kong ease its water supply problem. The supply of water from the PRC will increase to 690 million cubic meters in 1995, and to 840 million cubic meters in the year 2000 (Yeung, 1992).

Other milestones in Hong Kong's infrastructure development were the construction of the container terminal at Kwai

Chung port in 1970, the completion of the first cross-harbor tunnel in 1973, the opening of the mass transit subway in 1979, and the electrification and double-tracking of the Kowloon-Canton railway in 1983. However, the first systematic attempt to establish a coherent framework for the development of roads, railways, and ports came with the formulation of the Territorial Development Strategy (TDS) in 1984. The TDS partly addressed the lack of coordination between urban development and transport provision, notably in the towns which developed rapidly in the New Territories in the 1970s. This was followed by the Port and Airport Development Strategy (PADS) in 1988, designed to help the territory meet the projected growth in port and air traffic to the year 2001. Also in 1988, discussions on a "Metroplan" were initiated. The primary objective of the Metroplan was to enhance Hong Kong's role as an international port and airport. Thus the White Paper on Transport Policy in Hong Kong in 1990 called for (i) the replacement of Kai Tak airport with a new airport at Chek Lap Kok on Lantau Island, and (ii) the expansion of port facilities in Tsing Yi, Stonecutters Island, Tuen Mun, and North Lantau (Yeh, 1990; see Figure 1).

Although a memorandum of understanding between the Chinese and British governments was signed in 1991 on PADS, the ten core projects surrounding the new airport have been dogged by controversy, with disputes stemming initially from the rapid escalation of the total cost estimates from HK$98.6 billion in March 1991 to HK$112.2 billion in April 1992 at March 1991 prices. Differences over political reforms have called into question the validity of the contract award for Container Terminal 9, which was commissioned in 1993. Meanwhile, traffic between Hong Kong and South China has been on the rise, with the average daily traffic through the three border crossing points with Shenzhen increasing from 13,450 vehicles in 1990 to 15,900 in 1991. Vehicles carrying goods accounted for 95 per cent of the traffic, reflecting the massive relocation of manufacturing enterprises from Hong Kong (D. Chu, 1992).

Taipei,China

Not unlike Hong Kong, Taipei,China has been investing heavily in infrastructure development to bolster its economic growth. The

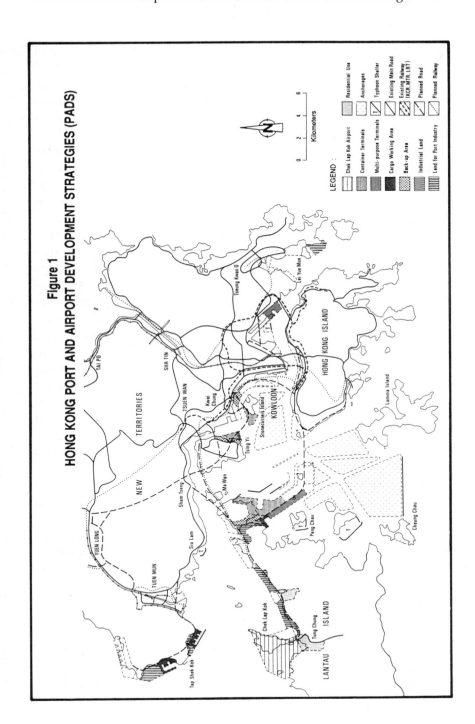

Figure 1
HONG KONG PORT AND AIRPORT DEVELOPMENT STRATEGIES (PADS)

LEGEND :

Chek Lap Kok Airport
Container Terminals
Multi-purpose Terminals
Cargo Working Area
Back-up Area
Industrial Land
Land for Port Industry

Residential Use
Anchorages
Typhoon Shelter
Existing Main Road
Existing Railway (KCR, MTR, LRT)
Planned Road
Planned Railway

most important breakthrough in this respect was the launching of the Ten Major Construction Projects in 1973 at a cost of NT$200 billion. Among the projects were six that focused on infrastructure development: the North-South freeway, Suao harbor, Taichung harbor, the railways electrification project, the Taoyuan International Airport, and the North-Link railway (see Figure 2). These projects contributed greatly to Taipei,China's economic takeoff in a number of ways. For example, the North-South freeway and the railway electrification projects linked the major cities along the west coast of the island, shortened the travel time between the north and the south and accelerated economic and social development in general. The North-Link railway provides the eastern part of the island with improved access to the Taipei metropolitan area, allowing greater population mobility. Taichung harbor facilitates the import and export of materials and products for Taichung's industrial development (Tsai, 1992). At the peak of Taipei,China's economic growth in 1977 and 1978, investment in the Ten Major Construction Projects accounted for 13 and 8 per cent, respectively, of total fixed asset investment (Executive Yuan, 1979). According to some estimates, the annual government expenditure on infrastructure may have been as high as 25 to 30 per cent of total fixed asset investment during the past 30 years (Kao and Lee, 1991). Whatever the actual figure, the Ten Major Construction Projects involved massive government outlays and were a critical factor in bringing Taipei,China out of an international recession and accelerating its economic and social development. This program was followed by the Twelve Major Construction Projects and the Fourteen Major Construction Projects, both of which emphasized infrastructure development.

More ambitious than any of the earlier infrastructure development schemes is Taipei,China's current Six-Year National Development Plan (1991-1996), which involves a total expenditure of $303 billion. It is a comprehensive strategy that seeks simultaneously "to rebuild economic and social order and to promote all-round balanced development." It includes 775 development projects that touch practically all aspects of economic and social life. For the transport sector, the plan provides for the construction of the Taipei Rapid Transit System, a second north-south highway, a high-speed railway along the island's western coast, and additional mass

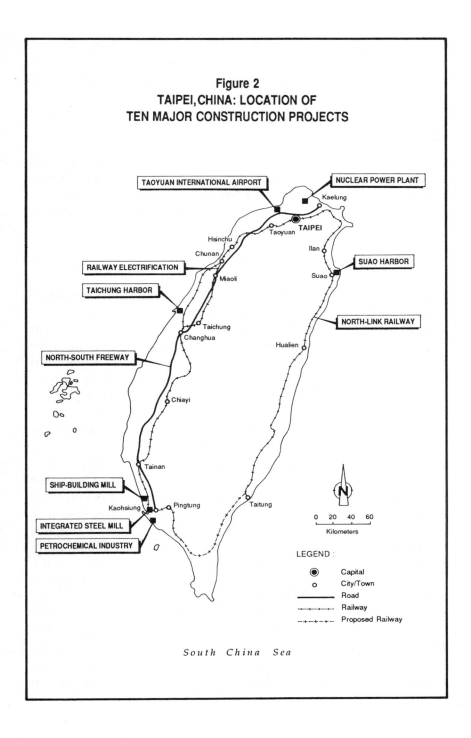

Figure 2
TAIPEI, CHINA: LOCATION OF
TEN MAJOR CONSTRUCTION PROJECTS

transit systems for the major cities of Kaoshiung, Taichung, Tainan, and others. There are also plans to build two additional nuclear plants, telecommunication facilities, and environmental protection projects (*Far Eastern Economic Review*, 15 October 1992).

South China

Guangdong and Fujian provinces have been attempting since 1978 to develop their infrastructure after many years of neglect. Development across sectors since 1978 has been uneven, but the past few years have seen feverish activity as the government has sought to keep pace with rapid economic growth.

Land Transport

In land transport, one of the most pressing needs is the extension of the railway network to unserved areas (see Figure 3). For decades the eastern and western parts of Guangdong have been inaccessible by rail. The national and provincial governments have in recent times tried to rectify this situation. Access to western Guangdong was improved in 1991 with the completion of the San-Mao (Sanshui and Maoming) railway. Double-tracking of the Hengyang-Guangzhou and Guangzhou-Shenzhen railways was also recently completed. The second Beijing-Kowloon railway, a 2,538 km line which will run parallel to the existing line to the east through nine provinces via Tianjin and Jiaojiang, is scheduled for completion in 1995 at a cost of 18 billion yuan (*Ming Pao*, 17 October 1992). However, the network in eastern Guangdong is still fragmented and awaiting the completion of lines to Meizhou and Shantou. At present the two provinces are not linked by rail, but there are plans to make them accessible to each other. Guangdong has agreed to finance the 80.3 km section from Meizhou to the border, while Fujian will construct the 44.2 km section from Longyan to the border as a joint venture between its government and Hong Kong investors at a cost of $55 million (*Ta Kung Pao*, 3 July 1992). The most impressive project is the proposed 280 km per hour bullet train, the first in the PRC, between Fuzhou and Xiamen, with the Itogawa Group from Japan jointly investing $2 billion with the Fujian government. The project, which is targeted for completion

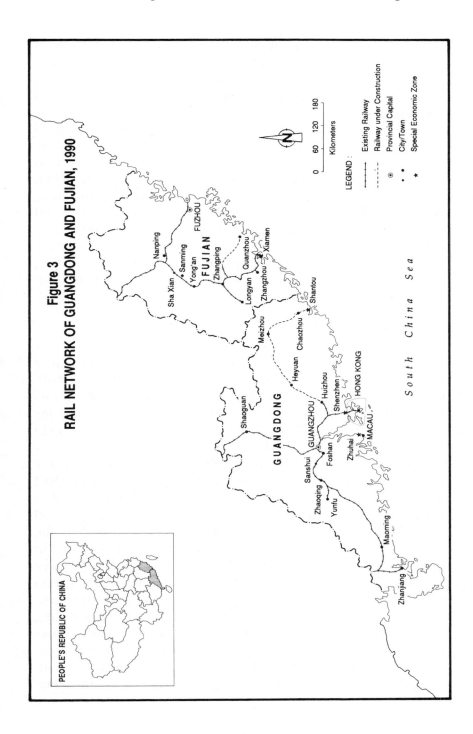

Figure 3
RAIL NETWORK OF GUANGDONG AND FUJIAN, 1990

by 1998, will shorten the journey between Fuzhou and Xiamen from the current six to seven hours by car to slightly over an hour (Chor, 1992).

Since 1978, Guangdong has built 3,100 km of highway and 1,748 highway bridges, bringing the total highway length in the province to 55,307 km in 1991 (see Table 1). At present, almost all towns and 85 per cent of the villages are linked by roads (*China Daily*, 1 December 1992). The road network in the two provinces is shown in Figure 4. The coverage by road is superior to that by rail, and highway construction has continued at a brisk pace. In Fujian, efforts have been made to accelerate the highway network centered around Fuzhou, with eight highways either being planned or now under construction. These are Fuzhou-Fuding, Quanzhou-Xiamen, Fuzhou-Quanzhou, Fuzhou-Minqing-Jianyang, Jianyang-Sanming, Putian-Meizhou Dao, Zhangzhou-Longyan, and Changting-Longyan (*Wah Kiu Yat Po*, 20 September 1992).

Water Transport

The long coastline in both Guangdong and Fujian makes marine transport viable. The presence of many rivers in both provinces also encourages the development of inland water transport (see Figure 5). Since 1978, Guangdong has built 109 berths along its coastal areas, 33 of which can accommodate ships of up to 10,000 deadweight tons (dwt). Its port handling capacity has expanded during that period from 44 million to 78 million tons a year (*China Daily*, 1 December 1992). By the end of 1990, Guangdong had 140 berths capable of accommodating ships of 1,000 dwt, with a total throughput of 0.12 billion tons, or 2.2 times the capacity in 1980 (Yuan, 1992). As Figure 5 indicates, there are more ports along the coast of Guangdong than in Fujian, and three ports–Yantian in Shenzhen, Daya Bay's Oatou port, and Gaolan port in Zhuhai–have been approved by the central authorities for development into large, deepwater container ports (Liu et al, 1992). In contrast, Fuzhou, Xiamen, and other ports in Fujian lack modern handling facilities and do not have regular shipping schedules, as a consequence of which many shippers prefer the more expensive three-day journey from Hong Kong's Kwai Chung port. Even in Guangdong, the major ports of Guangzhou, Zhanjiang, Shenzhen

Table 1. Transport and Telecommunication Indicators in Guangdong Province, 1985-1991

	Unit	1985	1986	1987	1988	1989	1990	1991	Per Cent Change 1990-1991
Operating Railways	Km	1,026	1,027	1,145	1,128	1,149	1,287	1,366	6.1
Highways	Km	51,228	52,785	53,218	53,820	54,361	54,671	55,307	1.2
Navigable Inland Waterways	Km	10,775	10,782	10,785	10,792	10,795	10,857	10,857	0.0
Civil Aviation Routes	Km	53,668	64,059	78,852	81,706	88,180	107,979	123,472	14.3
Ship Berths	Number	1,219	1,243	1,235	1,167	1,293	1,938	2,018	4.1
10,000 Ton Berths	Number	36	34	37	38	49	61	66	8.2
Berth Length	Meters	42,497	42,702	43,893	42,930	50,666	81,605	84,651	3.7
Permanent Road Bridges	Number	9,797	10,113	10,412	10,709	10,851	10,996	11,228	2.1
Civil Motor Vehicles	Number	219,649	244,588	271,763	324,195	366,505	402,086	476,170	18.4
Mechanized Boats	Number			36,405	37,775	42,371	40,473	35,950	-11.2
	Net tons			4,959,470	4,944,417	5,218,409	7,611,980	6,168,202	-19.0
Civil Aviation Aircraft	Number	87	82	74	68	73	73	78	6.8
Post Offices	Number	2,549	2,539	2,534	2,541	2,537	2,573	2,619	1.8
Direct-Dial Long Distance Tel. Lines	Circuits	1,665	2,835	6,645	16,042	19,822	38,030	46,470	22.2
Telephone Lines	10,000 ports	40.0	48.2	66.9	92.7	129.6	180.7	218.7	21.0
Urban Telephone Lines	10,000 ports	19.7	25.2	39.0	58.1	76.8	108.9	128.6	18.1
Telephones	Number	365,792	471,770	655,532	871,224	1,169,033	1,554,259	2,014,435	29.6
Telephones per 100 Persons	Number	0.62	0.78	1.12	1.47	1.94	2.45	3.17	29.4
Long Distance Telephone Circuits	Number	3,346	4,576	6,419	10,211	14,157	20,845	27,220	30.6
Road Passenger Traffic	10,000 persons	38,603	34,742	36,185	37,476	34,633	34,152	36,720	7.5
Road Passenger Volume	100 million person-km	233.85	222.18	255.60	298.79	292.16	301.08	349.89	16.2
Road Freight Traffic	10,000 tons	15,004	15,660	17,287	19,173	19,434	18,792	20,800	10.7
Road Freight Volume	100 million ton-km	1,607.96	1,700.16	1,877.86	1,953.57	2,090.81	2,214.38	2,752.17	24.3
Seaport Cargo	10,000 tons	8,811	9,120	10,332	11,582	11,855	11,904	13,219	11.0
Seaport Passengers	10,000 persons	2,704	2,977	2,953	3,166	2,933	2,686	2,750	2.4
Airport Passengers	10,000 persons	318	435	571	638	546	687	846	23.1
Total Operating Volume of Transport and Communications (at 1990 prices)	100 million yuan	3.63	4.50	6.18	13.46	18.30	26.30	38.89	47.9

Source: Guangdong Statistical Bureau.

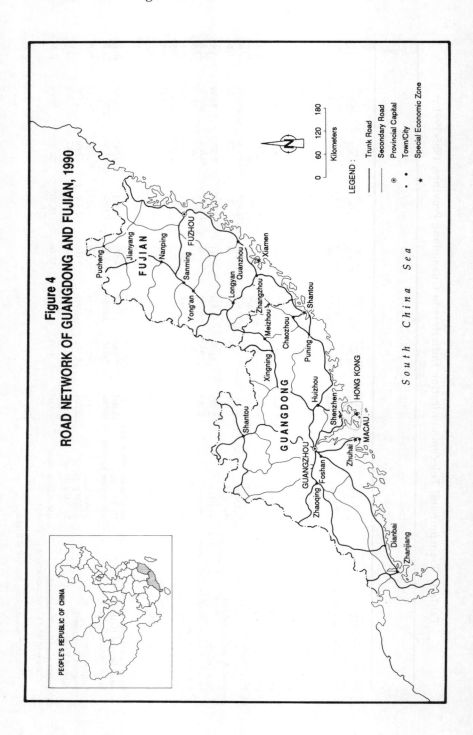

Figure 4
ROAD NETWORK OF GUANGDONG AND FUJIAN, 1990

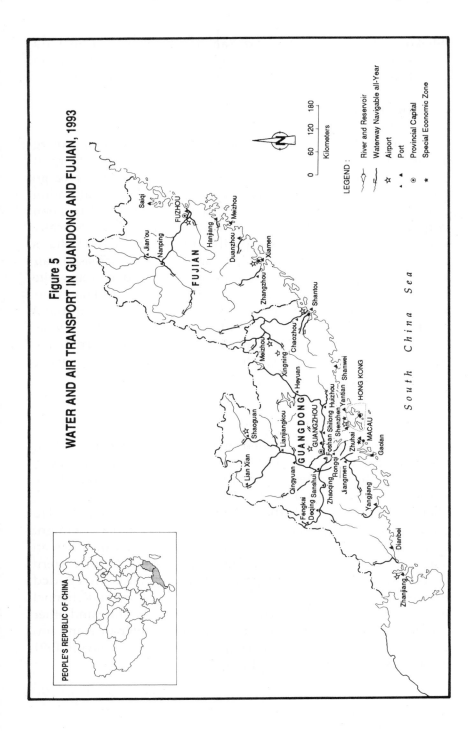

Figure 5

WATER AND AIR TRANSPORT IN GUANDONG AND FUJIAN, 1993

(Shekou, Chiwan, Mawan, and Yantian), Zhuhai, and Shantou were able to handle a total throughput of only 63 million tons in 1990, leaving another 13 million tons unserviced (Yuan, 1992).

Air Transport

Figure 5 also shows the location of major airports in Guangdong and Fujian. Guangzhou's Beiyun Airport is the PRC's third largest based on passenger traffic and the largest based on air cargo handling. With only a single runway, it may reach the saturation point before the end of this century. Shenzhen's large Huangtian Airport, which began operations in 1991, may not be critically needed in the short run, as capacity in the Pearl River Delta is already high. Nonetheless, to cope with the rapid increase in air travel, existing airports are being expanded and modernized, while new ones are being planned or constructed. What is most noteworthy for Guangdong is the explosion of air passenger traffic and civil aviation routes between 1985 and 1991 (see Table 1). In 1991 alone, Guangdong inaugurated six domestic routes and four international routes, in addition to two scheduled chartered routes (*Guangdong Yearbook 1992*).

Water Supply

As South China is situated in a subtropical climatic belt, it normally gets plenty of water from rainfall and rivers. However, there are periodic water supply shortages in the burgeoning large cities on the eastern side of the Pearl River Delta. Guangzhou, Shenzhen, Huiyang, and other cities must plan for the long term to ensure a steady supply of water. It has been suggested that it might be possible to divert water from the West River, which has an annual channel flow of 2,300 billion cubic meters, to the eastern parts of the delta (Cai, 1992). Significant progress has been reported in Guangdong over the past few years in irrigation and channel improvement engineering works, but because of silting and other problems, and despite seemingly incessant maintenance and improvements, the total length of navigable inland waterways in 1991 is still at the 1985 level (see Table 1).

Electricity

Hydroelectric power still constitutes a major source of power for the two provinces. In 1992, of the total power generation capacity in Guangdong of 8,070 MW, some 3,330 MW was accounted for by hydroelectricity from the existing grid. The major power stations were Shajiao A (1,200 MW), Shajiao B (700 MW), Whampoa Addition (300 MW), Shaoguan Addition (200 MW), Conghua Pumped Storage (300 MW), Zhanjiang (600 MW), and Panyu (1,200 MW). Most of these are coal-fired or thermal power stations built with substantial investments from Hong Kong (To, 1992). In December 1992, Hopewell Holdings and other Hong Kong companies concluded a joint venture with a subsidiary of the Guangdong General Power Company to develop three coal-fired generating units of 668 MW each at Shajiao C. Due for completion in 1994, these will boost Guangdong's electricity supply by 13 per cent (Manuel, 1992). Meanwhile, the first nuclear plant at Daya Bay, with a capacity of 1,800 MW, began operation in 1993, while another nuclear plant in Guangdong, the PRC's fifth, will be located in Dongping in Yangchun County, some 230 km southwest of Hong Kong. Construction will begin in 1995 and the plant should start operating in 2000 (Chen, 1992).

Even with these major projects, power shortages are likely to remain a problem in the Pearl River Delta because of the increasing power requirements of the large number of manufacturing plants that have relocated there during the past decade. It is estimated that demand will soon outstrip supply by at least 40 per cent (To, 1992). By 1995, Guangdong's electricity generating capacity is expected to reach 15,000 MW. In Fujian, the authorities have realized the importance of tapping hydro and thermal sources, while preparations are also being made for the building of nuclear plants. In the more remote areas, and particularly in places not covered by the provincial power grid, attempts are being made to generate electricity from nonconventional sources such as wind and tides (Chen, 1991).

Housing

A policy ensuring low-rent worker housing has been in existence in the PRC for decades. Since 1949, the government has viewed housing as a component of state welfare to be provided to all at nominal cost. Rents are in general the equivalent of only slightly more than 1 per cent of the average household income, but prolonged subsidization has led to huge problems of poor maintenance, overconsumption, and limited incentives for home ownership (Chiu, 1992).

The government has of late been encouraging home ownership, particularly since savings realized from the rapid post-1978 economic growth in Guangdong and Fujian can be harnessed for housing development. At the same time, housing projects aimed at Hong Kong and overseas Chinese buyers have mushroomed in the Pearl River Delta. In the first six months of 1992, as many as 12,956 housing units in the delta cities were offered for sale in Hong Kong. The majority of these were in Huiyang, Guangzhou, and Shenzhen (Ka, 1992).

Special Economic Zones

A survey of infrastructure development in South China would be incomplete without noting the status of the special economic zones (SEZs) at Zhuhai, Shenzhen, Shantou, and Xiamen. The four SEZs were designed to spearhead national modernization efforts, and their success was predicated on the provision of adequate infrastructure to attract foreign investment. When the SEZs were established in 1980, the infrastructure was rudimentary; since then many projects have been completed (see Table 2).

DEVELOPMENT OF THE PEARL RIVER DELTA

The Pearl River Delta, which has been a critical part of the rapid economic development in Guangdong, could further boost its rate of growth if its infrastructure were better developed. A total of $1.5 billion was invested there in 1991 by Taipei,China (Goldstein, 1992a). Hong Kong investors have more than 10,000 joint ventures and full subsidiaries in Guangdong. Nearly 60 per cent of Hong Kong's re-exports in 1990 consisted of raw materials or semi-manufactures destined for factories in South China, while 61 per cent of Hong Kong's imports from the PRC came from these factories (Cheng and Taylor, 1991).

Table 2. Infrastructure in Special Economic Zones (SEZs)

	Zhuhai	Shenzhen	Shantou	Xiamen
Seaports	Jinzhou deepwater port opened in 1987.	Total 78 berths in 4 ports: Yantian, Chiwan, Shekou, and Mawan.	7 berths as of 1988.	4 deepwater berths, 1 designed for ontainer traffic.
	Xiangzhou port with 11 berths for fishing and trading.	Two 350 TEU container terminals completed in Shekou.		
Airports	Zhuhai heliport completed in 1983.	Huangtian Airport opened in 1991.	Shantou Airport expanded at 60 million yuan.	Xiamen International Airport opened October 1983.
	New airport being planned in Sanzao Island in western Zhuhai.	Heliport at Nantou providing air service for oil exploration in South China Sea.	8 routes, including 1 international, by 1988.	
Railways		Train service scheduled between Shenzhen and Zhaoqing in 1990. Second Beijing-Kowloon railroad being constructed. Shenzhen West Branch railway linking Shekou container terminal to Guangzhou-Kowloon Railway. Construction began in 1991. Guangzhou-Shenzhen railway. Construction began in 1991.	Guangzhou-Meizhou-Shantou railway to be completed in Eighth Five-Year Plan period.	Electrification of Ying-Xia (Yingtan-Xiamen) under construction.
Roads	373.5 km of roads and 105 bridges constructed by 1988.	302 km Zhuhai-Guangzhou-Shenzhen superhighway to be completed in mid-1990s at a total cost of 3,500 million yuan.	50 km of roads built by 1988. Highway linking Shenzhen and Shantou being constructed.	A new causeway to link Xiamen Island to mainland planned.
Communications	151 telephone lines linking Hong Kong and Macau established by 1988. Linked to 150 countries by IDD.	3,526 long distance telephone lines by 1990.	153,000 telephones in urban area by 1992.	Digitalized telephone exchange introduced and microwave telecommunication system installed.
Electricity	Nanping supply station with 35 KW began operation in 1988.		10 KW power line linking urban district with SEZs built in 1991. 110 KW power station completed in Lunghu in 1985. Thermal power plant approved for construction in 1988.	Thermal power plant approved for construction in 1990.
Water Supply		7 reservoirs with holding capacity of over 1 million m³ in city. New reservoir completed in Kuichong with holding capacity of 952,000 m³.	2 km pipeline linking urban districts with SEZs constructed in 1982. 25.8 km of water pipelines available by 1988.	

Sources: Various publications.

Current Plans

Factories in the delta can no longer operate at full capacity for lack of adequate electricity, roads, railways, and ports. However, in the current Eighth Five-Year Plan (1990-1995), Guangdong plans to invest heavily to alleviate present inadequacies. Of the 39 major construction projects being planned, 13 involve infrastructure development. Five involve energy supply (Shajiao C, Guangzhou Pumped Storage Phase II, Taishan, Zhuhai, and Humen), six involve transport construction (Guangzhou-Meizhou-Shantou railroad; Foshan-Kaiping, Shenzhen-Shantou, and Guangzhou-Shenzhen-Zhuhai highways; a circular highway in Guangzhou; and Yantian port), one will develop telecommunications facilities in Guangzhou, and one will increase water supply from Dong Jiang-Shenzhen to Hong Kong (Zheng and Ni, 1992).

Electricity

As there is still a critical shortage of electricity in the delta, the establishment of many large-scale power stations has attracted Hong Kong investors. Many small-scale generation stations are also being developed, such as in Shenzhen, Dongguan, Humen, Foshan, Shunde, Huizhou, and Nanhai. These will ease the power supply bottleneck, although they will be more costly to operate because of their reliance on oil and their small size (Liu et al, 1992).

Land Transport

To alleviate bottlenecks in land transport, many highway and railway projects have been proposed or are now being implemented (see Figure 6). When completed in 1995, the new Beijing-Kowloon railway will increase traffic and greatly improve north-south rail service. A second new line, the Guang-Zhu railway, will connect Guangzhou with Zhuhai through seven counties and bring a large part of the western part of the delta within reach of rail service. The direct rail service between Foshan and Hong Kong, inaugurated in January 1993, reflects the growing demand in many cities of the delta for more frequent and direct contacts with Hong Kong.

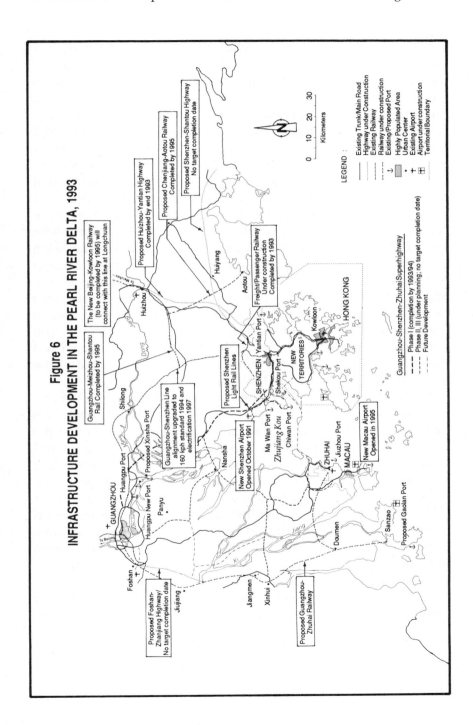

Figure 6

INFRASTRUCTURE DEVELOPMENT IN THE PEARL RIVER DELTA, 1993

Ongoing highway construction plans could reshape the nature of land transport in the delta. The most important of these is the Guangzhou-Shenzhen-Zhuhai superhighway, whose six lanes will link Guangzhou with the two SEZs of Shenzhen and Zhuhai. The first phase, covering 123 km between Guangzhou and Shenzhen, is due for completion in mid-1994 at an estimated cost of $1.2 billion. Dubbed the "spine of the province," the road will reduce travel time between Guangzhou and Shenzhen from the present four hours to only 90 minutes. The contract for the construction of the second phase (146 km linking Guangzhou with Zhuhai) was signed in October 1992, with Hopewell Holdings as one of the seven contracting parties (*Economic Journal*, 26 October 1992; Goldstein, 1992b). The contract also provides for the construction of the 33 km Boca Tigris Bridge, which will span the Pearl River and connect Nansha in Punyu with Humen in Dongguan (see Figure 6). The bridge, which is on one of two routes being envisaged, should also facilitate the delivery of water from the West River to the eastern flank of the delta (Cai, 1992). Along with the superhighways on either flank of the delta, the bridge will dramatically cut the travel time between the two sides of the estuary. The second phase will be implemented at a cost of $1.4 billion.

A car-ferry service was launched in 1991 linking Nansha and Humen. Jointly financed by Henry Fok, Lee Shau-kee of Henderson Land in Hong Kong, and Guangdong Enterprises, it halved the travel time across the delta by bypassing Guangzhou (Taylor and Cheng, 1991). An ambitious project to further improve the link between the two flanks of the estuary has been proposed by Hopewell, which plans to build a bridge-tunnel, one of the longest in the world, to link Zhuhai with Shekou, with a possible extension to the western New Territories in Hong Kong. The travel time between Hong Kong and Macau would be less than an hour along this bridge-tunnel link (Marriage and Chu, 1992). Besides the circular highway around Guangzhou referred to earlier, there are at least seven more major highway construction projects, with two involving links to cities outside the delta in Guangdong (see Tables 3 and 4).

Table 3. Planned Highway Construction Projects in Guangdong, 1992-1998

	Length (km)	Total Cost (million yuan)	Completion Year
1. Yantian - Huizhou	64 (4 lanes)	600	1992
2. Foshan - Sanshui	32 (4 lanes)	4,200	1993
3. Guangzhou - Zhuhai (Eastern lane)	76 (6 lanes)	3,400	1996
4. Foshan - Kai Ping	80 (4 lanes)	1,000	1996
5. Huizhou - Heyuan	67 (2 lanes)	800	1996
6. Guangzhou - Shaoguan	360 (4 lanes)	5,000	1997
7. Shenzhen - Shantou	286 (4 lanes)	3,200	1998

Source: K. Chu (1992).

Table 4. Types of Highways in Guangdong, by Length (km)

	1990	1995 (projected)	2000 (projected)
Superhighways (3 lanes)	23	316	1,300
Class I Highways (2 lanes)	106	1,130	2,500
Class II Highways (1 lane)	1,900	4,600	7,000
Roads	52,571	58,954	65,200
Total	54,600	65,000	76,000

Source: K. Chu (1992).

Ports and Airports

Port facilities in the Pearl River Delta are relatively well developed. There are currently 15 deepwater ports (including both Guangdong and Hong Kong), with another three being planned (Nansha in Punyu, Shatin in Dongguan, and Gaolan in Zhuhai). Every city or county along the coast of the delta nonetheless still aspires to have at least one port, even though the density of container ports in the delta is already the highest in the PRC. Apart from Huangpu port in Guangzhou, ports in Shekou, Chiwan, Zhuhai, and others contribute to the container traffic. Their main function is to feed containers to Hong Kong's Kwai Chung port. In 1990, 281,000 twenty-foot equivalent units (TEUs) were ferried to Hong Kong by riverine vessels and lighters from different ports of the delta. This compares with 805,000 TEUs through Shenzhen border checkpoints to Hong Kong in the same year (Chu, 1991). In 1991, Hong Kong handled 104 million tons of cargo and 6.16 million TEUs, representing two-fold and four-fold increases over the 1979 figure, respectively. Of the total number of containers handled in Hong Kong, approximately one-fourth was handled in midstream (D. Chu, 1992; Yuan, 1992).

As with port facilities, there is a high density of airports in the delta area. Within a 200 square kilometer area, there are eight airports, including the international airports of Hong Kong, Macau, Guangzhou, and Shenzhen, as well as regional airports at Zhuhai, Huizhou, Foshan, and Jiangmen. These airports are relatively close to one another, thus raising questions about duplication and efficiency (Liu et al, 1992).

PRC-Hong Kong Integration

For much of the ongoing and planned infrastructure development in the delta area, the return of Hong Kong to the PRC in 1997 looms large. Hong Kong is already being integrated with the delta area and beyond, both economically and in terms of infrastructure. Every day, an estimated 50,000 Hong Kong residents cross the border to manage factories in South China. The number of Chinese officials and other visitors who travel to Hong Kong for business is increasing rapidly (Cheng and Taylor, 1991). Some 2,700 containers and 11,000 truck cross the Shenzhen-Hong Kong border daily. The authorities are still struggling to cope with the growing traffic between the two territories. The increasing importance of Hong Kong in the delta and in the Asia-Pacific region is reflected in the fact that over the past five years 50 multinational corporations (MNCs) have established their regional headquarters in the crown colony. In 1990 alone, 62 MNCs opened new offices in Hong Kong to penetrate the Chinese and Asian markets (Szeto, 1992).

FINANCING INFRASTRUCTURE DEVELOPMENT

Hong Kong and Taipei,China

One of the key requirements for the success of infrastructure development is access to adequate capital to finance projects. Both Hong Kong and Taipei,China have generously funded their infrastructure development programs over the years, and their present systems of infrastructure provision are very sound. Looking toward the future, Hong Kong has the ambitious PADS that will make it ready for the 21st century. Financing of the far-reaching PADS (and especially the new airport at Chek Lap Kok) from local and international capital markets would not have been a problem had the British and Chinese governments not been mired in diplomatic problems stemming from the political reform proposals of Governor Patten in October 1992. Even before the political impasse, the Hong Kong government had made a commitment to spend HK$78 billion on capital projects over the 1992-1997 period, exclusive of the airport core projects. This represents a 42 per cent increase (HK$23 billion) over the expenditure for the previous five-year period (Wong, 1992).

In Taipei,China, attention has focused on the huge sums programmed for the Six-Year National Development Plan (1991-1996). The exact scope and justification for parts of the plan is still being debated, but with foreign exchange reserves of $90 billion, the country definitely has the means to raise funds through loans, bonds, and other channels (*Far Eastern Economic Review*, 15 October 1992). But problems of allocative inefficiency and cost overruns have been identified by Cai (1991), who pointed out that even in the

Ten Major Construction Projects of the 1970s cost overruns had been a major problem. Of the six projects on transport infrastructure, four incurred costs of more than twice the original budgeted figures, and the North-South freeway cost 51 per cent more. Only the expenditure for Taichung Harbor was close to the original cost estimate.

South China

Infrastructure development needs in South China are enormous, and dependence on foreign capital to finance these plans will be great. To put the problem in perspective, Guangdong spent 1.5 times as much on fixed asset investments in the Seventh Five-Year Plan (1986-1990) as it did in the Sixth Five-Year Plan (1981-1985) (*Guangdong Yearbook*, 1991). In the Eighth Five-Year Plan (1991-1996), an estimated 20-30 billion yuan will be required for transport, raw materials, and technical upgrading (Taylor and Cheng, 1991). For the next 20 years, Guangdong will need $190 billion in foreign investment for its infrastructure projects and high-technology industries (Zheng, 1992). The capital requirements for infrastructure development in South China are thus escalating, and as the PRC moves more toward a market economy, it should diversify its sources of finance.

At the beginning of the open-door policy period, Guangdong and Fujian were equally dependent on government funds for infrastructure development. During the next ten years, as economic growth in the two provinces accelerated, other sources of funding became relatively much more important. Since 1985 self-financing in infrastructure has been the most important financing modality. Nonetheless, the amount of foreign capital for infrastructure development has continuously increased (see Table 5).

Local Investment

Government funding for large-scale infrastructure projects has traditionally been determined at the central and provincial levels, where competing demands are weighed against one another and decisions are not always made strictly on the basis of a project's

**Table 5. Financing Modalities for Infrastructure Development
in Guangdong and Fujian**
(per cent)

	1980		1985		1990	
	Guangdong	Fujian	Guangdong	Fujian	Guangdong	Fujian
Government Funds	48.6	52.2	13.6	29.3	6.4	18.9
Domestic Loans	10.9	11.5	22.2	31.7	16.7	19.0
Self-Financing	34.3	35.7	38.6	33.1	33.9	41.8
Foreign Capital	6.2	0.6	15.7	1.5	21.4	10.7
Other Sources	0.0	0.0	9.9	4.4	21.6	9.6

Sources: *Statistical Yearbook of Guangdong 1992; Statistical Yearbook of Fujian 1992.*

own merits. Consequently, an attitudinal change has come about at
the local level. Local governments have adopted a strategy of self-
reliance, following the dictum "using road to sustain road, using
port to sustain port, and using bridge to sustain bridge." Under this
strategy, funds are raised locally and user charges are utilized to
recoup initial investments. Many of the roads and bridges in the
Pearl River Delta were constructed and paid for in this way.

In the mid-1980s, local governments showed creativity in
meeting their transport, energy, and telecommunications needs.
However, this would not have been possible without the devolu-
tion of decision making to their level. For example, Shunde has
since 1980 invested 1.35 billion yuan in transport, telecommunications, and other infrastructure development, so that it now has its
own electricity generation station of 130 MW, a container port at
Rongqi, and many bridges and roads (Guo and Chen, 1992). Another good example of local initiative is provided by Dongguan,
which made significant infrastructure improvements on large tracts
of land in this manner. Similar local initiatives have been encouraged in Fujian, as substantial Hong Kong interests have invested in
Meizhou Bay and Fuzhou. In Fuzhou, the Lippo Group has set up
a HK$1 billion joint investment company with the city government
to work on infrastructure development. As far as cooperative

ventures are concerned, two modalities are usually considered: build-operate-transfer (BOT) and build-operate-own (BOO) (Tyson, 1992).

Foreign Investment

For large-scale projects, more conventional sources of funding from overseas are needed. Thus, multilateral agencies such as the World Bank and the Asian Development Bank (ADB) have been approached for various projects. The World Bank, for instance, funded several projects in Guangdong and Fujian, including the Foshan-Kaiping and Shenzhen-Shantou highways, for $200 million (*Wah Kiu Yat Po*, 17 September 1992), and the Xiamen-Quanzhou highway, for 100 million yuan (*Wen Wei Po*, 30 May 1992). The ADB has lent $200 million for the construction of the Changping-Shantou single-track railroad (*Wen Wei Po*, 26 June 1992). Likewise, ADB has financed the second phase of the Conghua Pumped Storage Power Station (*Wen Wei Po*, 27 February 1992). Soft loans, which are preferred by the Chinese government and by end users, and other foreign investments are estimated to meet up to one-third of the financial needs of infrastructure development in Guangdong in the Eighth Five-Year Plan period. Noteworthy, too, is the fact that almost half of the $12 billion which the World Bank has lent to the PRC has been spent on roads, highways, and power plants (*Far Eastern Economic Review*, 12 November 1992).

Bonds constitute another vehicle for raising funds. This can be done through the local banking system, as has been reported by Taylor and Cheng (1991). Money can also be raised through overseas bonds. For instance, Guangdong International Trust and Investment Corporation was reported to have floated 15 billion yen worth of bonds in Japan (Zheng, 1992). Since 1986, Guangzhou has issued $343 million in infrastructure-related bonds in the financial markets of Hong Kong, Tokyo, and London.

Another more direct way of raising funds overseas is simply by setting up new banks or by purchasing existing ones. Guangdong Development Bank, a local provincial bank, negotiated with several nongovernmental financial institutions in Taipei,China for the purchase of a bank in Hong Kong (Zheng, 1992). Many Chinese banks are already operating successfully in Hong Kong, and local provincial banks could also gain access to the thriving Hong Kong financial market.

Yet another source of foreign funding is bilateral aid from countries such as Japan, France, and Germany. The Conghua Pumped Storage Power Station, the first of its kind in the country, is now being built at a cost of $450 million, of which $200 million has been lent by the French government. French firms are also involved in the construction of the Daya Bay nuclear plant.

Western commercial banks, on the other hand, are reported to have avoided lending for infrastructure development because of the PRC's poor legal climate and the perceived long-term risk of investing in large-scale projects. For example, Hopewell Holdings faced considerable difficulty in raising $800 million for the first phase of the Guangdong-Shenzhen-Zhuhai superhighway, ultimately tapping the resources of 29 international banks. Viewed from the perspective of the overall development of Guangdong, foreign investment has thus far been inadequate. In the period 1979-1990, Guangdong had 501 infrastructure projects involving foreign investment, with infrastructure ranking fifth in attracting such investment after industry, agriculture, real estate, and commerce (Zheng and Ni, 1992).

Resources of overseas Chinese have also emerged as an important source of capital, particularly in Guangdong, where Hong Kong investors such as Gordon Wu of Hopewell Holdings, Cheng Yu-tung, Lee Shau-kee, Li Ka-shing, Henry Fok, the S. K. Pao family, and others have invested heavily in infrastructure and related projects.

Outstanding Needs

More highways are needed, as by one estimate more than 1,600 towns in Guangdong are still not accessible to motor vehicles. Highway construction projects invariably need intricate financing packages. Construction of the seven highway projects emanating from Guangzhou require an estimated 19 billion yuan (K. Chu, 1992; see Table 3). In addition, six other high-speed highways, i.e., Shanwei-Shantou, Shantou-Raoping (Huanggong), Guangzhou-Hai'an, Qingyuan-Shaoguan, Guangzhou-Huizhou, and Guangzhou-Huaxian-Qingyuan, totalling 1,104 km, are to be built mainly with foreign investment. This investment is to be attracted by favorable terms, including the right to operate a highway for 30 years, with the profits in the first ten years accruing to the investor. The profits in the following ten years would go to the investor and the local government at a 60:40 ratio; for the last ten years, the ratio would be 30:70 (*Wah Kiu Yat Po*, 17 September 1992).

The four SEZs in South China were able to greatly improve their infrastructure within a relatively short period through self-financing and the use of foreign capital. When the SEZs were just starting up, the government allocated only limited funds for infrastructure development; this appropriation has shrunk progressively over the years. The pattern of financing for infrastructure development in the SEZs differed from that of the larger administrative areas where they are located (see Table 6). Sustained infrastructure development over the past 14 years in these relatively small areas has, however, yielded impressive results.

POLICY CONCERNS

Since 1978, but especially since 1990, there has been significant progress in infrastructure development in South China. The demand for infrastructure far outstrips supply, however, raising numerous questions about the formulation of policy.

Planning Coordination

While local governments have been lauded for taking the initiative for infrastructure improvement, there is a serious problem of duplication of work resulting from lack of coordination. Every local government essentially plans for itself, yet provincial governments lack the mechanisms to coordinate local efforts. This problem manifests itself in duplications such as the simultaneous construction of deepwater container ports in Shenzhen (two ports), Zhuhai, and Daya Bay. It would be more efficient to have one large container port to complement Hong Kong's Kwai Chung port, rather than four facilities within a relatively small area. Not surprisingly, the port projects have attracted less foreign investment than power plants, highways, railways, and telecommunications. This also highlights the sensitivity of foreign interests to the long-term eco-

Table 6. Financing Modalities for Infrastructure Development in Special Economic Zones (SEZs)
(per cent)

	1981				1985				1988			
	Zhuhai	Shenzhen	Shantou	Xiamen	Zhuhai	Shenzhen	Shantou	Xiamen	Zhuhai	Shenzhen	Shantou	Xiamen
Government Funds	10.7	8.4	0.0	64.1	1.6	1.6	0.0	6.3	4.5	0.8	2.7	14.8
Domestic Funds	22.9	11.7	0.0	–	27.6	20.4	–	–	26.8	16.2	–	25.3
Self-Financing	5.9	17.5	100.0	29.6	41.9	45.8	30.2	20.5	47.0	42.2	35.9	25.3
Foreign Capital	7.5	50.0	0.0	–	26.2	13.1	11.7	–	16.7	15.0	32.6	6.7
Other Sources	0.0	12.4	0.0	6.3	2.7	18.1	58.1[a]	73.2	5.0	25.9	28.8[a]	27.9

[a] Bank loans.

Note: Data for Zhuhai refer to the entire city and those for the other SEZs pertain to the special territorial units.

Sources: Statistical yearbooks for the SEZs, various years.

nomic prospects of different infrastructure subsectors (Liu et al, 1992).

There is also a glut in airports, with Shenzhen's Huangtian airport now operational and new airports being constructed in Hong Kong, Zhuhai, and Macau. The recently-released Twenty-Year Socioeconomic Development Profile of Guangdong indicates that the largest international airport in South China will be situated in Guangzhou, with airports in Zhuhai, Shenzhen, and other areas taking secondary roles (*Wah Kiu Yat Po*, 2 February 1993).

Environmental Impact

As noted in the previous section, two of the present bottlenecks in South China's infrastructure development, land transport and power supply, have attracted considerable foreign interest and investment. It is doubtful whether due consideration has been given to environmental concerns, however. In Guangdong, congestion on the railroads is very serious, with loaded railway cars queuing up to hundreds of miles to enter Guangzhou, from as far away as Hunan province (*Wen Wei Po*, 8 June 1992). Such congestion leads to higher production costs and forces shippers to use other means of transport. Increased land transport also causes environmental degradation and puts pressure on limited energy reserves.

In a similar vein, Cai (1992) emphasizes that, because of the rush to meet power demands, there is now an unusually large concentration of electric power generating stations in the Pearl River Delta. On two sides of Humen in Dongguan there are five large-scale, coal-fired stations and one oil-fired station, with total capacity of 6,000 MW. The Daya Bay nuclear plant, which began operation in 1993, will bolster this capacity. Hong Kong's power stations, with a capacity of 5,000 MW, are also located on the eastern flank of the delta, giving a combined power generation capacity of 13,000 MW. The large number of power stations and their geographical concentration has raised concerns about air pollution, acid rain, and the risk of environmental disasters in densely populated areas.

Competition for Resources

Infrastructure development has to compete for funding with other key economic sectors such as agriculture, industry, and state enterprises in need of restructuring. Crowding out of investment does not seem to pose a serious problem, however, as Guangdong and Fujian have been lessening their dependence on government funds for infrastructure development, as previously noted (see Table 5). Nor are other sectors within the two provinces adversely affected by infrastructure projects. At the national level, South China with its SEZs has traditionally not received heavy investments from the central government. Thus, there is no question of other provinces being adversely affected by infrastructure development in South China.

Other Concerns

The general policy concerns pertaining to infrastructure development in the delta area, and which are also applicable to South China as a whole, have been summarized well by Pryor (1991):

> Development within the Special Economic Zones has generally been well planned but elsewhere in the Delta much new development has been opportunistic and, at best, loosely coordinated. This has led to difficulties in upgrading transport networks, in the control of pollution and in the provision of utility services, especially power supplies.... Within the Delta area itself it would seem that the principal needs in the medium term will be the expansion of power supplies, the extension and upgrading of road networks and cross border links, the expansion of feeder port and domestic air service facilities, the rationalization of urban development patterns and the wider implementation of environmental protection measures.

Pricing and subsidizing infrastructure projects must be viewed within the context of broader economic reforms and policies related to those reforms. By and large, it may be observed that with price liberalization and the gradual development of free markets, explicit subsidization of infrastructure services has been declining. This is especially true of many of the local initiatives where repayment is contingent on the use of user charges, as well as of projects depending on foreign investment. Pricing questions are more complicated because, on the one hand, the costs of raw materials and other inputs are rising faster than returns on infrastructure projects, and, on the other, prices cannot be raised drastically without general and fundamental price reforms in the Chinese economy.

CONCLUSIONS

The experience in infrastructure development in the Southern China Growth Triangle can yield important lessons not only for the economies concerned but also for other nations wishing to engage in cross-border collaborative productive enterprises. Hong Kong and Taipei,China have shown wisdom and foresight in their massive investment in infrastructure development, which has in turn enabled their economies to take advantage of new opportunities as the world economy has moved toward greater integration. Infrastructure development enabled both places to attain their preeminent status as transport, communication, manufacturing, and service centers in the region. Their experiences also provide a good example of effective partnership between the government and the private sector.

In South China, infrastructure investments were neglected until recently. In 1982 in Guangdong, for example, modern highways were only a very minor part of the total road network. It was only recently that plans were drawn up for road development to 2010, when it is projected that there will be over 90,000 km of highways, of which 2,800 km will be superhighways, 5,000 km Class I and Class II highways, and 83,000 km roads (*China Cityscape*, 21 June 1992).

Annually, the Chinese government provides only 6 million yuan to Guangdong for transport infrastructure development. This is a pittance considering that it costs 2,000 yuan to build a one-meter portion of a bridge and 200,000 yuan to build one kilometer of roadway. It is therefore impressive that in the period 1981-1990,

Guangdong built more than 1,200 bridges, a rate of construction that was unimaginable during the earlier command economy period. This may be attributed partly to the efficacy of devolving decision making to the local level, and partly to savings from the agriculture sector, which have proved to be an important source of funds for investment not only for infrastructure but also for schools, hospitals, and housing (Cheng and Taylor, 1991).

Another important lesson from Guangdong relates to the potential for infrastructure development to help reduce sectoral or geographical income imbalances. As the province's coastal areas attained a measure of success in economic development, efforts were directed toward helping poorer mountainous areas, effecting, in essence, a redistribution of wealth. The 49 mountain counties, which account for 65 per cent of Guangdong's land area and 40 per cent of its population, saw an increase in agricultural output from 8.9 billion yuan in 1980 to 44.9 billion yuan in 1990. In 1991, coastal cities and counties assisted the mountainous areas in 318 projects, with capital investment of almost 200 million yuan. This was accompanied by a transfer of technology.

The foregoing analysis of infrastructure development in the Pearl River Delta and beyond has highlighted the problem of lack of coordination in certain key sectors. While this problem always existed among cities and counties within the delta area, the need for coordinated infrastructure development has of late assumed greater importance because Hong Kong and Macau will revert to Chinese rule in 1997 and 1999, respectively. There have been various proposals on how to better coordinate infrastructure development across the territories by forming expert groups, joint management structures, and joint investment companies (*Wen Wei Po*, 16 March 1990). To complement each other's strengths and weaknesses, there is a wide scope for cooperation not only among the governments, but also among private enterprises and nongovernmental organizations (Lei and Chen, 1990). Cooperation is not uncomplicated, however, particularly given the different political systems and administrative cultures that prevail in the territories. The challenge of collaboration is further compounded by recent political controversies.

On the whole, infrastructure development in South China still lags behind overall economic development. Infrastructure standards are uneven, but they are constantly being improved. Infrastructure development presents opportunities for foreign investors as well as local entrepreneurs. The main goal in the 1990s will be the systematic development of large-scale projects to take infrastructure development to a higher level, with wider networks, more modern facilities, and increased scope for international trade and cooperation.

One conclusion that can be drawn from the foregoing analysis is that bilateral and multilateral foreign assistance and investment is obviously necessary in Guangdong and Fujian provinces. Development at the national and provincial levels has many competing demands, and infrastructure development using government funds in the two provinces must necessarily be accorded a low priority. Local initiatives are therefore important, but there is a limit to what local resources can finance and build.

International assistance is needed for a wide range of highway, railway, port, airport, and telecommunications projects in Guangdong and Fujian. Already, the World Bank and the ADB are providing loans for a number of projects, but more needs to be done. Foreign assistance is particularly critical for projects such as power stations and nuclear plants, which must take account of the environmental concerns of neighboring territories and the Asia-Pacific region at large. Since environmental concerns are not yet high on the agenda of planners in the PRC, bilateral and multilateral donors might include environmental conditions with the assistance they render.

Priorities also need to be established within the PRC regarding the development needs of South China in relation to those of other provinces; further, infrastructure projects must be weighed against projects in other sectors. Even within South China, and in the Pearl River Delta especially, external assistance might prompt the local authorities to evaluate their infrastructure needs in a more rational and holistic manner. Individual cities and local authorities should be dissuaded from their present practice of planning within narrow territorial perspectives, with decisions driven by concerns about prestige rather than the economic viability of projects. External assistance can provide the impetus for large projects to be better coordinated and harmonized.

Endnotes:

1.   Director, Hong Kong Institute of Asia-Pacific Studies and Professor of Geography, The Chinese University of Hong Kong.
2.   Thanks are due to Professor Lei Qiang and Hu Xiaoliang for providing reference materials on South China, and to Irene Lai and Fung Lok-sang for research assistance in the preparation of this paper. All the maps in the original paper were drawn by Too See-lou.

Bibliography

Cai, Jiayuan, "Evaluation of the Administrative Implementation Ability in Promoting the Six-Year National Development Plan," in *Proceedings of the Seminar on Evaluating the Six-Year National Development Plan* (in Chinese), Vol. II (1991), pp. 74-81.

Cai, Renqun, "On Some Projects of Infrastructure Construction in the Zhujiang Delta," in *Tropical Geography* (in Chinese), Vol. 12, No. 3 (1992), pp. 214-20.

Chen, Jiayuan, ed. *Economic Geography of Fujian* (in Chinese). Beijing: New China Press, 1991.

Chen, Kent, "Go-ahead for New Nuclear Power Plant," in *South China Morning Post*, 18 July 1992.

Cheng, Elizabeth and Michael Taylor, "Delta Force: Pearl River Cities in Partnership with Hong Kong," in *Far Eastern Economic Review*, 16 May 1991, pp. 64-67.

China Daily, "Guangdong Builds Infrastructure," 1 December 1992.

Chiu, Rebecca, "Trends of Public Housing Development in Asia: The Cases of Singapore, Hong Kong and China," paper presented at the Conference on Hong Kong Public Administration in Transition, Hong Kong, 10-12 December 1992.

Chor, Yan, "Fujian's Bullet Train Dream," in *Wide Angle Monthly* (in Chinese), October 1992, pp. 86-89.

Chu, David K.Y., "Containerization of Hong Kong and Pearl River Delta-Opportunities and Constraints," paper presented at the Transportation and Urban Development in Pacific Rim Conference, Vancouver, 6-10 October 1991.

_____ , "Transportation," in Joseph Y.S. Cheng and Paul C.K. Kwong, eds., *The Other Hong Kong Report*. Hong Kong: Chinese University Press, 1992.

Chu, Kennis, "Guangdong in Cash Call for Road Network Projects," in *South China Morning Post*, 27 December 1992.

Executive Yuan, Council for Economic Planning and Development. *Evaluation of the Ten Major Construction Projects*. Taipei, 1979.

Far Eastern Economic Review, "Aims are High, Funds are Low," 12 November 1992, pp. 44-46.

Far Eastern Economic Review, "Big-budget Spending on Infrastructure," 15 October 1992, pp. 41-42.

Fujian Statistical Bureau. *Statistical Yearbook of Fujian 1992*. Yichun: Chinese Statistical Publishing Co, 1992.

Goldstein, Carl, "It's All Go in the South," in *Far Eastern Economic Review*, 12 November 1992a, p. 47.

_____ , "Skirting the Potholes: Hopewell Wins Chinese Vote of Confidence," in *Far Eastern Economic Review*, 3 December 1992b, pp. 62-63.

Guo, Zuoyi, and Chen Jianhua, "Local Government-led Economy," in *Asia-Pacific Economic News* (in Chinese), 12 July 1992.

Guangdong Yearbook 1991 (in Chinese). Guangzhou, 1992.

Guangdong Statistical Bureau. *Statistical Yearbook of Guangdong 1992*. Yichun: Chinese Statistical Publishing Co., 1992.

Ka, Yu, "Competing for `Sphere of Influence' by Hong Kong Entrepreneurs in China," in *Contemporary Monthly* (in Chinese), 15 September 1992, pp. 70-71.

Kao, Charles, and Joseph S. Lee. *The Taiwan Experience: 1949-1989* (in Chinese). Taipei: Commonwealth Publishing Co., 1991.

Lei, Qiang, and Chen Li, "Strengthening the Cooperative Development of Infrastructure Provisions in Guangdong, Hong Kong and Macau," in *Hong Kong and Macao Economic Digest*, No. 5 (1990), pp. 9-12.

Liu, Pak-wai, Wong Yue-chim, Sung Yun-wing, and Lau Pui-king, "China's Economic Reform and Development Strategy of Pearl River Delta," a research report by Nanyang Commercial Bank Ltd., 1992.

Manuel, Gren, "US$750 Power Deal for Hopewell," in *South China Morning Post*, 19 December 1992.

Marriage, Paul, and Kennis Chu, "Wu Plans to Transform Pearl Delta," in *South China Morning Post*, 28 June 1992.

Pryor, E.G., "The Role of Hong Kong's Infrastructural Development in the Modernization of Southern China with Particular Reference to the Pearl River Delta," in *Planning and Development*, Vol. 7, No. 1 (1991), pp. 2-10.

Szeto, Wai-fun, "New Blueprint of Cooperation Between Hong Kong and Guangdong," in *Wide Angle Monthly*, March 1992, pp. 54-57.

Tan, Yangbo and Yang Haim, "The Past and Future of Guangdong's Open Policy," in *Asia-Pacific Economic News* (in Chinese), 29 March 1992.

Taylor, Michael, and Elizabeth Cheng, "The Way Ahead: Guangdong Plan Puts Emphasis on Transport Links," in *Far Eastern Economic Review*, 16 May 1991, p. 68.

To, Eva, "Dreams of Power," in *South China Morning Post*, 8 March 1992.

Tsai, H.H., "Globalization and the Urban System in Taiwan," paper presented at the Workshop on The Asian Pacific Urban System: Towards the 21st Century, Hong Kong, 11-13 February 1992.

Tyson, Laura, "Lippo and Fuzhou in $1b Deal," in *South China Morning Post*, 25 November 1992.

Wong, Fanny, "Government Commits $78b for Capital Works Projects," in *South China Morning Post*, 17 November 1992.

Wu, Yu-wan (ed.). *Economic Geography of Guangdong* (in Chinese). Beijing: New China Press, 1986.

Yeh, Anthony G. O., "Urban Development of Hong Kong in the 21st Century: Opportunities and Challenges," paper presented at the Commonwealth Geographical Bureau Workshop on Geography and Development in Pacific Asia, Hong Kong, 10-14 December 1990.

Yeung, Yue-man, "China and Hong Kong," in Richard Stren, Rodney White and Joseph Whitney, eds., *Sustainable Cities: Urbanization and the Environment in International Perspectives*. Boulder: Westview Press, 1992.

Yi, Zuoyi, and Chen Jianhua, "Local Government-led Economy," in *Asia-Pacific Economic News* (in Chinese), 12 July 1992.

Yuan, Geng, "The Transport Relation Between Hong Kong and the South China Region in the 1990s Revisited," in *Economic Reporter* (in Chinese), 30 March 1992, pp. 5-9.

Zheng, Caixiong, "Guangdong Determined to be Asia's Next Dragon," in *China Daily*, 18 July 1992.

Zheng, Tianxiang, and Ni Xiyuan, "Large-scale Infrastructure Projects in Guangdong, Hong Kong and Macau in the 1990s," unpublished research report (in Chinese). Zhongshan University, 1992.

Expansion of the Southern China Growth Triangle

■ Wang Jun[1]

INTRODUCTION

Since 1980, the Southern China Growth Triangle, consisting of Hong Kong, Macau, Taipei,China, and South China (Guangdong and Fujian provinces), has gradually evolved to attain prominence in the Asia-Pacific region. The complementarities among the members have formed a solid basis for subregional economic cooperation. Such cooperation has not only provided an impetus for the economic development and structural transformation of South China, especially the Pearl River Delta area of Guangdong (Yasukuni, 1991), but it has also accelerated structural adjustment in Hong Kong and Taipei,China (Lin, 1992).

Economic cooperation between Hong Kong and Guangdong (particularly the Pearl River Delta) is closer and older than that between other participants in the growth triangle. This cooperation began when Hong Kong invested in Guangdong's special economic zones (SEZs), mainly in labor-intensive export-oriented manufacturing industries. As the Pearl River Delta gradually opened up to the outside world, foreign investments flowed heavily into the area. With the rapid economic development in the delta, labor and overall production costs there began to rise, while investments in northern part of Guangdong and in other provinces (e.g., Fujian, Guangxi, and Hainan) significantly increased.

This paper attempts to analyze the process of expansion of the Southern China Growth Triangle, especially with respect to economic cooperation between Hong Kong and the Pearl River Delta.

It also attempts to examine the expansion of economic cooperation to other areas in South China, and looks into possible developments in the future. The paper is organized into three main sections. The first section examines the foundations of economic cooperation in Southern China. The second section describes the different types of economic cooperation that have resulted. The final section examines public policies and the reasons for the expansion of the growth triangle area.

EVOLUTION OF ECONOMIC COOPERATION IN SOUTHERN CHINA

"Tiers" of the Growth Triangle

Currently, the Southern China Growth Triangle includes five economic regions: Hong Kong; Taipei,China; Macau; the Pearl River Delta area of Guangdong province; and a part of Fujian province of the People's Republic of China (PRC). One may divide the area into three economic "tiers" based on per capita GDP (see Table 1).

The first tier includes Hong Kong, Macau, and Taipei,China, with an average per capita GDP of $8,950 in 1990. The second tier is made up of the special economic zones (SEZs), with an average per capita GDP of $1,508. The third tier is made up of the Pearl River Delta (excluding the Shenzhen and Zhuhai SEZs), with an average per capita GDP of $889.

Foundations for Cooperation

The people in the growth triangle share a common heritage of culture and language. More than 90 per cent of the Hong Kong population can trace its origins to Guangdong, while about 85 per cent of the population of Taipei,China is originally from Fujian and Guangdong. This, along with geographical proximity and economic complementarity, have provided a solid foundation for economic cooperation. Guangdong and Fujian provinces can offer a large pool of cheap labor and large tracts of land, but suffer shortages in capital, technology, and management and marketing skills.

Table 1. Major Economic Indicators, 1990

	Population (million)	Land (sq km)	GDP ($ million)	Per Capita GDP ($)	Population Density (per sq km)
Hong Kong	5.8	1,071	71,260	12,389	5,371
Taipei,China	20.4	36,000	162,740	7,997	565
Macau	0.5	17	3,710	8,100	26,941
SEZs	2.0	636	3,366	1,508	3,165
Shenzhen	1.0	328	2,162	2,143	3,081
Zhuhai	0.5	121	674	1,357	4,105
Shantou	0.1	56	102	1,202	1,511
Xiamen	0.4	131	428	1,011	3,234
Pearl River Delta[a]	18.0	36,015	16,022	889	501
Guangzhou	6.3	7,435	7,260	1,153	847
Zhongshan	1.2	1,683	1,007	814	735
Dongguan	1.7	2,465	1,838	1,055	706
Jiangmen	3.5	9,418	1,985	566	368
Huizhou	2.3	11,200	1,063	464	205
Fuoshan	3.0	3,814	2,896	965	787
Total	46.6	73,735	257,099	5,516	632

Note: GDP is calculated at the exchange rate of $1=4.7 yuan.
[a] Excluding Shenzhen and Zhuhai.
Sources: Statistical Yearbook of Guangdong (1991); Statistical Data of "Four Dragons" (1980-1990).

The labor-intensive light manufacturing industries which supported Taipei,China's high-growth economy for more than 20 years have started to move off the island because of high land and labor costs and an appreciating currency. It is only by gaining access to low-cost land and labor that these industries have been able to maintain their international competitiveness.

As for Hong Kong, its further growth has been constrained by the tight supply of labor and land, which has driven up the production costs of many of its industries. To reduce these costs, production facilities have been relocated to low-cost areas.

The decision of the People's Republic of China (PRC) to open up to the outside world, along with other reforms it enacted to

establish a market-oriented economy, was critical to the establishment of the growth triangle. Since 1979, when special rights and
privileges were granted to Guangdong and Fujian to encourage
foreign trade and investment, these provinces have become attractive low-cost production bases for manufacturing concerns from
Hong Kong and Taipei,China (see Table 2). Of the four SEZs
initially set up, three (Shantou, Shenzhen, and Zhuhai) were located in Guangdong and one (Xiamen) was located in Fujian.

Extent of Economic Cooperation

The growth triangle has expanded from the SEZs to the Pearl River
Delta area because (i) the numerous municipalities, counties, towns,
and villages in the delta have themselves attracted large amounts of
foreign investment; and (ii) companies already set up in the SEZ have
transferred many of their labor-intensive activities to the delta area.

The Pearl River Delta area has absorbed much of the foreign
investment in the PRC. Table 2 shows the amount of FDI in the delta,
with the exception of Shenzhen and Zhuhai. The share of investment has been accelerating in the Pearl River Delta since the mid-
1980s, while the relative share of investment going to the SEZs has
been declining gradually. There are several reasons for this.

**Table 2. Foreign Investment in the Pearl River Delta Area,
Selected Years**
($ million)

	1980	1986	1987	1988	1989	1990	1991
Guangzhou	30.1	179.7	85.8	255.2	298.5	267.4	377.4
Zhongshan	8.8	14.4	36.3	28.2	41.2	54.5	102.7
Dongguan	9.3	18.8	30.5	66.9	88.6	101.8	148.6
Jiangmen	4.2	45.1	76.8	102.6	96.5	78.6	127.7
Huizhou	0.5	18.1	32.6	52.1	78.9	157.1	152.1
Fuoshan	5.7	81.5	72.9	198.3	189.4	223.1	226.3
Total	58.6	357.6	334.9	703.3	793.1	882.5	1,134.8

*Sources: Statistical Yearbook of Guangdong Province (1991); Statistical Data of National Economy
in the Municipalities and Counties of Guangdong 1980-1990.*

First, when the PRC opened its door to the outside world, businesses from Hong Kong which invested in the SEZs did so conservatively. The scale and magnitude of their investments were rather modest, amounting to only about HK$100,000 per investment. But as they gained confidence, especially in Shenzhen SEZ, they started increasing their investments. Manufacturing industries in Hong Kong, suffering from labor shortages and increasing land costs, found the unexploited territories of the SEZs attractive and transferred their factories and equipment there. Eventually the SEZs could not accommodate the growing number of Hong Kong investors, leading to an increase in investment in other parts of Guangdong and a decline in the SEZs' share.

Second, the delta was one of the first areas to open itself up to the outside world. Guangzhou, the capital of Guangdong and an important trading port for the delta, was designated as one of 14 "open coastal cities" when the SEZs were set up. After Guangzhou opened its doors, foreign investors were attracted in large numbers. In 1985, the Pearl RiverD elta and the Minnan Delta in Fujian were also designated economic development areas. In particular, the Pearl River Delta area, with its center in Guangzhou, has become the most open region in the PRC, attracting large foreign investments.

Third, the market economy in the delta is already highly developed. The labor and real estate markets there have been relatively effective, and the financial market and trade within and outside the delta have been proceeding smoothly. Initiatives by municipal governments in the delta to develop and improve their infrastructure have also been strong attractions for foreign investors.

Fourth, the disparities in labor cost between the SEZs and the municipalities in Pearl River Delta area have been on the rise since the mid-1980s (see Table 3). Finally, it has been easier for workers from the inland provinces to move to the Pearl River Delta Area than to SEZs as the Frontier License System and other restrictive policies have limited their access to the SEZs. Thus, the ratio of the new migrants to local inhabitants in the Shenzhen SEZ has been lower than that in the Pearl River Delta area.

Table 3. Nominal Average Annual Wages in Eight Cities in the Pearl River Delta Area, 1980-1990
(yuan)

	Shenzhen	Guangzhou	Zhuhai	Huizhou	Dongguan	Zhongshan	Jiangmen	Fuoshan
1980	1,033	961	927	789	750	758	842	843
1981	1,196	1,040	1,146	857	887	946	965	1,023
1982	1,408	1,112	1,311	950	1,095	1,085	1,079	1,125
1983	1,610	1,170	1,375	1,002	1,197	1,182	1,114	1,273
1984	2,266	1,363	1,776	1,228	1,383	1,265	1,237	1,599
1985	2,524	1,658	1,912	1,252	1,456	1,587	1,535	1,645
1986	2,628	1,843	2,105	1,444	1,616	1,735	1,678	1,714
1987	2,796	2,087	2,297	1,573	2,067	2,259	1,838	1,953
1988	3,540	2,742	2,835	2,377	2,757	2,884	2,356	2,644
1989	3,924	3,343	3,659	2,781	3,320	3,232	2,861	3,335
1990	4,464	3,571	4,046	3,218	3,552	3,499	3,177	3,531

Source: *Statistical Data of National Economy in the Municipalities and Counties of Guangdong 1980-1990.*

ECONOMIC COOPERATION IN THE PEARL RIVER DELTA

Foreign Investment Flows

The rapid expansion of the Pearl River Delta area is shown in Table 4. The area's growth has surpassed that of both Guangdong and the country as a whole. On the other hand, the share of foreign investment to total fixed asset investment in the delta has consistently been lower than that in the SEZs, although it surpassed the average in Guangdong after 1989 (see Table 5).

In terms of the composition of foreign investment coming from Hong Kong and Taipei,China in the 1980s, four characteristics are quite interesting.

(i)   Most of the investments from Hong Kong and Taipei,China in the delta are in the form of foreign direct investment (FDI). During the period 1979-1991, cumulative total foreign investment in the PRC was $82.487 billion, of which only 32.7 per cent was FDI, while two-thirds of the total foreign investment in the delta was in the form of FDI;

Table 4. Comparison of Annual Average Growth Rates of Major Economic Indicators, 1980-1990
(per cent)

	Pearl River Delta	Guangdong	PRC
GDP	16.5	12.3	9.0
National Income	14.6	11.4	8.4
Total Exports	19.8	17.0	13.1
Fiscal Revenue	14.2	13.8	10.6

Source: *Statistical Yearbook of Guangdong* (various issues); *Statistical Yearbook of China* (various issues).

Table 5. Share of Foreign Investment
in Total Fixed Asset Investment in Guangdong, 1985-1991
(per cent)

	1985	1986	1987	1988	1989	1990	1991
SEZs	23.17	27.50	21.67	25.40	33.97	34.77	38.72
Shenzhen	31.27	42.26	34.42	27.37	29.38	31.23	30.39
Zhuhai	27.49	22.10	21.11	39.48	40.82	34.79	42.31
Shantou	10.77	18.18	9.49	9.36	31.72	38.28	43.46
Pearl River Delta	10.99	9.45	9.71	12.08	23.53	27.11	27.39
Guangzhou	10.43	9.91	5.16	10.50	10.76	15.72	16.13
Zhongshan	16.90	9.29	8.60	5.92	14.48	21.53	29.76
Dongguan	9.33	4.67	7.38	13.03	39.49	39.05	35.74
Jiangmen	7.85	8.01	11.68	11.48	23.54	22.16	23.91
Huizhou	10.32	12.75	15.65	17.28	23.10	32.98	27.21
Fuoshan	11.16	12.09	9.77	14.25	29.86	31.21	31.68
Guangdong	14.59	17.42	15.21	21.45	20.36	23.65	22.26

Sources: Statistical Yearbook of Guangdong (1992); Statistical Data of National Economy in the Municipalities and Counties of Guangdong 1980-1990.

(ii)   Most of the investments are in labor-intensive and light
       industries. A survey conducted by the Hong Kong
       Industrial Consolidated Association (HKICA) indicated
       that, of the 1,256 member companies, 511 had invest-
       ments in the Pearl River Delta area. This included 69.4
       per cent of the electronics companies and 58.3 per cent
       of the toy companies. Other manufacturing companies
       were in plastics, electrical appliances, hardware, and
       machinery. The survey also showed that 75 per cent of
       the products of the 511 companies were manufactured
       in the delta, including 93 per cent of the toys, 84 per cent
       of the electrical appliances and optical instruments, and
       79 per cent of the electronic products (HKICA, 1991);

(iii) Most investors from Hong Kong and Macau have in-
       vested in small and medium enterprises. A survey by the
       HKICA showed that (a) the average number of employ-
       ees of Hong Kong enterprises in the delta was 787;
       (b) 58 per cent of the enterprises had less than 500
       employees; (c) 18 per cent had between 500 and 1,000
       employees; and (d) 22 per cent had over 1,000 employ-
       ees. The average investment per enterprise was
       $1.84 million for foreign enterprises compared to $7.05
       million for state-owned and collective enterprises (see
       Table 6); and

(iv)   Most of the products of the foreign enterprises in the
       Pearl River Delta area are for export because the govern-
       ment restricts foreign manufacturers from selling their
       products on the domestic market. Foreign manufactur-
       ers in the delta have mainly taken advantage of its
       abundant and cheap labor, low land rents, geographical
       proximity to markets or corporate bases, rich natural
       resources, and improved infrastructure. Finished or
       semifinished products are often transported back to
       Hong Kong or Macau for re-export under contractual
       arrangements (Yasukuni, 1991).

Table 6. Ownership of Enterprises in Cities in the Pearl River Delta Area, 1991

	State-Owned and Collective Enterprises		Foreign Enterprises	
	Number of Enterprises	Investment per Enterprise (million yuan)	Number of Enterprises	Investment per Enterprise ($ million)
Guangzhou	4,452	7.30	1,985	1.96
Shenzhen	2,765	5.54	4,053	2.76
Zhuhai	964	5.29	1,726	1.07
Huizhou	1,692	2.40	608	2.06
Dongguan	1,213	4.71	1,110	1.54
Zhongshan	634	31.24	470	1.87
Jiangmen	1,998	5.89	867	1.44
Fuoshan	1,846	10.04	1,360	2.04
Pearl River Delta Area	19,775	7.05	12,179	1.84

Source: Statistical Yearbook of Guangdong (1992).

Forms of Economic Cooperation

Economic cooperation between the Pearl River Delta and Hong Kong and Macau has come in three main forms: (i) combining the existing financial resources of the participating areas; (ii) channeling the financial resources of Hong Kong and Macau through processing and assembly operations and compensation trade in the delta; and (iii) increasing the technical and productive capacity of the delta by borrowing from foreign sources.

In the first form, Hong Kong-Macau's financial resources, technology, management capability, and marketing skill are combined with the delta's own funds, manpower, and existing capital equipment. The Shenzhen SEZ is a classic example of this arrangement. Because of its favorable policies and geographical proximity to Hong Kong, the SEZ has served both as a "window" and a "tunnel" for domestic enterprises entering the world market. A number of Chinese enterprises have invested in the Shenzhen SEZ by establishing companies, opening offices, and establishing linkages with the international market. By the end of 1990, a total of 3,975 inland-connected enterprises had been registered in the SEZ, with real investment amounting to 4 billion yuan. In addition, over 40 ministries of the central government, 29 provinces, and 152 districts and cities had set up representative agencies in the zone (Luo, 1991).

The second form of cooperation is through export processing and assembly production. Dongguan City, which is located in the Pearl River Delta, provides the best example of this approach. During the period 1979-1990, the cumulative foreign investment actually utilized by Dongguan amounted to $1.068 billion, 61 per cent of which was in processed and assembled products. The city produced more of those products than any other city in the delta in 1990.

The third form of cooperation involves the introduction of advanced technology financed through foreign borrowing. This is best exemplified in Fuoshan City, which is situated at the fringe of the Pearl River Delta, adjacent to Guangzhou. At the start of PRC's open door policy, Fuoshan's processing and assembly plants, along with compensation trade, were the main avenues through which foreign investment was attracted from Hong Kong and Macau. During the period 1979-1982, 67.6 per cent of Fuoshan's total foreign investment went into these activities. Fuoshan's authorities were aware that the city was farther away from Hong Kong and Macau than were Dongguan City, Baoan County, and the Shenzhen SEZ, and that transportation costs were therefore higher. Yet Fuoshan had a relatively well-developed economy, with a strong light industry sector and a busy commercial network. Fuoshan shifted from processing and assembly production and compensation trade to direct foreign borrowing to purchase advanced technology and equipment. Foreign businesses did not actually invest in these enterprises; their funds flowed into Fuoshan mainly through commercial bank loans. As a result, these enterprises enjoyed the favorable treatment granted by the Chinese government to enterprises with foreign investment. During the period from 1979-1986, total foreign investment amounted to $100 million, of which about $86.44 million was accounted for by Fuoshan's own enterprises (Tangtao and Zhang, 1990).

EXPANDING THE TRIANGLE: POLICIES AND ISSUES

Wage and Labor Policy

Low-cost labor is the most important factor in attracting investment. Shortly after its establishment in the early 1980s, Shenzhen SEZ established a wage distribution program for foreign-funded enterprises, setting the average wage of workers at 240 yuan a month (approximately HK$800), which was 20-25 per cent of the average wage in Hong Kong at the time. Although the average wage rate in Shenzhen SEZ increased by 12 per cent annually in terms of the Chinese currency during the 1980s, the labor cost barely increased in terms of the Hong Kong dollar due to the devaluation of the yuan.

Average wages in the other municipalities of the Pearl River Delta area were much lower than those in Shenzhen SEZ, for two reasons. First, many municipalities in the delta did not formulate a special wage standard for enterprises with foreign investment. The average wages of workers in the delta outside Shenzhen ranged from HK$400 in Dongguan to HK$700 in Guangzhou. Second, Shenzhen did not encourage the development of labor-intensive industries, and restricted the inflow of unskilled labor into the SEZ. This also led to the rapid increase of workers' wages in Shenzhen. Other municipalities in the delta did not restrict the inflow of unskilled labor from other parts of the PRC. The existence of a large pool of labor in the delta restrained the growth in workers' wages (see Table 7).

**Table 7. Per Capita Income in Selected Cities
of Guangdong Province, 1978 and 1990**
(yuan)

	Shenzhen	Guangzhou	Zhongshan	Dongguan	Shaoguan	Shantou	Heyuan	Maoming
1978	486	625	463	498	348	220	203	283
1990	4,785	3,721	3,511	4,078	1,620	1,130	715	1,238

Source: Statistical Data of National Economy in the Municipalities and Counties of Guangdong 1980-1990.

A reliable supply of quality labor is required if the triangle is to continue expanding. There are at present some 8 million surplus rural laborers in Guangdong province, and 186 million throughout the country. Because of the difficulty in transferring them to industries in local areas, a proportion of the labor force has moved to the relatively high income centers in the Pearl River Delta area.

Although the supply of unskilled labor is always enormous, shortages of skilled labor (including technicians) are becoming serious. Recently, the Pearl River Delta tried to promote heavy and high-technology industries, making it imperative to formulate policies to attract skilled labor. These included the provision of housing, the establishment of relatively high salary levels, and the reduction of restrictions on labor mobility. The Shenzhen SEZ has made arrangements with Hong Kong investors for its students abroad to be assured of employment once they return to Shenzhen. However, the number of skilled workers and technicians is still not high enough to meet the demand. The shortage is aggravated by administrative restrictions on the employment of technicians and skilled workers.

Land Policy

After more than thirty years of free land use, land use charges are now imposed in the Pearl River Delta and throughout the PRC. At present, these charges vary from locality to locality. In accordance with the existing regulations on foreign investment, the charge for land development and land use may be set at about 5-20 yuan per square meter per year, but a number of municipalities in the delta have pegged it at 5 yuan per square meter per year.

The SEZs levy the lowest charges on land use. For example, land for industrial use is charged 1 to 1.6 yuan per square meter annually in SEZs, while land for cultivation, animal husbandry, and marine cultivation is leased at 0.2 to 0.3 yuan. Enterprises initiated and funded by overseas Chinese from Hong Kong, Macau, and Taipei,China are exempted from the charge for five years starting from the date of ratification, and are allowed a 50 per cent reduction for five years thereafter. Projects which produce high-technology items are exempted from the charge for five years starting from the date of ratification, and are allowed a reduction of 50 per cent of the land use charges for three years thereafter. Projects which involve even more advanced technology are likewise exempted from the charge, and while a new enterprise is being established, the charge on land use is anywhere from 20 to 30 per cent of the standard amount.

By the end of the 1980s, restrictions on real estate development by foreign investors had been lifted in some municipalities of the Pearl River Delta. Enterprises with foreign investment were permitted to invest in the real estate sector, develop tracts of land, transfer land use rights, and engage in real estate projects. On 19 May 1991, the State Council promulgated interim administrative measures governing the development and management of land tracts by firms with foreign investment. There remains, however, a wide disparity in the price of land between the Pearl River Delta and Hong Kong. For example, the rental expense for factory space per square meter per month in the delta is approximately HK$25-30, which is approximately one-eighth to one-tenth of that in Hong Kong. Factory space per square meter in the Pearl River Delta also ranges from HK$1,500 to HK$2,000, or about one-sixth to one-eighth of that in Hong Kong. With the continual improvements in infrastructure and the refinement of laws and regulations, the real estate sector will probably attract further investments from Hong Kong.

Trade Policy

Beginning in 1979, the PRC gradually but sporadically reduced the rate of tariff protection. The biggest tariff reductions or exemptions were given in the SEZs. Enterprises with foreign investment were exempted from import duties and the consolidated industrial and commercial taxes levied on imported machinery, equipment, parts, components, raw materials, fuels, and vehicles for construction and production. Guangzhou, as an open coastal city, and the Pearl River Delta, as an open economic zone, also enjoyed some preferential treatments in trade. In Guangzhou City, imported equipment, building appliances, communication equipment, vehicles, and office equipment for use by foreign participants, as well as raw materials, assembly parts, components, and packing materials, were all exempted from customs duties and consolidated industrial and commercial taxes. Open economic zones also enjoyed roughly the same preferential treatment.

Furthermore, local governments were given greater leeway by the national governments in organizing local companies, attracting business and forging economic cooperation schemes, engaging in foreign economic activities, staging fairs and exhibitions abroad, and holding trade negotiations in Hong Kong and Macau. As a result, the opportunities for economic cooperation among Hong Kong, Macau, Taipei,China, and the Pearl River Delta area greatly increased.

Tax Policy

Foreign-funded enterprises in the SEZs are normally subject to a 15 per cent income tax, but all enterprises with foreign investment are exempted from the local income tax. In economic and development zones, only productive enterprises with foreign investment enjoy the privilege of a 15 per cent income tax. In the open coastal cities and open economic zones, the standard income tax rate for productive enterprises with foreign investment is 24 per cent. The rate is 15 per cent for those enterprises engaged in technology-intensive projects with foreign investment of over $30 million which have long gestation periods, and for activities related to energy, communication, or port construction. For enterprises engaged in technology-intensive exports, the income tax rate is only 10 per cent. Enterprises investing in projects that will last more than 10 years enjoy tax-free treatment for two years, and a tax reduction by one-half for a further three years. The income tax rates in the SEZs, the open coastal areas, and the open economic zones are lower than those in many countries of Asia.

The preferential treatment in the SEZs is more favorable than in the open economic zones and coastal cities. However, because of the limited land area of the SEZs and the high labor costs, enterprises with foreign investment have been moving their factories from the Shenzhen SEZ to the outlying cities of Dongguan, Guangzhou, Zhongshan, and Zhuhai. More and more factories from Hong Kong have been attracted to the areas alongside the expressways and highways of Guangzhou, thus accelerating the expansion of the growth triangle area.

Industrial Policy

As expansion continues, it will be necessary for the countries involved in the growth triangle to coordinate their industrial policies. For example, the industrial relationship between Hong Kong and the Pearl River Delta has given rise to the pattern of "Hong Kong shop and Pearl River Delta factory." Tertiary industry in Hong Kong has been dependent on secondary industry in the Pearl River Delta, while the "factory" in the delta has encouraged the development of the tertiary industry in Hong Kong. The complementary economic relations have propelled the growth of both economies. Yet with the gradual increase in living standards in the 1990s, the Pearl River Delta has been devoting more effort to developing its tertiary industry, so much so that the rate of growth in the subsector has surpassed that in primary and secondary industries. This change in the division of labor will certainly have an impact on the economic relations between the members of the triangle.

Some scholars now worry that the further development of tertiary industry in the Pearl River Delta will weaken economic complementarity and result in intensive competition between the two regions. This is not likely to happen, however. In 1991, the share of tertiary industry in the total GDP of the Pearl River Delta was 39 per cent, which was not only far below that of Hong Kong and Taipei,China (75 and 53 per cent, respectively) but also below that of Thailand, Indonesia, and the Philippines (50, 40, and 42 per cent, respectively). Although the delta's tertiary industry share of GDP will catch up with that of Hong Kong in the future, their functions will likely remain dissimilar. Tertiary industry in the Pearl River Delta caters to the needs of local and domestic production, trade, and consumption. Hong Kong, in contrast, serves as a center for regional and international finance and trade. Moreover, with the gradual opening of the domestic market and the transfer of labor-intensive industries from the Pearl River Delta to the internal areas of the PRC, the "shop" will become the dominant industry in the delta. For purposes of penetrating the Chinese market, businesses from Hong Kong will need to make full use of the Pearl River Delta's tertiary industry, which provides services relating to finance, information, real estate, trade, and tourism. Consequently, the pattern of "Hong Kong shop and Pearl River

Delta factory" will be replaced by cooperation among the tertiary industries.

Infrastructure Policy

The development of infrastructure must be coordinated in the triangle. Every municipality in the Pearl River Delta is attempting to develop a full range of infrastructure locally. This could lead to a duplication of power, ports, telecommunication, and airport projects. Although there has been some cooperation between Hong Kong and the delta in the building of highways, customs facilities, and ports, and in the supply of electric power, focused infrastructure planning is necessary. This will require regular discussions and an exchange of information among the organizations concerned.

Financial Policy

An improvement in the financial environment will be essential for the further development of the triangle. Financial cooperation began in the early 1980s mainly for foreign trade. After the mid-1980s, international financial institutions and Hong Kong's banks began to provide credit and finance for enterprises with foreign investment. Meanwhile, every municipality in the Pearl River Delta channeled foreign capital and technology through their enterprises and offices in Hong Kong. The means of financial mobilization affected not only the scale and speed of construction, but also the potential for expansion of the growth triangle. Public funds as well as credit from domestic banks and capital generated by enterprises themselves remained important.

THE FUTURE OF THE GROWTH TRIANGLE

Geographical Expansion

In the 1990s, with the continued development of the Chinese economy and the opening up of more regions, the growth triangle will likely expand to the mountainous areas of Guangdong and to neighboring provinces such as Guangxi, Fujian, and Hunan. There are several reasons for this. One is the presence of natural resources in Guangdong's neighboring provinces. Mineral resources are lacking in Guangdong, and forest and water resources are becoming more and more limited. In the 1980s, industrial cooperation between Guangdong (especially the Pearl River Delta) and Hong Kong-Macau was concentrated in the field of light industries. Because most of the raw material components and equipment were imported, there was not much demand for the natural resources of the neighboring provinces. But with vast improvements in infrastructure and with the establishment of more heavy industries and chemical projects in Guangdong, imported raw materials alone may not meet the needs of these industries. It may thus be necessary to get some of these materials from domestic sources.

Fujian province has more than 100 large and medium-sized mineral deposits that have been explored. Its main mineral deposits are iron, coal, and tungsten. The province has harnessed hydropower of about 10,460 MW from its many rivers. Further, it has a forest area of 4.5 million hectares, with timber resources amounting to some 400 million cubic meters. Guangxi province has abundant mineral deposits, including a great variety of nonferrous metals. Guangxi has hydropower resources with a potential of 21,330 MW, of which 17,370 MW is exploitable. Its forest area covers 55.15 million hectares, which is 23.3 per cent of the total land area. Hunan province has very similar endowments.

The rapid increase in land and labor costs in the Pearl River Delta also exert pressures for the growth triangle area to expand. In 1978, the average per capita income of the four delta cities (Shenzhen, Guangzhou, Zhongshan, and Dongguan) was 517.8 yuan, which was nearly twice as high as that of the cities of Shaoguan, Shantou, Heyuan, and Maoming (263.5 yuan). In 1990, the gap grew even wider. The gap between incomes in Guangdong and neighboring provinces also widened after 1978 (see Table 8).

In addition, land costs and the price of real estate in the Pearl River Delta are also higher than those in the neighboring provinces. In the Shenzhen SEZ, the cost of land per square meter increased from 90 yuan in 1990 to approximately 150 yuan in 1992. In Guangzhou, the cost of land was roughly 130 yuan in 1992, but in Guangxi the cost was only about 15 yuan. The prices of buildings

**Table 8. Average Nominal Wages
in Guangdong and Neighboring Provinces in Selected Years**
(yuan)

	1978	1980	1985	1990
Guangdong	612	792	1,375	2,928
Jiangxi	552	708	996	1,728
Hunan	564	720	1,056	2,016
Guangxi	540	720	1,080	2,052
Fujian	564	708	1,056	2,160
Sichuan	588	744	1,068	2,016
Average of Neighboring Provinces	562	720	1,051	1,994

Source: Statistical Yearbook of the People's Republic of China (various issues).

in the cities of Shenzhen, Guangzhou, Zhuhai, Shantou, Fuzhou, and Xiamen have also risen. For instance, in Shenzhen, a villa now goes for HK$1,174 per square foot, while a luxury house can be had for HK$1,640 per square foot. Guangzhou is the next most expensive. The least expensive location is Fuzhou.

There has also been an improvement in the investment environment in neighboring provinces. In recent years, with the opening of coastal areas and the establishment of economic development zones, the preferential treatment enjoyed by investors in Shenzhen and the Pearl River Delta became less important, particularly as higher costs in these areas have offset the initial savings. For example, the cost per square meter of land charged by the government of Guangxi on foreign enterprises was not more than 1 yuan; in Fujian, the cost was not more than 2 yuan, while in Guangzhou city the cost was 2.5 yuan. The government of Guangxi issued a temporary provision to encourage the introduction of foreign investment in April 1991. For a project valued below 10 million yuan, a 1.5 per cent commission could be drawn by the sponsor. For a project valued at 10 to 100 million yuan, a 0.5 per cent commission was permitted. Hainan, the largest SEZ in the PRC, offered several incentives in addition to the preferential policies granted by the central government. Land development on a large scale was encouraged at low prices, and long rental periods of up to 70 years were given to foreign enterprises. Foreign banks were permitted in Hainan, and local enterprises with more than 25 per cent foreign funding enjoyed the same preferential treatment as foreign enterprises.

The approval process for projects with foreign investment was simplified in these provinces, making it more convenient for foreign businesses to invest. At the same time the physical infrastructure of the neighboring provinces has gradually improved.

Cooperation Within South China

While economic cooperation between Hong Kong-Macau-Pearl River Delta and the surrounding areas started only in the mid-1980s, cooperation between the delta and the interior areas in Guangdong has a longer history. The Guangdong authorities formulated two specific economic policies to strengthen such cooperation. First, they encouraged foreign-funded enterprises in the delta to employ workers from the mountainous and backward areas in the province. Second, they set policies to encourage long-term economic cooperation. For example, Shenzhen is financially assisting Meizhou City in more than 20 projects and has provided loans of over 30 million yuan. It is also assisting in the establishment of more than 10 factories, e.g., Dapu Pharmaceutical Factory, Automobile Component Factory, Wuhua Electrical Power Station, and Meixian Country Textile Factory. Shenzhen has also set up enterprises with the "head" in the interior and the "tail" in the SEZ, i.e., in which raw materials undergo primary processing in the interior before being moved to the SEZ for further processing and export. There are now more than 300 enterprises in Shenzhen, capitalized at approximately 450 million yuan, that have invested in the inland areas.

Power generation projects have also created closer ties between the coastal and interior regions of the country. Under the guidance of the Ministry of Energy and the PRC's Energy Investment Company, the South Electrical Integrated Company (jointly managed by Guangdong, Guangxi, Guizhou, and the Energy Investment Company), will invest in three large-scale hydropower stations in Guangxi. The Changzhou hydroelectric hub in Wuzhou, with an installed capacity of 620 MW, was jointly established by Guangdong and Guangxi, and has recently begun operations. Guangdong and Guangxi have also signed an agreement to construct a highway from Liuzhou in Guangxi to Fengkai in Guangdong, and to improve the road from Xindu in Guangxi to Huaiji in Guangdong. These projects are now underway.

Guangdong and Hainan, which have common historical roots, have launched projects in manufacturing, electric power, textiles, chemicals, transportation, finance, telecommunication, commerce, science, education, and agriculture. They have also set up a number of multi-provincial cooperative networks to lay the foundation for greater economic integration. Finally, the Guangzhou Fair and other periodic regional commodity exhibitions provide opportunities for economic exchanges between Guangdong and neighboring provinces.

CONCLUSIONS

Economic cooperation in Southern China is based on economic complementarities and facilitated by the common cultural heritage of the vast majority of the populace. The Pearl River Delta has absorbed much of the foreign investment coming to the area. Most of the investments are from Hong Kong and Taipei,China and are in labor-intensive light industries. This paper has examined the issues involved in the expansion of the Southern China Growth Triangle into the interior of South China and surrounding provinces. A number of conclusions can be drawn from a decade of experience and experimentation.

First, the shift in the relative comparative advantages of the different areas included in the growth triangle area has prompted the cooperation to expand to areas where labor and land costs are lower. The common heritage of the people of Hong Kong and of the Pearl River Delta has also facilitated the shift in emphasis to new areas.

Second, government policies are a major driving force in the expansion of the growth triangle. Since 1979, the open door policy in the PRC and the "special policy, flexible measures" granted to Guangdong and Fujian by the central government have made economic cooperation between Hong Kong and the Pearl River Delta possible.

Third, further expansion of the Southern China Growth Triangle from the Pearl River Delta to the inland area of Guangdong and to the neighboring provinces of Guangxi and Hunan is underway. However, past experience shows that policy cooperation and administrative coordination will be crucial for the success of this expansion.

Endnote:

1.   Professor, Department of Economics, Lingnan (University) College, Zhongshan University, People's Republic of China.

Bibliography

Antonio, Ramon D., "China, Hong Kong and Taiwan: The Growing Economic Strength of Three China," No. 19 (April-May 1992).

Chen, Wei-hong, "The Cooperative Relationship Concerning the Investment of Taiwan and Hong Kong in the Mainland, based on the Experience of Hong Kong," in *Trust and Finance Monthly*, Vol. 186 (September 1992).

Chia, Siow-yue, and Lee Tsao Yuan, "Subroutine Economic Zones: A New Motive Force in Asia-Pacific Development," paper presented at the 20th Pacific Trade and Development Conference, 10-12 September, Washington, D.C., 1992.

Chow, Gregory C., "The Integration of China and Other Asian Countries into the World Economy," paper presented at the International Academic Conference on Outward-Looking Strategy and Development of the Economy in Guangdong, 1992.

Garschagen, Harry, "The Status and Outlook of the Guangdong-Hong Kong-Macau-Taiwan Economic Cooperation," paper presented at the International Academic Conference on Outward-

Looking Strategy and Development of the Economy in Guangdong, 1992.

Heng, Tian-Gao-ming, "Economic Region and Southern China," paper presented at the International Academic Conference on Outward-Looking Strategy and Development of the Economy in Guangdong, 1992.

Hong Kong Industrial Consolidated Association, "Hong Kong's Investment in the Pearl River Delta," in *Information of International Economy*, Vol. 5 (1992).

Kyoko, Yasukuni, "Complementary Economic Relations Between Guangdong Province and Hong Kong," in *Pacific Business and Industries*, Vol. 111 (1991).

Lee, Tsao Yuan. *Growth Triangle: the Johor-Singapore-Riau Experience.* Singapore: Institute of Southeast Asian Studies, 1991.

Liao, Be-wei, ed. *China's Reform and Open to the Outside World and Development of the Pearl River Delta.* Hong Kong: The Southern Commercial Bank Press, 1992.

Lin, Tzong-biao, "Economic Nexus Between the Two Sides of the Taiwan Straits with Special Emphasis on Hong Kong's Role," paper presented at the International Academic Conference on Outward-Looking Strategy and Development of the Economy in Guangdong, 1992.

Luo, Mu-sheng, "The Effects of Shenzhen SEZ on the Economic Development in Guangdong," in The Office of Hong Kong-Macau, ed., *The Economic Reform and Open in Guangdong.* Panyu City Press, 1991.

Qi, Wen-jun, ed. *Shenzhen SEZ's Ten Years.* Shenzhen SEZ: Haitian Press, 1991.

Tangtao, and Yue Liang Zhang, "The Analysis of the Form of the Industrial Cooperation Between Guangdong and Hong Kong," in Ding Li-shong, ed., *New Stage of the Economic Cooperation Between Guangdong and Hong Kong.* Guangzhou: Guangdong People's Press, 1990.

Toh, Mun-heng, "Asian Growth Triangles: Experiments in Coopera-
    tion, Complementarity or Competition?" Paper presented at the
    International Center for the Study of East Asian Development
    Model Comparison Conference on Trade Development and Re-
    gion Groupings in East and Southeast Asia, 1992.

Zhou, Da-ming, "The Non-Native Laborers of the Pearl River Delta: An
    Analysis of Its Distribution Characteristics and Migration Ten-
    dencies," in Research Center of the Pearl River Delta Economic
    Development and Management, ed., *Economic Development of the
    Pearl River Delta: A Retrospect and Prospects*. Guangzhou: Zhongshan
    University Press, 1992.

Johor-Singapore-Riau Growth Triangle: A Model of Subregional Cooperation

■ Sree Kumar[1]

INTRODUCTION

The emergence of growth triangles is a recent development in economic cooperation in Southeast Asia. The growth triangle idea is not really new, as similar arrangements have existed for several years in places such as Guangdong-Shenzhen-Hong Kong, western Europe, and North America. The basic concept is simple: three geographically proximate areas with different factor endowments and comparative advantages are linked to form an economically dynamic region.

Within the Association of Southeast Asian Nations (ASEAN), however, the growth triangle is a relatively new area of interest. For instance, the Johor-Singapore-Riau (JSR) Growth Triangle has been widely discussed as a model for cooperative economic development. The triangle's early success has spurred the development of a northern growth triangle, encompassing the northern states of Malaysia (including Penang), southern Thailand, and northern Sumatra. Other triangles, such as one consisting of parts of the Philippines, Malaysia, and Indonesia, are now being considered as possible zones of economic activity.

At this writing, the JSR triangle is approaching its third year. Industrial estates have sprung up in Riau, and Johor is enjoying an economic boom. While these developments have been very well-received, various operational, social, and political problems have surfaced in their wake. Most of these problems have been acknowledged by policy makers in the different countries, and a number of remedial measures have been taken. In this light, JSR can be seen as a crucible for understanding the policy implications of joint economic development. The lessons to be learned from this experience can form a useful guide for the development of other triangles in the region.

This paper will review the developments within the JSR triangle, attempting to identify areas in which policies can be strengthened and suggesting ways in which development institutions can play a catalytic role. It begins by providing a brief review of Singapore's development. Next it examines the general rationale and requirements for growth triangles. The next section reviews current developments in Johor and Riau; this is followed by an evaluation of the policy framework supporting the growth triangle. The following section discusses some of the problems arising out of joint development ventures. A look at the lessons and prospects for the triangle follows, while the final section deals with ways in which development institutions can support the evolution of the triangle.

EVOLUTION OF THE GROWTH TRIANGLE

Singapore is one of Southeast Asia's so-called "dragons." Its rapid progress over the last 20 years has been phenomenal compared to that of other developing countries with better natural endowments. At the time of independence from Britain, its economy was based on commerce and low value-added manufacturing and services for the British forces stationed in the Far East. In the early 1960s, Singapore, then a part of newly formed Malaysia, pursued an import-substitution industrialization strategy.

Rapid Industrialization of Singapore

In 1967, two years after Singapore left the Federation of Malaysia, the British Labor government announced a pullout of all its forces in Asia. The need to absorb unemployed labor arising from this pullout, coupled with a rapidly growing population, meant that Singapore had to embark on industrialization swiftly. With a small domestic

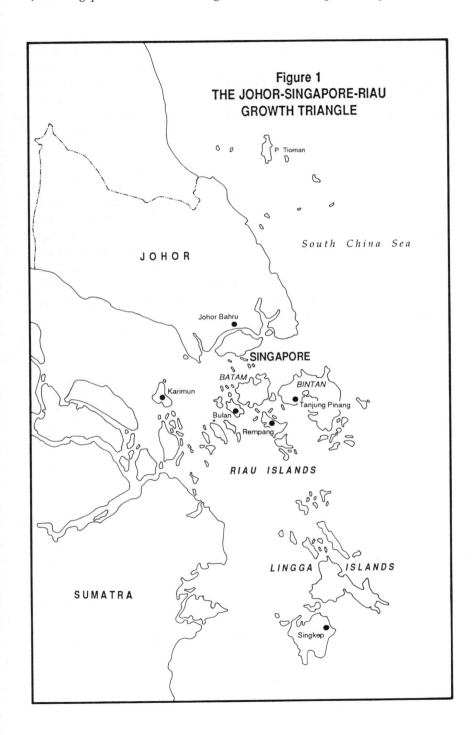

Figure 1
THE JOHOR-SINGAPORE-RIAU
GROWTH TRIANGLE

market, and in light of the inward-looking strategies being pursued by its neighbors, Singapore decided to adopt an export-led industrialization strategy. During the 1970s the country's low value-added manufacturing industries thrived, with ship repair and servicing as the main components. However, with rapid advances in technology and changing demands for products, the need to insulate the economy from wide swings in product markets prompted the creation of backward linkages in manufacturing and services.

As Table 1 shows, the structure of the Singapore economy changed markedly between 1980 and 1990, with financial and business services becoming more prominent. At first, high value-added manufacturing and higher value-added services were seen as the necessary ingredients for a more resilient and robust economy. Then, during the second half of the 1980s, industrial and service restructuring became the order of the day, as the gross domestic product (GDP) actually declined in 1985-1986 (Ministry of Trade and Industry, 1986).

Table 1. Singapore: Sectoral Shares of GDP in Selected Years
(per cent)

	1970	1980	1990
Agriculture and Fishing	2.3	1.3	0.3
Quarrying	0.3	0.3	0.1
Manufacturing	20.4	29.1	29.0
Utilities	2.6	2.2	2.0
Construction	6.8	6.4	5.3
Commerce	28.2	21.7	17.6
Transport and Communication	10.8	14.0	16.2
Financial and Business Services	14.1	19.7	27.8
Miscellaneous	14.5	5.3	3.6

Note: Miscellaneous includes "Other Services" and import duties less inputed bank service charges.

Sources: Singapore Department of Statistics; Singapore Ministry of Trade and Industry.

Growing Pressures in Singapore

Economic restructuring created pressures on the factors of production. First, average wages in the labor market rose significantly as a result of deliberate policies designed to effect industrial and service sector upgrading. This was exacerbated by a declining pool of skilled labor. Second, land constraints became critical, especially since modern manufacturing required vast tracts of open land for factories, warehousing, and distribution. Nevertheless, industrial restructuring efforts required that (i) infrastructure be built to a very high standard; (ii) labor be well-trained and productive; and (iii) economic diversification be achieved to some extent.

Previous development strategies had been designed to ensure strong domestic manufacturing and service sectors. Resource constraints such as water, land, and labor supply, however, severely limited the domestic expansion of these sectors. Meanwhile, the external environment had also changed. Competition from other industrializing economies such as Malaysia, Thailand, and Mexico had intensified, driving Singapore out of its traditional export-oriented production niches. This was compounded by protectionist tendencies in the Organization for Economic Cooperation and Development (OECD) countries. All of this made the exports of undifferentiated products from Singapore increasingly unprofitable (Ng and Wong, 1991). In the short term, therefore, there were pressures on manufacturing firms to relocate some of their activities to other lower-cost locations in order to stay competitive. In the longer term, there was a need for Singapore firms to have greater forward linkages and to gain control over key activities to retain its competitive advantage.

While international vertical linkages slowly took root, with the Singapore government and its associated companies investing heavily in the developed countries and Hong Kong, horizontal linkages became more visible in and around Singapore. The JSR growth triangle is an example and an outgrowth of this process.

Birth of the Triangle

In 1989, the then Deputy Prime Minister of Singapore, Goh Chok Tong, stated that Singapore, Johor, and Batam (in Riau) could form a "triangle of growth." The Johor-Singapore link was not new, having been driven initially by market forces. The Singapore-Riau link, however, was created by government-led initiatives. Thus it can be said that JSR was formed as a result of both economic imperatives and the political will of the participants.

The triangle had to contend first with land and labor constraints that resulted in sharp increases in the cost of doing business in Singapore. This was compounded by the appreciating Singapore dollar. For example, nominal average earnings in manufacturing increased by an annual average of 12 per cent in 1980-1990 when denominated in Singapore dollars (see Table 2), and by 21 per cent when denominated in US dollars. However, during this same period labor productivity increased by only 4.6 per cent, implying that the real unit cost of labor had increased (see Table 3). In addition, rents for industrial and commercial property rose by an average of 13 per cent over the period (see Table 4). A tight labor market also made the hiring of foreign workers expensive because of increases in the foreign worker levy and quotas on the numbers that could be employed in each factory.

Thus, firms had to decide whether to upgrade their activities in Singapore, redistribute their labor-intensive operations elsewhere, or do both. The growth triangle facilitated such redistribution, and proximity became a key factor as it implied lower travel and transportation costs.

Comparative Advantages

Comparative advantages arising from differences in factor endowments are complementary rather than competitive within the three areas of the triangle (see Tables 5 and 6). Johor has land and skilled medium-cost labor, Singapore has well-developed infrastructure and highly skilled (but expensive) labor, and Riau has land and low-cost labor. When the triangle was first being considered, unskilled labor cost $90 a month in Batam, $150 in Johor, and $350 in Singapore. Singapore, with its developed infrastructure and skill base, was still attractive to multinational companies (MNCs) for their capital-intensive and high technology operations, while labor-intensive and spatially driven operations were attracted to Johor or Batam. The proximity of these areas to Singapore facilitated moni-

Table 2. Singapore: Average Monthly Earnings, 1980-1990
(S $)

	1980	1981	1982	1983	1984	1985	1986	1987	1988	1989	1990
Nominal											
All Workers	692	789	910	991	1,083	1,191	1,210	1,231	1,295	1,427	1,561
Annual Change (per cent)	-	14.0	15.3	8.9	9.3	10.0	1.6	1.7	5.2	10.2	9.4
Manufacturing	575	670	740	842	907	980	989	1,025	1,095	1,225	1,377
Annual Change (per cent)	-	16.5	10.4	13.8	7.7	8.0	0.9	3.6	6.8	11.9	12.4
Real											
All Workers	782	824	915	985	1,049	1,149	1,182	1,198	1,240	1,335	1,420
Annual Change (per cent)	-	5.4	11.0	7.7	6.5	9.5	2.9	1.4	3.5	7.7	6.4
Manufacturing	650	700	744	816	879	945	967	997	1,048	1,146	1,253
Annual Change	-	7.7	6.3	9.7	7.7	7.5	2.3	3.1	5.1	9.4	9.3

Note: Real earnings refer to the nominal earnings deflated by the corresponding year's consumer price index (June 1982 to May 1983 = 100).

Source: Kumar and Lee, in Lee, ed. (1991).

Table 3. Singapore: Changes in Productivity and
Value-Added per Worker, 1980-1990
(per cent)

	Changes in Productivity		Value-Added Per Worker Adjusted for Hours Worked	
	All Workers	Manufacturing	All Workers	Manufacturing
1980	5.7	4.6	5.5	4.6
1981	5.2	9.2	5.9	9.0
1982	1.6	-0.7	2.0	0.3
1983	5.3	9.1	4.9	8.0
1984	6.9	7.2	6.9	7.8
1985	3.1	-1.5	5.3	1.2
1986	6.3	13.6	5.2	11.0
1987	4.8	3.7	3.9	2.2
1988	4.5	2.0	4.3	4.1
1989	4.8	3.8	2.5	1.2
1990	3.4	4.6	3.6	4.8

Source: Ministry of Trade and Industry (1990).

toring and control of operations, and kept down costs of transshipment of intermediate and final goods. Figure 2 gives an example of industrial redistribution done by a multinational company with a history of operations in Singapore.

JSR's wide manufacturing base and different factor endowments have drawn MNCs both to the triangle itself and to nearby areas. In Riau, this has resulted in the development of islands such as Bintan, Karimun, and Singkep. In Johor, industrial activity has expanded toward Melaka.

Spillover Effects

Both manufacturing and services benefit from the activities in a growth triangle. Singapore's financial and business services sector

Table 4. Singapore: Property Price Trends, 1980-1990
(S$ per sq m)

	Prime Flatted Factory		Prime Flatted Warehouse	
	Monthly Rental	Sale Price	Monthly Rental	Sale Price
Industrial Properties				
1980	6	1,292	10	1,830
1981	11	2,691	17	3,767
1982	10	2,422	16	3,122
1983	10	2,045	15	2,691
1984	9	1,776	13	2,260
1985	8	1,453	11	1,830
1986	7	1,076	9	1,345
1987	8	1,345	10	1,453
1988	9	1,453	11	1,561
1989	17	2,368	19	3,014
1990	27	3,014	30	3,875
Commercial Properties				
1980	49	13,347	183	31,205
1981	86	18,300	323	53,820
1982	76	16,038	269	45,208
1983	65	13,563	237	39,826
1984	54	10,226	227	36,597
1985	49	8,073	215	26,910
1986	43	6,351	194	25,833
1987	46	8,073	215	31,215
1988	59	11,840	431	53,820
1989	92	16,146	592	91,493
1990	140	22,066	626	107,639

Source: Ng and Wong (1991).

Table 5. Factor Costs in Johor, Singapore, and Batam, 1989
($)

	Johor	Singapore	Batam
Land (per sq m)	4.08	4.25	2.30
Labor (per month)			
Unskilled	150	350	90
Semi-Skilled	220	420	140
Skilled	400	600	200

Source: Mann (1990).

can achieve economies of scale in serving a wider economic and geographic base. Industries in the neighboring areas are tied to Singapore through managerial, operational, and logistics systems, and these ties spill over into other sectors of the domestic economy. For example, the expansion of the industrial park in Batam has required offshore funding from Singapore's financial market. Similarly, support industries such as packaging and freight forwarding have grown because of increased demand from Batam. For Johor and Batam, to the extent that they have adequate infrastructure and an elastic supply of the factors of production, this represents a cost-effective development strategy.

Internationalization

The JSR growth triangle can be seen as a launching pad for Singapore's internationalization strategy. The redistribution of industrial and service activities to Johor and Riau gives local entrepreneurs the opportunity to understand different business and cultural norms prevalent within the region. Although there are concerns that Singapore's role may diminish if or when the Straits of Malacca become congested, such fears seem unfounded given the strong and growing need for sophisticated shipping services in the region. And while it is conceivable that Singapore's internationalization strategy could choke off investments within the triangle, it

Table 6. Comparative Advantages in JSR

Business or Activity	Singapore	Johor/Riau
Electronics	Major regional base for manufacturing; major international procurement office	Lower labor/land costs for labor/land-intensive assembly operations
Oil	Refining/petrochemical processing, trading, storage, and distribution	Riau islands (e.g., Karimun Island) offers environmentally isolated space for oil storage
Maritime Services	Full range of ship-building, repair, and maintenance activities	Johor and Riau islands (e.g., Singkep) offer sites for shipbuilding/repair
Telecommunications and Business Services	World-class information technology infrastructure and wide range of business services; operational headquarters of many large MNCs	Many manufacturing, marketing, marketing, procurement and technical support activities by MNCs requiring coordination
Logistics and Distribution	Excellent telecommunication/transportation facilities and logistics management services	Wide range of export manufactures requiring transportation and logistics management support
Research and Development	Large pool of R&D scientists and engineers; R&D manpower training facilities & supporting infrastructure	MNC products requiring applied R&D and design for local market adaptations; MNC operations requiring process improvement R&D
Tourism	Excellent air travel gateway for tourists; emerging regional sea-cruise center; cosmopolitan shopping center; multicultural city	Abundant leisure resources such as beach resorts, golf courses, etc.; cultural diversity
Agribusiness	Food processing technology and biotechnology R&D capability	Abundant land resources for agriculture and animal husbandry

Source: Wong (1992).

Figure 2
REDISTRIBUTION OF FISHHOOK MANUFACTURING IN THE
JOHOR-SINGAPORE-RIAU TRIANGLE

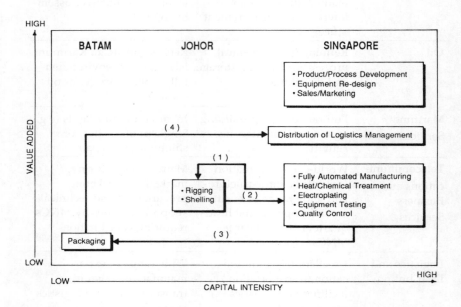

must be understood that such internationalization is being carried out primarily to strengthen Singapore's pivotal role in the region and in the growth triangle.

Competition for Investment

It is likely that some investment diversion from existing sources of foreign direct investment (FDI) will occur as a result of intensive competition from the Pearl River Delta area in the People's Republic of China and the low-cost production bases in Viet Nam. In fact, the movement of industries to Johor and Riau has the potential to cause an industrial hollowing-out in Singapore, and it is in this light that current strategies to foster capital-intensive manufacturing to replace such redistributed industries should be seen. Singapore's objective has been, and continues to be, to have a strong manufacturing base within its territory.

Tourism Development

Both Johor and Riau have excellent beaches and recreational facilities for tourists. Singapore, which is an airline hub with annual tourist traffic of around five million, could be the gateway to these areas once the necessary infrastructure is in place. Singapore is now developing a ferry terminal near its international airport to allow direct transfers to Riau and Johor. Likewise, hotels, resorts, and marine landing terminals are being constructed in Bintan and Johor.

Public and Private Sector Roles

The public sector has played an important role in the development of Riau, where both the Indonesian and Singaporean governments have been actively involved in developing infrastructure and managing resources such as labor. Infrastructure development in Batam has been undertaken by government-linked companies (GLCs) from Singapore in cooperation with an Indonesian private company. Similarly, the development in Bintan is being spearheaded by GLCs and private companies from Singapore, along with the Indonesian Navy Foundation and Indonesian companies.

The private sector has been the main engine of growth on the Johor side of the triangle, where companies have relocated as a result of "push" factors such as rising business costs in Singapore and "pull" factors such as lower land and labor costs in Johor.

Ethnic Chinese family links and cultural affinities in all three areas of the triangle have also been particularly important in the flow of Singaporean private investments. Furthermore, all three areas have a common Malay heritage which dates back to the precolonial period (Tate, 1971).

CURRENT DEVELOPMENTS IN JOHOR

Johor (population 2.2 million), which is peninsular Malaysia's southernmost state, contributes about 10 per cent to Malaysia's

GDP ($31.6 billion in 1990) (Kamil et al, in Lee, 1991). State GDP has grown by around 8 per cent over the last three years. The ratio of the state's GDP per capita to the national average is expected to increase from 0.91 in 1990 to 1.01 in 1995 under the Sixth Malaysia Plan.

Investments

Johor's economic structure is similar to that of the entire country except that it has a higher proportion of agro-based businesses. Investments in Johor constituted 22 per cent (7.5 per cent in value) of the total number of investment commitments (906) in Malaysia in 1990 (Sixth Malaysia Plan, 1991-1995). This compares with around 12 per cent of the total investments in Malaysia at the beginning of the decade (see Table 7).

The most interesting feature of the growth in investment is that foreign equity has surpassed domestic equity, to where it is now almost twice the domestic level on a cumulative basis (see Table 8). Along with this growth, there has been rapid employment creation. On average, some 30,000 jobs have been created annually over the last three years. A wide variety of industries have relocated to Johor, producing textiles, electronics, rubber products, processed

Table 7. Approved Investments in Johor and Malaysia, 1984-1990

	Approved Investments in Malaysia (M$ million)	Approved Investments in Johor (M$ million)	Johor as % of Malaysia
1984	3,801.1	457.3	12.0
1985	5,686.9	827.5	14.6
1986	5,163.2	439.9	8.5
1987	3,933.9	703.0	17.9
1988	9,093.9	1,829.5	20.1
1989	12,215.4	2,736.1	22.3
1990	28,168.1	2,090.0	7.4

Source: Malaysian Industrial Development Authority, various years.

Table 8. Johor: Approved Manufacturing Projects, 1981-1990

	1981	1982	1983	1984	1985	1986	1987	1988	1989	1990ᵃ	TOTAL
Number of Approvals											
Johor	69.0	79.0	66.0	129.0	102.0	80.0	82.0	183.0	208.0	204.0	1,202.0
Malaysia	596.0	468.0	490.0	749.0	625.0	447.0	333.0	732.0	784.0	906.0	6,130.0
Johor Share (per cent)	11.6	16.9	13.5	17.2	16.3	17.9	24.6	25.0	26.4	22.5	19.6
Potential Employment	6,028.0	5,436.0	7,337.0	12,920.0	7,450.0	8,910.0	12,829.0	27,815.0	36,226.0	28,413.0	153,364.0
Proposed Paid-Up Capitalᵇ (M$ million)	157.1	152.3	118.7	161.5	292.7	184.7	265.0	728.0	1,004.6	841.7	3,906.3
Malaysian Equity (M$ million)	81.6	100.2	86.5	90.5	242.2	82.6	65.3	170.4	193.4	182.8	1,295.5
Bumiputra	34.8	59.6	47.6	43.3	184.2	52.9	27.6	69.5	74.3	91.0	684.8
Non-Bumiputra	46.8	40.6	38.9	47.2	58.0	29.7	37.7	100.9	119.1	91.8	610.7
Foreign Equity (M$ million)	75.5	52.1	32.2	71.0	50.5	102.1	199.7	557.6	811.2	658.9	2,610.8
Loans (M$ million)	260.3	238.9	184.1	295.8	534.8	255.2	438.0	1,101.4	1,697.9	1,248.3	6,254.7
Total Proposed Capital Investmentᶜ (M$ million)	417.4	391.2	302.8	457.3	827.5	439.9	703.0	1,829.4	2,702.5	2,090.0	10,161.0

ᵃ January to December
ᵇ Proposed paid-up capital = Malaysian equity + foreign equity
ᶜ Total proposed capital = Proposed paid-up capital + loan

Source: Malaysian Industrial Development Authority.

foods, and wood products. Investments in excess of $0.8 billion from Singapore alone over the last decade have created some 75,000 jobs (*Straits Times*, 21 May 1992). Overall, investments worth some $4.0 billion are expected to be attracted to Johor over the next five years (*New Straits Times*, 25 August 1992). It is expected that the manufacturing sector will become more prominent in Johor's economy, with chemicals, metal products, and electronics as the leading products (see Table 9).

Infrastructure Development

The Johor state government is actively promoting the growth triangle in a number of ways. First, it is increasing the number of industrial estates from 14 to 21 in the next five years. The current 3,000 hectares allotted to the estates will be increased by 7,440 hectares (*Business Times*, 15 April 1992). Second, the industrial

**Table 9. Johor: Projected Growth Rates of Manufacturing
Subsectors, 1990-1995**
(per cent)

	Average Annual Growth Rate
Manufacturing	10.41
Food Processing	7.23
Apparel	4.49
Wood Products	4.02
Paper Products	10.52
Chemicals	43.82
Electronics & Nonmetal Products	30.15
Rubber Products	1.07
Metal Products	34.50
Machinery	15.98
Other Manufacturing	2.15
Utilities	7.57
Construction	15.74
Service	3.87
Government	0.37

Source: Malaysian Institute of Economic Research.

estates are being sited close to rural areas to assure employment for rural workers. The dispersal of industries was confined initially to the state capital of Johor Bahru, but now the dispersal is across the state. Third, some industries are being sited close to the sources of raw materials, such as rubber or oil palm, which have transport links to urban areas and ports (see Table 10).

Pasir Gudang port, which services trade in southern Malaysia, is being upgraded not only to accommodate more vessels but also for faster turnaround times. In line with port upgrading, industrial facilities in the free trade area in and around the port are also being improved. Customs procedures are likewise being streamlined to allow faster processing time at the wharves, and to make possible re-exports with Singapore across the causeway.

Table 10. Industrial Estates Developed by Johor State Economic Development Corporation

Industrial Estate (distance from Johor Bahru)	Total Planned Area (ha)	Total Developed Area (ha)	Total Saleable Area (ha)	Price Per Square Foot (M$)
Kluang (118 km)	51.80	51.80	36.70	4.00
Kota Tinggi (45 km)	12.14	12.14	10.20	4.00
Parit Raja (107 km)	28.33	28.33	23.07	4.00
Pasir Gudang (36 km)	808.50	808.50	687.23	7.00
Pasir Gudang (Extension) (36 km)	545.00	545.00	463.25	7.00
Pontian (55 km)	35.00	–	–	4.50
Segamat I (180 km)	39.46	39.46	36.42	n.a.
Senai I (30 km)	40.47	40.47	37.98	n.a.
Senai II (30 km)	70.01	70.01	55.85	n.a.
Senai III (32 km)	134.00	133.00	–	7.00
Sri Gading (117 km)	124.64	58.48	20.91	4.50
Tanjung Agas (179 km)	79.72	79.72	60.12	n.a.
Tebrau II (16 km)	89.00	80.00	68.00	8.00
Tongkang Pecah (130 km)	15.18	15.18	13.27	n.a.

Note: All estates have 60-year tenure plus 30-year options, except Pasir Gudang, Pasir Gudang (Extension), Senai III, and Tebrau II, which have 30-year tenure plus 30-year options.

Source: Industrial Development-Johor State Economic Development Corporation

In line with those developments, the state government also intends to set up a technical training institute and a business park with the support of the Singapore government (*Straits Times*, 19 June 1992). The training institute will upgrade the skills of Malaysian labor and management, while the business park will allow businesses investing in Johor to have a base from which to expand further into the state and beyond.

Singaporean GLCs have been actively involved in developing infrastructure such as industrial townships on a joint-venture basis with Malaysian companies. A township is now being put up north-west of the state capital of Johor Bahru. Other townships east of the capital are also being planned. The private sector, meanwhile, has invested not only in industries but also in large-scale resort development. Japanese and local investors have committed large sums for the development of hotels, golf courses, and seaside facilities in the state. Traditional, low value-added and labor-intensive industries are being displaced by larger investments in manufacturing such as electronics, assembly of consumer products, air conditioners, automobile parts, surgical gloves, and processed foods.

Prospects and Problems

Johor's economy is booming, but infrastructure development has not kept pace. This means that start-up costs have increased, since companies have had to incur the costs of housing, transportation, and their own auxiliary power plants for continuous operations. With increased industrial and commercial traffic, the road network has also been strained to full capacity. These bottlenecks are being addressed but private sector involvement will be crucial in alleviating them in the near future. Tight labor market conditions in Johor are also compounding problems. Two competing factors have contributed to this. The first is the flow of workers seeking higher wages from Johor to Singapore. The second is the overall shortage of labor throughout Malaysia as a result of its successful industrialization efforts. In view of all this, some segments of the labor market prefer to stay in their own regions rather than migrate.

As a result of this labor market rigidity, industries have moved to other states, such as Pahang and Trengganu, where labor is more abundant. This movement of industries, however, has to occur within the overall framework of Malaysian development plans, which call for balanced development and equitable resource allocation with regional and sector specificity (Kamil et al, in Lee, 1991). For example, Trengganu's offshore oil and gas makes it a potential downstream processing center to reduce bulk transportation costs. The establishment of industries in certain locations will impinge on the labor supply, which is being attracted to other sectors. Furthermore, wages in the petroleum industry will tend to drive up wages in the non-trading and manufacturing sectors.

CURRENT DEVELOPMENTS IN RIAU

Riau province is rapidly being transformed into an industrial center and tourist destination. Batam Island has become an industrial enclave, while the islands of Singkep and Karimun are being developed as oil service and ship repair centers. The economic indicators for Batam show that there has been a rapid increase in population, tourist arrivals, and ship transit (see Table 11). Similarly, exports from Batam have also grown and diversified, with electronic products surpassing oil equipment in importance in 1991 (see Table 12).

The natural early outcome of the Singapore-Batam link has been a widening of the industrial base, with location-specific industries taking root. While Batam has been industrializing rapidly, the neighboring island of Bintan is being developed for tourism, as well as for agro-business and industry. Batam will be linked by bridges to Rempang and Galang islands. Bulan's agro-businesses such as pig raising and orchid farming take advantage of plentiful land and low-cost labor. Similarly, Singkep and Karimun have deep waters for the establishment of ship repair services, while the northwestern shore of Bintan also has deep waters and is easily accessible to ships passing through the Riau Straits.

Batam Island

In line with the goals in the province's development plans, infrastructure is being expanded in Riau. The airport in Batam can take wide-bodied aircraft, while its port has begun to service more ships

Table 11. Batam: Key Indicators in Selected Years

	1973	1983	1985	1988	1989	1990	1991
Population	6,000	43,000	58,000	79,400	90,500	106,800	107,600
Local Workers	–	–	6,159	9,478	11,041	16,085	22,942
Foreign Workers	–	–	230	153	140	251	295
Annual Flights	–	481	1,545	2,887	3,511	6,487	8,003
Annual Port Calls	–	5,029	5,592	9,066	10,258	37,802	54,351
Tourists	–	–	60,161	227,981	359,497	579,305	606,251

Source: Batam Industrial Development Authority

Table 12. Major Exports from Batam, 1986-1991
($ million)

Product	1986	1987	1988	1989	1990	1991
Fish	.45	.48	.43	3.32	1.94	2.75
Live Pigs	0	.27	1.88	5.75	7.78	5.66
Garments	0	3.25	4.21	4.76	4.74	6.06
Metal Pipes	.24	1.03	4.92	2.74	30.66	12.25
Chemicals	.15	0	.01	.16	1.19	1.11
Electronic Components	0	0	1.81	2.29	17.00	78.12
Oil/Mining Equipment	0	0	23.48	9.04	63.90	53.78
TV Modules	0	0	0	5.74	2.54	0
Transport Equipment	0	0	0	.31	7.47	3.04
Cordless Phones	0	0	0	0	5.28	61.66
Construction Frames	0	0	0	.73	.78	7.83
Spare Parts	0	0	0	.20	.89	.25
Sawn Wood	.18	.28	.91	.19	.66	2.68
Chip Wood	0	0	0	.95	1.35	1.19
Polyethelene Barges	0	0	0	0	0	.51

Source: Batam Industrial Development Authority, cited in Ahmad (1992).

of greater tonnage. At the end of 1990, total investments in Batam stood at over $2.5 billion, with private investment comprising some 75 per cent of the total. Government investment went mainly into infrastructure development. Private sector investments channeled through the Indonesian Board of Investment were given incentives such as duty-free imports of capital equipment and accelerated depreciation (Pangestu, in Lee, 1991). The largest investors in Batam as of the end of 1990 were Singapore with 45 per cent and the United States with 26 per cent (see Table 13). One-fourth of the investments was channeled to real estate, while another quarter went to tourism projects (see Table 14).

Bilateral cooperation has been the hallmark of development in the southern axis of the growth triangle. The best example of this is the Batam Industrial Park (BIP), a $400 million joint venture between Singapore and Indonesia which was set up in January 1990 and officially opened in 1992. The industrial park, which is owned by PT Batamindo Investment Corporation, is a joint venture between Singapore GLCs (40 per cent) and an Indonesian private concern (60 per cent). The park initially encompassed 500 hectares; 1,000 hectares will be added later. Facilities in the park include two 9 MW electric generators, a labor recruitment agency, a direct telecommunications link with Singapore, and dormitories for workers. Ultimately, the park will house around 50,000 workers. As of the end of 1991, some 27 companies had become tenants of the industrial park (Lee, 1992). These include Thomson Electronics (assembling TV tuners and modulators), Phillips (assembling channel selectors), Smith Corona (making electric typewriters), and Sumitomo Electric (producing wire harnesses for automobiles). Other MNCs, most of which are based in Singapore, have also signed letters of agreement to move to BIP to take advantage of the lower operating costs there. These include corporations such as Western Digital, Sony, and Toshiba; most are 100 per cent foreign-owned.

Other industrial parks being built include the Kuang Hua Industrial Park (with Taiwanese investment) and the Kabil Industrial Estate for the oil industry. Six more industrial estates will take shape in the coming years.

Table 13. Cumulative Approved Foreign Investment in Batam by Origin in Selected Years
($ '000)

	1980	1983	1985	1988	1989	1990	1991	Indonesia 1991 ($ billion)	Batam Share in Indonesia 1991 (per cent)
Japan	4,000	4,000	4,000	24,000	54,000	54,000	61,780	10,343.6	0.6
Singapore	31,564	31,564	31,564	34,564	139,364	347,164	409,830	1,235.1	33.1
US	–	151,765	167,991	167,991	167,991	172,591	177,596	2,220.5	8.0
Hong Kong	–	–	–	–	–	14,500	38,500	3,954.0	1.0
Netherlands	–	9,450	9,450	14,450	18,950	18,950	34,574	1,947.9	1.8
Sweden	–	–	–	16,300	16,300	16,300	16,300	49.5	32.9
Bahamas	6,443	6,443	6,443	6,443	6,443	6,443	6,443	31.2	20.7
Panama	3,000	3,000	3,000	3,000	3,000	3,000	3,000	420.5	0.7
UK	–	–	–	22,066	22,066	22,066	22,066	1,036.8	2.1
Others	–	–	–	–	48,000	69,725	96,567	18,543.1	0.5
Total Indonesia ($ billion)	6,980	12,134	14,320	21,038	25,757	34,507	39,782	39,782.2	
Total Batam	45,007	206,222	222,448	288,814	476,114	724,739	866,656		2.2
Batam Share in Indonesia(%)	0.6	1.7	1.6	1.4	1.8	2.1	2.2		

Source: Batam Industrial Development Authority, cited in Ahmad (1992).

Table 14. Cumulative Approved Foreign Investment in Batam by Sector in Selected Years
($ million)

Sector	1980	1983	1985	1988	1989	1990	1991
Electronics	–	–	–	.50	.50	26.00	88.20
Chemicals	–	–	3.50	3.50	3.50	3.50	3.50
Oil/Mining Equipment	9.44	98.19	108.93	108.93	113.43	113.43	113.43
Steel and Iron	4.00	76.47	76.47	77.47	125.47	127.67	131.90
Plastic and Paper	–	–	–	–	–	5.60	11.54
Food and Agriculture	–	–	–	17.30	43.60	53.60	53.60
Real Estate	–	–	–	1.50	1.50	193.23	222.85
Tourism	31.56	31.56	31.56	73.63	134.13	187.13	221.33
Equipment Services	–	–	2.00	6.00	6.00	8.60	9.60
Toys and Others	–	–	–	–	48.00	6.00	10.66
Total	45.01	206.22	222.49	288.81	476.11	724.74	866.66

Source: Batam Industrial Development Authority, cited in Ahmad (1992).

Other Islands

In Bintan, an Indonesian partner, Salim Group, together with Singapore's Wah Chang International and Keppel Corporation, is in the process of developing a tourist resort with hotels, golf course, and marinas. In the first phase, seven world class hotels with a total of 2,000 rooms will be built. A ferry link will enable tourists from Singapore to reach the island within an hour. There are also plans to put up an olefin plant close to Pertamina's shipping and storage facilities on the island. An industrial park, which will cater to land-intensive manufacturing such as textiles, toy making, wood products, food processing, and packaging, is also on the drawing board.

Bulan has a number of agro-businesses, ranging from pig and orchid raising to crocodile and poultry farming. The island has become a supplier of pork to Singapore and of flowers to the European Community (EC), and is also exporting crocodile skin to Hong Kong and Taipei,China through Singapore.

Singkep and Karimun are more recent additions to Riau's development. Karimun came into the spotlight when it was announced that the Sembawang Group, a Singapore GLC, had embarked on an ambitious joint venture project with an Indonesian group to make the island a major petroleum processing and shipyard center. This facility will enable the oil and marine industries in Singapore to expand and better serve the region. Singkep, an island whose tin mines are slowly being depleted, will be developed as a ship-breaking center.

Prospects and Problems

The Singapore-Riau of the growth triangle is becoming more than an industrial, agro-business, and tourism zone. With Singapore's oil trading activities and its large quantities of oil products, the area is emerging as an important oil center on the global energy map. In 1990, a total of $38 billion in oil stocks were traded in the Singapore International Monetary Exchange (SIMEX). Links in the oil industry involving trading, distribution, processing, and extraction are now being closely integrated in the growth triangle.

Despite the rapid growth in the triangle, problems remain. Infrastructure is inadequate, bureaucratic procedures for investors have not been fully streamlined, and labor is in short supply, particularly for industries in Batam. Skilled workers have been recruited from Java and Sumatra on two-year contracts, but there are fears that they may not stay on after two years, or that they may be subject to poaching by other companies. More critical is the lack of trained technical staff to supervise and manage the factories. When found, skilled workers demand wages on par with those being received by their counterparts in Singapore, which raises the overall cost of conducting business in Batam. Infrastructure development has lagged; for example, dormitory facilities for workers are still inadequate. Compounding this is the fact that housing for executives is limited. Overall, these supply restrictions have led to high operating costs in the initial stages.

POLICY FRAMEWORK AND EVOLVING ISSUES

Appropriate public policies can facilitate the formation of a growth triangle. Some of these policies require coordinated action by all the parties concerned, while others can be determined by the national priorities of the individual members.

Development of Industrial Infrastructure

The development of the JSR triangle, as well as the more general need to attract investors to the region, has required public sector investments in basic infrastructure. These include industrial estate development, housing, transportation, electricity, water, and telecommunications. In Johor, both the federal and state governments have developed the basic infrastructure as called for in their five-year plans. Nonetheless, the movement of industries to Johor from Singapore and the recent, rapid inflow of foreign investments there have stretched the capacities of the existing infrastructure. In many instances, investors have had to set up auxiliary plants and provide transportation and basic housing for their workers. This has brought into sharp relief the need for even greater public sector investment in infrastructure if bottlenecks and delays are to be avoided. This problem, however, is not unique to Johor, as rapid industrialization is taking place across most of peninsular Malaysia.

In Riau – and Batam in particular – the drive toward industrial and tourism development was set in motion long ago. This allowed infrastructure development to take place before investments began flowing. The development process in Batam was led by initiatives from both the Singaporean and Indonesian governments. Singapore GLCs such as the Singapore Technologies Industrial Corporation and Jurong Engineering formed a joint venture with the Salim Group, an Indonesian private company, to develop the BIP. The Indonesian government, through the Batam Industrial Development Agency (BIDA), improved road, airport, and port facilities, as well as the delivery of electricity and water (Ahmad, 1992). Specifically, some 264 km of minor roads and 70 km of main roads have been developed, and the delivery of treated water has been expanded from 850 liters per second to over 3,000 liters per second. The current power generating capacity of just over 25 MW will increase to 100 MW over the next three years. A gas-fired station will also be built and its output will be shared with Singapore.

In Bintan, infrastructure development is programmed to include large-scale water resources in addition to other basic infrastructure. The potable water produced in Bintan will be sold to Singapore, while also meeting the requirements of local consumers. A total capacity of 121 million gallons of water per day is expected to be generated, with infrastructure costs to be borne by the Singapore government and the Salim Group. Recently, it was proposed that water resources elsewhere in Riau should be developed and that potable water should be sold to Singapore, thereby ensuring that the latter's water resource needs will be served over the long term. This is over and above Singapore's similar arrangement for water resource development with the Johor government. These moves are part of the overall strategy of building ahead to avoid shortages and bottlenecks later. Further, these actions indicate that cross-border investments by governments can be mutually beneficial. Similarly, the involvement of the private sector in infrastructural development is a welcome change from traditional approaches where only governments are expected to undertake such capital-intensive endeavors. From a public policy perspective, what is more important are the benefits which such development could bring to all the communities involved in the process. This will, to a certain extent, depend on the pricing policies to be adopted, including subsidies. These are still unclear at the present time. It is, however, apparent that companies in the private sector have concentrated on infrastructural development in Riau because the returns on investment appear to be attractive.

Labor Market

Singapore has restrictions on the entry of unskilled workers. The policy in force since the early 1980s has favored skilled workers, with the objective of enhancing capital-intensive manufacturing. This has contributed to a tightening of the labor market in Johor, as industries have expanded while skilled labor has migrated in response to higher wages in Singapore. Labor turnover has increased, forcing factories to spend more time training new workers.

In Batam, labor migration into the island is being controlled by a recruitment agency. Only migrants with residence permits are allowed in; permits are only issued to people who have secured employment. The residence permit and employment contract are normally valid for two years and subject to renewal. In order to prevent high labor turnover, returning workers must be assured of employment with their previous employers. This centralized management of labor prevents poaching by different employers and encourages the payment of uniform wages across the manufacturing sector. Nonetheless, the illegal population on the island (i.e., those without residence permits) is growing.

To prevent employers from bringing in low-cost labor to work in factories in Singapore, the government imposes a stiff levy on all foreign workers. This extends to workers who are receiving training in Singapore. Recent complaints by the private sector about the need for training for workers in Batam have led to case-by-case exemptions from this rule. Skilled workers such as engineers and technicians, however, commute regularly to Batam from Singapore. To speed up the entry of workers through immigration, the use of "smart cards" has been implemented (*Straits Times*, 9 June 1992).

Training facilities where workers can upgrade their skills are of critical importance within the triangle for a number of reasons. First, there is an urgent need for skilled and semi-skilled workers to fill the manufacturing and service jobs being created. Second, to maintain competitiveness with other parts of the region, the skills of workers must be improved continuously. Both these imperatives imply public sector involvement in funding and providing facilities for skills training. While on-the-job training will be important, other formal training programs will also be necessary to supplement and improve labor mobility across sectors. While Singapore has enough resources to provide training opportunities, companies operating in Johor and Batam do not. The "public good" nature of skills training calls for a larger role for individual governments. Fiscal incentives such as lower taxation or higher tax write-offs for skills training may also have to be introduced to induce companies to offer formal training and skills upgrading programs.

In Singapore, policy makers have had to consider waiving foreign worker levies for those brought in for genuine on-the-job training from Riau or Johor. In line with this, it has also been necessary to consider providing a two-tiered worker levy scheme to alleviate the current shortage of labor in manufacturing. These measures have to be seen in the light of a possible industrial hollowing-out if many industries relocate rapidly as a result of labor shortages. A coherent policy environment to phase out labor-intensive manufacturing has therefore been designed to prevent this.

In the short term, there are problems associated with the overheating of economies. In Johor, attempts are underway to reduce high labor turnover and prevent excessive cost increases in the labor market. This has required new compensation schemes which have a higher variable component tied to length of service. Similarly, hiring schemes and contracts have had to be designed with a view to reducing high labor turnover. For example, employment contracts with conditions on exclusive employment in one factory for a fixed period of two years and high penalties for breach of contract have been considered by some companies. These, unfortunately, introduce rigidities in the labor market and can only be considered as short-term measures.

Land Tenancy and Property Rights

Land regulations and property rights policies are different in Singapore and Johor than in Riau. Both Singapore and Malaysia were once under British colonial rule, and their legal systems and land laws are similar in many respects. In general, their land laws allow for freehold acquisition and long-term leases. Under Indonesian law, which was patterned after Dutch administrative practices, there is no freehold acquisition of land, and land tenancy normally exists for a 30-year period, with possibility for renewal. Negotiation is made difficult by the sheer number of laws covering land use in Indonesia. While industrial park managers have assumed property rights risk and insulated individual investors against it, industries intending to locate in Riau are vulnerable.

From a policy perspective, two major options emerge. The first is for the governments to harmonize property rights policies across the borders, to make investment risk more uniform throughout the triangle. The second is for the dominant partner in the triangle to assume the property rights risk and insulate investors. This would provide a more level playing field for investors and also reduce financing costs considerably.

Housing and Health

Johor and Riau have had to consider rural development with a view to improving health, providing basic services, and controlling fertility. This is all the more important given the social and economic inequities which arise as a result of rapid development. Unless planned development can proceed in line with market-driven growth, social problems can multiply rapidly. In Batam, for instance, the private sector has been called upon to ensure that adequate low-cost housing is provided in the industrial sites.

Housing development is dependent to a large extent on the property rights regime. If governments can insure against compulsory acquisition or nonmarket pricing policies, then the private sector can be induced to undertake housing programs. The growing pressure on housing has been occasioned mainly by the inability of public authorities to provide shelter to skilled and unskilled migrant workers and their families. Thus, both in Batam and Johor, the authorities have promoted the private development of low-cost housing for workers and others living close to the industrial townships.

One unwanted effect of in-migration is the proliferation of shantytowns on the peripheries of industrial townships. As this may be difficult to stem in the short term, the need for basic health care and sanitation in such areas cannot be ignored. In order to prevent an overwhelming demand for such services later, in-migration has to be controlled. The use of residence permits in Batam has been one way of achieving this, but this is unworkable in Johor because workers are mobile across the peninsula.

Related to the growing pressure on services and to the increase in population is the need for fertility control. This is a serious issue associated with low value-added manufacturing, where incoming workers tend to be young female school leavers. Many workers are finding it difficult to adjust to changing environmental conditions and to the uprooting of traditional lifestyles. There is therefore a need to provide affordable health care and family planning counseling.

Planners have also had to be aware of the consequences of urbanization on the rural population. Household patterns are changing as more and more women leave their homes to work in industries. Similar concerns have been raised in the tourism sector, where changing lifestyles can create social unrest and lead to political tensions. For example, the workers migrating to islands which are predominantly tourist resorts will experience culture shock, while at the same time bringing their own culture to bear on the community.

Regional Policy Coordination

A growth triangle is attractive to investors for its ability to redistribute industrial and service activities across borders. This redistribution can be expedited if investment policies in the different countries are similar. In the case of the JSR triangle, Singapore's investment incentives allow 100 per cent equity ownership and full repatriation of profits, as do Malaysian investment policies in Johor following the Promotion of Investments Act in the mid-1980s. In Riau, investors were originally required to divest 5 per cent of their equity within five years, but this requirement has now been removed, so 100 per cent foreign equity ownership is permitted.

Attracting businesses to the region and providing investment incentives should also be a regional effort. To this end, Indonesian and Singaporean officials have held joint investment conferences in

Japan, Hong Kong, Taipei, and Seoul, and have been fairly successful in generating interest. Although there is a joint Johor-Singapore
committee for the promotion of investments, no formal international organization has yet been formed to carry out this task.

The current policy focuses on two areas: the Johor-Singapore
link and the Singapore-Riau link. Malaysians are concerned that
there is no formal Johor-Riau link despite several official discussions between the two sides.

There must also be cooperation in the redistribution of manufacturing and tourism projects around the triangle. To prevent
excess capacity, the developments in each area will have to be
considered within the context of the region's development. For
example, the proliferation of golf courses and tourist resorts must
be controlled.

AREAS OF CONCERN

In many respects, the JSR growth triangle has been a success. But
this success has been accompanied by a number of operational,
social, and political problems.

Operational Problems

Malaysian labor policy is biased toward the hiring of local skilled
labor, thus putting Singaporean professionals stationed in Johor at
a disadvantage. High labor turnover has surfaced in the state, in
part due to the flow of Malaysian workers to Singapore for higher
wages. These difficulties have prompted calls to restrict labor
movement from Johor to Singapore.

In Singapore, employers have frequently voiced dissatisfaction with the imposition of the foreign worker levy on workers
brought from Johor and Batam for training. The Labor Ministry has
stated that each case will be decided on its own merits, as employers
previously abused the system by rotating workers every six months
from Johor under the guise of training. As Singapore's labor costs
have increased significantly and labor is in short supply, the government has provided a two-tier worker levy with a 45 per cent
ceiling for foreign workers in any one factory. While the initial

impetus for the formation of the triangle had been the availability of low-cost labor and land, greater investments have caused labor costs to increase, thereby diminishing the original comparative advantage. Labor in Batam has had to be trained, and this has increased labor costs. Furthermore, controlling the supply of labor into the island has also had the undesirable effect of causing further wage increases. In effect, the policy of managed migration into Batam has inadvertently caused labor costs to increase.

The movement of MNCs and large local companies to Johor and Batam has meant that supporting industry has to move to those locations, or transport networks must be upgraded to deal with manufacturing systems that maintain low stocks and assemble items from materials they have just received. These systems obviate the need for holding large buffer stocks and reduce operating costs significantly. Yet many supporting industries have not moved because of the high set-up costs, and have continued to produce inputs in Singapore and send them to Johor. However, customs procedures for these small and medium enterprises tend to be lengthy and, at times, arbitrary. These procedures, as well as the restricted hours of operation at the customs checkpoints, have impeded the free movement of intermediate goods across the border to Johor.

Social Problems

The most urgent social problem is the rising cost of living in Johor and Batam. In Johor, the lure of employment in Singapore has driven up labor costs significantly. This has further been affected by increased housing costs resulting from shortage. The influx of Singaporeans who shop in Johor to take advantage of the weaker Malaysian ringgit has also contributed to rising costs of living. Recent surveys indicate that Johor is now a more expensive place to live in than Kuala Lumpur. In 1991, Johor had an annual inflation rate of around 6.8 per cent, which was much higher than the national average (*Business Times*, 15 April 1992). Similar problems exist in Batam, where the Singapore dollar is accepted for business transactions.

The migration of labor to urban centers and industrial town-ships has exerted enormous pressures on the existing infrastructure. In Johor and Batam, housing and basic amenities have been stretched to the limit and rents have escalated. Consequently, shantytowns have mushroomed in and around the industrial townships.

A more pressing problem has to do with the changing cultural-ethnic mix in towns and urban centers. In Batam, the influx of workers from Java and Sumatra brings into play ethnic and religious differences which have to be managed carefully. Similarly, the migration of mostly Malay single female workers to industrial locations in Johor may create problems in both the rural and urban centers.

Another issue that has emerged of late is the ethnic exclusivity of the jointly developed projects in Riau and, to a lesser extent, in Johor. Most of the joint development efforts by the private sector in both Johor and Riau are being led by ethnic Chinese businesses with their counterparts from Singapore. This has raised questions relating to the sharing of the economic pie with other communities – particularly the *pribumis* in Indonesia and the *bumiputras* in Malaysia. Government leaders have, however, sought to play down these issues, and a tacit understanding has been reached that all ethnic groups will enjoy similar benefits in the triangle.

Political Problems

In an arrangement involving three countries, political problems are likely to arise. A case in point is the Malaysian government's view of the close relationship between Johor and Singapore. While Singapore is a sovereign state, Johor is a part of the Federation of Malaysia, and any development in Johor has to be seen within the context of overall Malaysian development. The need for balanced development has meant that resources have had to be allocated to the less well-endowed states in the northeast. Johor's aggressive drive for its industrial growth to match that of Singapore has therefore been viewed with some dismay from the center. Johor has been a node of labor-intensive manufacturing within the JSR triangle, while the overall Malaysian goal has been to achieve higher value-added and more capital-intensive industrialization. From the perspective of the federal government, these are conflicts in objectives over the short term.

Within Malaysia, there are also questions as to who will benefit most from the development of the triangle. The perception that Singapore enjoys significant benefits at the expense of Malaysia is not taken lightly. Likewise, Johor's rapid growth, which outpaces the growth in the other states, is also viewed with suspicion by other states.

In Riau province, questions have been raised about whether or not the benefits of the triangle will accrue to the local population. There is also some resentment outside the province that development should be concentrated in Riau, which has a smaller population base than parts of eastern Indonesia with more resources and larger populations.

LESSONS AND PROSPECTS

At this writing, the growth triangle has been in existence for a little over three years. During this time a number of lessons have emerged, foremost of which is that the most important requirement for the success of any cross-border arrangement is for the participants to be politically committed to their endeavor. Other important factors are the existence of comparative advantage, geographical proximity, cultural affinities, and business links.

Political Commitment

The development of the growth triangle was set into motion by a meeting between President Suharto of Indonesia and Prime Minister Lee Kuan Yew of Singapore in October 1989 (*Straits Times*, 7 October 1990). Following that meeting, investment regulations in Batam were relaxed to allow 100 per cent equity ownership for foreign investors for the first five years. The private sector was also encouraged to participate in the development of basic infrastructure.

Prime Minister Mahathir and President Suharto endorsed the growth triangle concept in mid-1990. This was followed soon after by two bilateral agreements between Singapore and Indonesia. The first agreement set the framework for the joint development of Riau province, while the second was an agreement to protect investments from being nationalized. A further agreement in June 1991 provided for the joint development of water resources in Riau, under which Singapore was assured of water supply for 50 years (*Straits Times*, 29 June 1991). Singapore also has a water agreement with Johor, and a Johor-Singapore Joint Committee on Business Cooperation has been set up for industrial development.

To strengthen their political commitment and encourage the participation of private investors, the governments concerned have undertaken joint ventures within the triangle. These joint development efforts, which may be in themselves quite minor, have given investors the confidence that the governments are serious about the growth triangle and willing to resolve any operational problems that might arise.

One area of cooperation has been the effort to facilitate the movement of goods and workers across national borders. Links with Johor were expanded and transfer formalities across the causeway were streamlined. In Batam, the movement of commuters from Singapore has been facilitated through the use of "smart cards." As Batam is considered a bonded free trade zone, customs formalities for the movement of goods have also been relaxed. Inward and outward shipments from Batam can now be done within a day, an important consideration for manufacturers who rely on suppliers from Singapore.

Another area for cooperation is marketing. Singapore and Indonesia have conducted two high-level joint marketing missions to generate interest in Batam and Bintan among investors from Japan, Hong Kong, Republic of Korea, and Taipei,China (Lee, 1992). The Malaysian government has also stated that it intends to promote the triangle jointly with Singapore (*Straits Times*, 30 September 1992). These joint marketing efforts will assume greater importance as competition increases from other low-cost production areas in the Asia-Pacific region. Nonetheless, the active interest of the three partners in joint marketing shows the seriousness with which they view the triangle and its development.

Comparative Advantage

The relative costs of land and labor in the three areas of the triangle are complementary, with industrial and commercial property costs being lower in Riau and Johor than in Singapore. This difference in cost structure enables the redistribution of manufacturing and service operations in the three areas, thus minimizing production and operating costs. Singapore has high-quality infrastructure, an efficient telecommunications network, a wide-ranging airline network and a trained labor force, all of which permit the retention of higher value-added activities. Johor has ample industrial land and a fairly elastic supply of labor. Similarly, Riau has industrial land, water resources, beaches, and a managed labor market which have made possible industrial relocation, agro-businesses, and tourism development.

Geographical Proximity

A key determinant in the success of the growth triangle is the close proximity of Singapore, Johor, and Riau to one another. Johor is connected to Singapore by a causeway, and a second connecting link is being designed. Travel time to Johor and its industrial estates is about one hour from Singapore by road. Batam is about 45 minutes by ferry from Singapore, while Bintan is about three hours away by boat. Once hydrofoil services begin, Bintan will be accessible from Singapore in about an hour's time. Thus, the proximity of the three areas allows daily travel from Singapore, which is an attractive feature for companies redistributing their activity within the triangle. Most chief executive officers and their key staff prefer to be based in Singapore and commute to factories in Johor or Batam (Kumar and Lee, in Lee, 1991).

Role of the Public and Private Sectors

Efforts to strengthen the formation of the growth triangle have mostly been undertaken by governments and their agencies, and the longstanding perception has been that the private sector should become more involved. The recent move of companies to the industrial park in Batam indicates the willingness of the private sector to invest if the institutional and infrastructural requirements are in place. The developments in Johor indicate that, in the provision of public infrastructure, government must catalyze private sector involvement if bottlenecks and delays are to be avoided. In

Batam, and Riau province in general, it is apparent that the provision of infrastructure by the government alone is insufficient. Transparent and clearly defined property rights are also essential for the private sector to become involved. As the growth triangle evolves, the role of the private sector in investment and the creation of a self-sustaining economy is likely to become relatively more important. Over time, the role of the government should diminish and be confined only to the provision and enforcement of property rights, the management of public infrastructure, and the provision of basic services.

CONCLUSIONS

Thus far, the development of the JSR growth triangle has hinged on the commitments made by the different governments and on their supportive policies. Growing populations, expanding townships, dynamic central government and state relationships, and the changing nature of competition with other low-cost production areas have evolved as points of concern as the triangle has evolved.

The most pressing external issue facing the JSR triangle today is competition from other developing countries with low-cost production bases. These include the special economic zones (SEZs) in the People's Republic of China, the export processing zones in Viet Nam, and, possibly in the near future, the free trade zones in the Philippines. The critical factors which will determine the competitiveness of the triangle will continue to be low wages, rents, and land costs, and superior infrastructure.

In order to keep wage costs down, current labor market policies in each of the three areas may have to be made more flexible. Managed labor in Riau and high training costs will have to be moderated if the ratchet effects of wage increases are to be contained. Similarly, the high cost of doing business in Singapore must be brought down to manageable levels. Policies to contain excessive infrastructure and service costs in Singapore also need to be introduced rapidly if its competitive edge is not to be lost. The current moves toward lower corporate taxation and the adoption of an expenditure-based tax system should provide some relief in the medium term.

Related to this is the strength of the Singapore dollar. Since the policy of the Singapore government is not to devalue the currency, any growth will have to come from higher productivity. For the triangle, therefore, productivity must be considered from a regional perspective rather than on an individual country basis. This will require all three governments and their respective investors to consider joint training and skills upgrading facilities. Nonetheless, a large portion of such development expenditure must come from the public sector if overall business competitiveness is not to be lost. Hence, fiscal incentives and funding for training infrastructure will be needed in the short term.

Expanding townships and growing populations, especially of different ethnic backgrounds, pose a challenge for economic planning. As infrastructure development has a long gestation, it would be judicious to provide basic health and sanitation facilities first. Steps should then be taken to reduce the rigidities imposed by a managed labor market to ensure a more elastic supply of labor. In this regard, the Malaysian pattern of industrial townships is preferable to the one developing in Riau, where there is a large nonresident population and a growing shantytown economy.

A further issue of concern is the nature of the relationship between the center and the periphery. In Malaysia, Johor is a state within a federal system. As such, issues related to investment policies, immigration, customs formalities, acquisition of land for development, etc., are considered to be within the domain of the federal government. Differences of opinion between the state and federal governments on political matters often have a bearing on the actions of the former. For Singapore, relations with the state and federal governments need to be delicately handled. There is less ambiguity in the relationship with Riau, as there is greater central direction from Jakarta. Within Malaysia, there are concerns that Johor has received more federal funding after growing rapidly within the triangle, to the detriment of other states with pressing infrastructural needs. There is also political concern at the center over the economic ties being forged between Johor and Singapore.

The formation and evolution of the JSR growth triangle has brought into sharp focus the difficulties involved in joint development. This study has traced the development of JSR and the policy framework underlying its evolution. As the triangle evolved, various operational, social, and political problems have emerged. Some have been addressed by the individual governments concerned but some have required coordinated action by all three parties. The need to strengthen some existing policies and also to institute new ones has become more apparent. The critical factor which faces the triangle today is competition from other areas within the Asia-Pacific region. In order to maintain competitiveness, policies must be instituted from a joint perspective rather than from the point of view of a single nation.

The issues highlighted above presage a slower development than participants may have hoped. If this deceleration is to be avoided, discussions to ensure the harmonization of labor, social, and legal regulations must be carried out at a high level rather than by low-level agencies. The need for sovereign responsibility over national issues precludes the possibility of a centralized body to oversee overall developments within the triangle. A more workable tack would be to provide the necessary leadership and political commitment through joint consultations.

While individual governments can implement those policies, it would help if development institutions could lend their assistance. Bilateral and multilateral institutions could alleviate some of the pressing problems confronting policy makers in the JSR triangle. Following are the four areas that require assistance.

Financing Infrastructure Development

The most important support which development institutions could provide to the growth triangle is in funding infrastructure development. An important lesson from the experience in the JSR triangle is that it is better to build for higher capacity than may appear warranted in the short term. This will require larger sums and a willingness to sustain initially lower rates of return.

Multilateral agencies can support governments by providing preferential financing and technical know-how. To expand and hasten the provision of basic infrastructure, multilateral agencies should also be in a position to facilitate build, own, operate, and transfer (BOOT) schemes so that private sector involvement in infrastructure development can be enhanced.

Establishing an Appropriate Property Rights Regime

The second and equally pressing task in which multilateral agencies can lend support is the formulation of an appropriate property rights regime in the areas being jointly developed. Multilateral agencies can provide unbiased support for a framework that would take into account environmental standards, pollution abatement, land regulations, investment incentives, and labor market policies. They can further assist in setting up the institutional requirements for operationalizing the framework by drawing up the regulations, training public servants, and playing an adjudicatory role. They can also be instrumental in preventing the emergence of monopolies and ensuring that the public interest is protected.

Providing Basic Services and Manpower Development

A third area in which development agency efforts would be welcome is in the provision of basic services such as health care, fertility control, and vocational training. The training of workers and skills formation should be considered as public benefits that promise substantial returns in the long run.

Lagging infrastructure, overheated economies, and political squabbles have begun to sap the energies of state and provincial governments in the triangle, leaving less time for training or skills development. Within the JSR triangle, therefore, multilateral agencies may be best suited to supporting and setting up training institutes and a business park in Johor, as well as vocational training facilities in and around Riau province.

Supporting Small and Medium Enterprises

While the respective governments have been concentrating on building facilities for large companies and MNCs, support for small and medium enterprises has waned. Development institutions could play a key role in promoting these enterprises and provide funding for the purchase of appropriate capital equipment. Such institutions could also finance the working capital requirements of small firms that provide subcontracting services to large companies and MNCs, assist in the building of workshops and factories, and help with the development of secondary transport networks.

Endnote:

1.   Fellow, Institute of Southeast Asian Studies, Singapore.

Bibliography

Ahmad, Mubariq, "Economic Cooperation in the Southern Growth Triangle: An Indonesian Perspective," paper presented at the Conference on Regional Cooperation and Growth Triangles in ASEAN, Centre for Advanced Studies, National University of Singapore, 23-24 April, 1992.

Growth Triangles in ASEAN. PITO Brief No. 10. Honolulu: East-West Center, 1992.

Kamil, Yuhanis and Associates, "A Malaysian Perspective," in Lee Tsao Yuan, ed., *Growth Triangle: The Johor-Singapore-Riau Experience*. Singapore: Institute of Southeast Asian Studies, 1991.

Kumar, Sree and Lee Tsao Yuan, "A Singapore Perspective," in Lee Tsao Yuan, ed., *Growth Triangle: The Johor-Singapore-Riau Experience*. Singapore: Institute of Southeast Asian Studies, 1991.

Lee Tsao Yuan, ed. *Growth Triangle: The Johor-Singapore-Riau Experience*. Singapore: Institute of Southeast Asian Studies, 1991.

Lim Chong Yah and Associates. *Policy Options for the Singapore Economy*. Singapore: McGraw Hill, 1988.

Mann, Richard I. *Batam: Step by Step Guide for Investors*. Toronto: Gateway Books, 1990.

Ministry of Trade and Industry. *Report of the Economic Committee*. Singapore, 1986.

Ng Chee Yuen, and Wong Poh Kam, "The Growth Triangle: A Market

Driven Response?" in *Asia Club Papers*. Tokyo: Tokyo Club Foundation for Global Studies, 1993.

Tate, D. J. M. *The Making of Modern Southeast Asia*, Vol. I. Kuala Lumpur: Oxford University Press, 1971.

Wong Poh Kam, "Economic Cooperation in the Southern Growth Triangle: A Long-Term Perspective," paper presented at the Conference on Regional Cooperation and Growth Triangles in ASEAN, Centre for Advanced Studies, National University of Singapore, 23-24 April, 1992.

Johor-Singapore-Riau Growth Triangle: Progress and Prospects

■ G. Naidu[1]

INTRODUCTION

Since the late 1980s, the economies of five of the six countries of the Association of Southeast Asian Nations (ASEAN) have grown extremely rapidly, with Singapore and Thailand occasionally posting double-digit growth rates. This remarkable economic performance is not attributable to economic cooperation among the member countries; such cooperation has in fact been rather minimal (Tan, 1992; Toh and Loh, 1992). Nonetheless, the ASEAN framework has provided a degree of political stability, which has fostered an atmosphere in which member countries have been able to concentrate on their own growth and development.

ASEAN economic cooperation was given a boost with the holding of the fourth meeting of ASEAN heads of governments in Singapore in January 1992, where, among other things, an agreement on the Common Effective Preferential Tariff (CEPT) scheme for the ASEAN Free Trade Area (AFTA) was signed by the economic ministers of the ASEAN countries. The agreement envisages the establishment of a free trade area covering all manufactured and processed agricultural products within a period of 15 years beginning on 1 January 1993, with tariff rates to be brought down ultimately to a range of 0-5 per cent.

The CEPT scheme in itself did not usher in an era of increased economic cooperation among ASEAN member countries. AFTA, after all, was to materialize only within 15 years' time. To hasten the process of international economic cooperation, some governments sought to establish localized economic cooperation zones outside the CEPT, ASEAN, or AFTA frameworks. These zones have variously been referred to as natural economic territories (Scalapino, 1992), extended metropolitan regions (McGee, 1992), transnational export processing zones, and, most commonly, growth triangles. A growth triangle involves the linking by various means of three areas with different factor endowments. Unlike trade blocs or major international groupings, growth triangles are "narrow" subregional economic zones that do not entail the integration of entire national economies (Chia and Lee, 1992).

SUBREGIONAL ECONOMIC ZONES IN THE ASIA-PACIFIC REGION

At present, the only substantive example of a growth triangle in the ASEAN region is the one that includes Singapore, the neighboring southern peninsular Malaysian state of Johor, and the Indonesian province of Riau. There are various names currently being used to denote the triangle: JSR (coined by Dr. Habibie, the Indonesian Minister of State for Research and Technology), the Johor-Singapore-Riau Growth Triangle (which is popular in Singapore), and Nusa Tiga (a label coined by Johor Chief Minister Tan Sri Muhyiddin Mohamed Yassin).

Other subregional economic zones have also been proposed in ASEAN. One proposal that has caught much attention is the so-called Northern Growth Triangle, encompassing the contiguous subregions of northern peninsular Malaysia, southern Thailand, and northern Sumatra. Another proposed growth triangle would link Davao in the southern Philippines, Madano in northern Indonesia, and Sandakan in Sabah, Malaysia (see Figure 1).

The slow pace of trade cooperation and trade liberalization in ASEAN, as well as the difficulty of securing consensus on all issues among the six member countries, were undoubtedly the main factors leading to the proposal on investment cooperation within the JSR growth triangle (Chia and Lee, 1992). Official statements of support by Indonesian President Suharto and Malaysian Prime Minister Dr. Mahathir Mohamed in June 1990 increased the

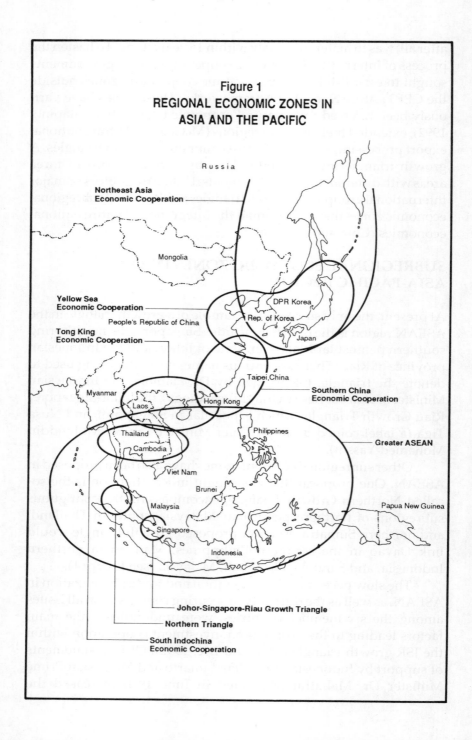

Figure 1
REGIONAL ECONOMIC ZONES IN
ASIA AND THE PACIFIC

Russia

Northeast Asia
Economic Cooperation

Mongolia

Yellow Sea
Economic Cooperation

DPR Korea

People's Republic of China

Rep. of Korea

Tong King
Economic Cooperation

Japan

Taipei,China

Southern China
Economic Cooperation

Myanmar

Laos   Hong Kong

Thailand   Philippines

Cambodia   **Greater ASEAN**

Viet Nam

Brunei

Malaysia   Papua New Guinea

Singapore

Indonesia

Johor-Singapore-Riau Growth Triangle
Northern Triangle
South Indochina
Economic Cooperation

momentum toward the realization of JSR. Finally, at the fourth ASEAN summit in January 1992, the growth triangle concept was formally endorsed. This endorsement, however, came about only after the member countries recognized the viability and usefulness of JSR (Ariff, 1992). It is important to stress that the triangle was not based on any formal agreement among the three member countries, but remained a loose alliance wholly independent of ASEAN.

As originally envisaged, the zone was to cover only Batam, Singapore, and Johor. However, under an Indonesian presidential decree issued in July 1990, the entire Riau archipelago officially became part of the JSR growth triangle, with subsequent development plans for the triangle including Batam, Bintan, and Singkep (Ahmad, 1992).

As currently configured, JSR covers a land area of nearly 23,000 square kilometers, and supports a total population in excess of five million. Table 1 shows that wealth and land resources are extremely unevenly distributed among the participating territories.

Table 1. Selected Indicators of the JSR Growth Triangle

	Johor	Singapore	Riau	Total
Area (sq km)	18,914	639	3,300[a]	22,853
Population (million)	2.2 (1990)	2.8 (1991)	0.1[b] (1991)	5.1 (approx.)
Per capita GDP ($)	3,594 (1991)	12,940 (1991)	500[b] (1988)	--
GDP at current prices ($ million)	4,300 (1990)	34,600 (1990)	45[b] (1988)	38,945 (approx.)

[a] Includes only Batam, Bintan, Bulan, Singkep, Rempang, and Galang dan Barelang.
[b] Batam only.
Source: Chia and Lee (1992).

RATIONALE FOR THE JSR TRIANGLE

The basic economic rationale for JSR is that it makes possible the joint development of the subregion by capitalizing on the resource complementarities of the three participating areas (Chia and Lee, 1992). Geographical proximity keeps down transaction costs and facilitates the flow of resources, workers, and products. A favorable political and policy environment is an important factor supporting the development of the triangle, as is the existence and promise of suitable infrastructure.

Complementarity

Each component area of the JSR triangle has its own comparative advantages. Singapore's advantage lies in its managerial and professional expertise and its developed transport and telecommunications networks. It has, however, lost its comparative advantage in labor-intensive and land-intensive activities. Singapore's real unit labor costs have escalated; increases in its foreign worker levy and a 40 per cent ceiling on foreign workers (effective since October 1987) have also adversely affected labor-intensive manufacturing industries (Lee, 1992). Property prices in Singapore have also risen sharply. Johor and Riau, in contrast, offer land and labor at lower costs. Table 2 shows the relative land and labor costs in JSR. The cost of land in Singapore is higher than in Johor, and the land costs in Batam are very much lower than in both Singapore and Johor. Similarly, labor costs in Johor are

Table 2. Factor Cost Comparisons in JSR, 1991

	Johor	Singapore	Batam
Land ($/sq m)	4.08	4.25	2.30
Labor ($/month)			
Unskilled	150	350	90
Semiskilled	220	420	140
Skilled	400	600	200

Source: Chia and Lee (1992).

between one-half and two-thirds of those in Singapore, while in Batam they are only about one-half to two-thirds of those in Johor. It has been suggested that the economic complementarity of the three areas has made the JSR triangle more attractive to investors as a whole than in its separate parts.

At the macroeconomic level, JSR should help Singapore achieve many of its objectives (see Chia and Lee, 1992; Lee, 1992). These include:

(i) *Economic restructuring.* By making it possible to relocate labor-intensive and land-intensive industries in Johor and Riau, the subregional grouping has provided Singapore the opportunity to move to new areas of comparative advantage in high value-added manufacturing and service industries. JSR thus constitutes a "borrowed economic space" for Singapore (Toh and Loh, 1992), or an opportunity to decant workers and enterprises in labor-intensive and land-intensive industries. As a result of the redistribution of industries to the three areas in accordance with their comparative advantages, Singapore should be able to solidify its position as a regional hub for trade, finance, transportation, telecommunications, and information, and as the regional headquarters of multinational companies (MNCs). This should allow its partners to exploit a rapid growth in land-intensive and labor-intensive manufacturing activities;

(ii) *Regionalization and internationalization of Singaporean enterprises.* For some time now, the government of Singapore has been urging its large government-linked companies (GLCs) and private companies to move into the international marketplace (Toh and Loh, 1992). Small and medium-scale enterprises have also been urged to regionalize their activities. JSR is seen as a first step in this direction;

(iii) *Access to recreational and leisure facilities.* The growing affluence of Singapore has led to an increasing demand for leisure and recreational facilities. In addition, as the transport hub of Southeast Asia, Singapore has emerged as an increasingly important tourism gateway for Johor. Meanwhile, Riau has come to the fore as a tourist destination with enormous potential. Thus, in the long run, JSR may be able to become a "mega resort" (Yeo, 1991); and

(iv) *Additional sources of water.* Singapore has been dependent on Johor for its water supply. By providing a pretext for an agreement with Indonesia to obtain water from the Riau islands, the triangle has enabled Singapore to diversify its water sources.

Although it is common knowledge that Singapore derives many benefits from JSR, the triangle has also been beneficial to both Johor and Riau. From the perspective of Johor and Batam (and the other Riau islands), the triangle means not only higher levels of investment, with consequential effects on GDP and employment growth, but also faster industrial growth and a shorter learning curve for their labor forces (Toh and Loh, 1992). Many observers believe it will take less time for Johor and the Riau islands to move up the value-added chain by being part of the triangle. In the case of the Riau islands, JSR has also brought a commitment by Singapore to conduct manpower training and undertake infrastructure development.

At the microeconomic level, firms in the triangle should have the opportunity to rationalize their production and distribution through vertical specialization, as they will be free to locate their production facilities according to the production factor intensity in the various areas. Labor-intensive processes could be located in areas with abundant labor resources (the Riau islands and perhaps Johor) while activities that require knowledge and skill inputs — engineering development, marketing, supply acquisition, finance, etc. — could be based in Singapore. This kind of locational distribution could create a wider manufacturing base in JSR, providing an incentive for multinational companies (MNCs) to locate in the region. It should be noted that the growth triangle will probably not induce much vertical specialization between Singapore and Johor.

Like other forms of subregional economic cooperation, JSR should benefit all its constituent parts. The export-oriented triangle approach should mean that domestic enterprises will not be threatened by competition from partner territories, as might be the case under, say, a free trade area arrangement. As investments in JSR are aimed at export markets, conflicts over trade creation and trade diversion should not arise.

Geographical Proximity

The proximity of the three participants is a key factor in facilitating industrial redistribution, contributing to low travel and transport costs, easy monitoring and control of production, and speedy transshipment of intermediate and final goods.

Geographical proximity also reduces transaction and information costs and, in the case of JSR, affords a certain measure of cultural bonding. The Chinese ethnic connection has no doubt fostered joint ventures between Singapore and the Indonesian businessmen in Batam. Ethnic links may also be a facilitating factor in the Singapore-Johor segment of the growth triangle. Therefore, it should not come as a surprise that some people have called the grouping a "Chinese Triangle," giving Singaporean, Indonesian, and Malaysian entrepreneurs of Chinese origin a chance to meet and do business with a minimum of interference or inconvenience (Ariff, 1992).

Policy Environment

While geographical proximity and differences in factor endowments are prerequisites for subregional economic cooperation, the formation of the JSR triangle would not have occurred had it not been for policy shifts on the part of Indonesia and Malaysia. Of particular importance was the move toward investment liberalization by both countries, which led to the growth of economic linkages with (and investment flows from) Singapore. The policy changes instituted by Indonesia to attract investments to Batam included the following:

(i) Beginning in 1989, 100 per cent foreign equity ownership was allowed for the first five years of operation, after which a 5 per cent divestment would be required.

In other parts of Indonesia, foreign firms must be major-ity-owned by domestic investors within 15 years;

(ii)   The processing of investment applications was made possible in Batam, rather than at the Investment Board (BKPMD) in Jakarta; and

(iii)   The private sector was allowed to set up industrial estates in Batam.

These major policy shifts have been instrumental in encourag-ing previously reluctant Singaporean investors and foreign MNCs based in Singapore to invest in Batam.

Malaysia, too, undertook radical policy reforms. Prior to 1986, only manufacturing concerns with shareholders' funds of less than M$250,000 and with less than 25 full-time paid employees were exempted from the requirement to obtain a license under the Investment Coordination Act of 1975. For larger manufacturing concerns, investors had to satisfy conditions relating to equity, employment structure, distributorship, etc., before they could be granted a manufacturing license. By the mid-1980s, the Investment Coordination Act had proved to be an impediment to both domestic and foreign private investment. Since 1986, however, the govern-ment has formulated a more liberal policy framework (see, for instance, Naidu and Tamin, 1992). The principal changes include the following:

(i)   The Investment Coordination Act was progressively liber-alized, to where it now exempts manufacturing activities with shareholders' funds of less than M$2.5 million or with less than 75 full-time employees from the requirement to obtain a license to engage in manufacturing;

(ii)   In the face of declining foreign investments in the mid-1980s, foreign equity rulings were relaxed. Since 1986, foreign investors have been allowed to hold up to 100 per cent equity in companies that export at least 80 per cent of their products. Full foreign ownership is also allowed when only 50 per cent of the output is exported, provided the company's products do not compete with products being manufactured locally for the domestic market; and

(iii)   Foreign and domestic investments have since 1989 been given additional encouragement through a reduction in the company tax rate from 50 to 35 per cent, while a progressive phasing out of the 5 per cent development tax began in 1990.

International Developments

A number of developments in the world economy also acted as "push factors" behind the formation of growth triangles such as JSR. These included the formation of large continental trading blocs such as the European Community (EC) and the North American Free Trade Agreement (NAFTA), which brought about a heightened sense of vulnerability among the ASEAN economies. Resource complementarities and the bigger markets generated by these large trading arrangements allowed a new vertical division of labor in the manufacturing and service industries in the member countries of the EC and NAFTA, significantly enhancing the potential competitiveness of companies operating within these groups. The vulnerability of the small-scale and medium-scale economies of ASEAN was amplified by the slow pace of progress of the Uruguay Round of the General Agreement on Tariffs and Trade (GATT). These developments were key factors in the impetus toward AFTA, the Asia-Pacific Economic Cooperation (APEC) forum, and the East Asian Economic Caucus (EAEC). Growth triangles such as JSR can be seen as a response to an increasingly protectionist international trading system.

Japan and the newly industrializing economies (NIEs) such as Taipei,China, South Korea, and Singapore are finding their competitiveness in land-intensive and labor-intensive industries being eroded. Efforts to maintain their competitiveness have resulted in huge investment outflows from these countries to the capital importing member countries of ASEAN. The formation of the JSR growth triangle was in part a response to this development, and the subregional economic grouping should be seen as an attempt to attract these investment funds and direct them to the labor and land surplus areas in Riau as well as in Johor.

A related issue is the phenomenon of globalization of production by MNCs. This has led to a regional distribution and redistribution of production processes in accordance with the comparative advantages of different regions. A regional production system such as that which has been made possible by JSR allows investors to improve their competitiveness through the exploitation of economies of scale and agglomeration economies (Wong, 1992).

Infrastructure

There is no question that infrastructure has an important bearing on the success of a growth triangle. In JSR, Johor's infrastructure is by and large adequate, Riau's is generally inadequate, and Singapore's is excellent. Indeed, the well-developed sea and air transport and telecommunications facilities in Singapore have been an important lure for investors, giving them easy access to world markets, and making the triangle an efficient transnational export processing zone.

PUBLIC POLICY INITIATIVES

On the basis of factor endowments, geography, policies, and infrastructure, the JSR growth triangle is probably as well placed as any other area in the Asia-Pacific region to develop into a vibrant subregional economic zone. Like the Southern China Growth Triangle, JSR is largely a private-sector endeavor, with governments and government-linked companies acting as catalysts. However, the importance of the catalytic role must not be overlooked. Public sector efforts to bring about cooperation and arouse private sector interest are evident in the following:

(i)   In August 1990, Singapore and Indonesia signed the Agreement on Economic Cooperation on the Framework of Development of Riau Province, which broadened the triangle to include the Riau islands and not just Batam. The main provisions of this agreement are simplification of product distribution, payment, and delivery procedures between Singapore and Riau province; joint tourism promotion and development; cooperation in the development and maintenance of infrastructure for joint development projects; cooperation in industrial and technological development in Riau province, including trade, agriculture, and warehousing; and simplification of the tax system to facilitate investment (Pangestu, 1991);

(ii) Also in August 1990, the two governments signed the Agreement on the Promotion and Protection of Investment, which affirmed the top-level political commitment on the part of Indonesia and Singapore to the idea of the JSR growth triangle;

(iii) A bilateral agreement in June 1991 provided for the joint development by Indonesia and Singapore of water resources in Riau (Bintan Island). Under a 50-year agreement, Bintan would supply Singapore with water. In the first project under the agreement, two joint venture companies were formed. The first, which is largely owned by Singaporean investors, will distribute water to Singapore, while the second, which is mostly owned by Indonesian concerns, will distribute water to Bintan;

(iv) An Indonesian-Singaporean ministerial committee has been set up to oversee and facilitate the development of the Riau islands;

(v) An ad hoc coordination board has been set up to assist countries investing in Riau. The board is made up of officials from Riau province's regional development agency (BAPPEDA), the provincial-level Board of Investment (BKPMD), and Singapore's Economic Development Board;

(vi) Two high-level Indonesian-Singaporean joint investment promotion missions were organized to promote investment opportunities in Batam and Bintan. The first visited Tokyo and Osaka in December 1990, and the second Hong Kong, South Korea, and Taipei,China in September 1991 (Ahmad, 1992);

(vii)   Government-linked corporations in Singapore have taken part in a $400 million Singapore-Indonesia joint venture to set up the Batam Industrial Park on Batam Island. The park is predominantly owned by PT Baramindo Investment Corporation, with shareholders including Singapore Technologies Industrial Corporation (with a 30 per cent share) and Jurong Environment Engineering (with a 10 per cent share). The latter is a subsidiary of Jurong Town Corporation, the main industrial estate developer in Singapore. The Indonesian partners consist of some of the major business groups in Indonesia, including the Salim Group, Bimantera, and Timmy Habibie. The participation of Jurong Town Corporation is clearly important in facilitating the relocation of investors originally based in Singapore; and

(viii)   Many other collaborative initiatives are being taken to forge greater cooperation in the Singapore-Batam segment of the JSR growth triangle. These include negotiations between the Batam Industrial Development Authority (BIDA) and Singapore to develop a compatible telephone system for the island, BIDA's proposal to build a gas-fired power plant and share its output with Singapore, and the establishment of the Bintan Development Coordinating Board, made up of officials from the Riau Regional Development Planning Agency, Riau Investment Coordinating Board, and Singapore's Economic Development Board. The introduction of "smart cards" in October 1991 to facilitate communication and travel between Singapore and Batam is an example of cooperation on immigration procedures. Likewise, ferry service between Singapore and the Riau islands has contributed to subregional cooperation and integration while promoting tourism in Riau province.

The aforementioned initiatives are by no means the only joint efforts between the governments of Indonesia and Singapore. What they demonstrate is that both countries want the growth triangle to succeed. There have been fewer cooperative endeavors between Singapore and Johor, however. As in the Singapore-Riau sector, smart cards have been introduced for travel between Singapore and Johor. And, to alleviate severe congestion on the causeway between Singapore and Johor, the Malaysian government has expanded immigration and customs clearance facilities at Johor Bahru. Significantly, Singapore has expressed its willingness to jointly develop water resources in Johor and to participate in the construction of a second link between the two territories. Although there is not much activity in the Singapore-Johor segment, the economic integration between the two areas predates JSR, and the economic and other links between the two areas are certainly broader and stronger than the present level of cooperation between Singapore and Riau.

IMPACT ON SUBREGIONAL DEVELOPMENT

A definitive assessment of the impact of JSR on the economic integration of the constituent territories cannot be made at this juncture. First, the JSR growth triangle is only slightly more than two years old, and any evaluation of its impact must be provisional. Second, data constraints on many aspects of the economic linkages are severe. For example, trade statistics between Johor and Singapore are not compiled on a regular basis. Even at the national level, certain key trade and investment statistics pertaining to economic linkages between the three countries are unobtainable. Finally, even if the required information were available, it would still be difficult to determine precisely to what extent an intensification of trade and investment between the three participants was due specifically to subregional cooperation and to what extent it was due to other influences. For these reasons, the following assessment is highly tentative.

Investment

Increased investment is a more important goal of JSR than an increase in trade between the participating countries. Evidence suggests that the formation of the growth triangle has indeed led to an increase in investment, particularly by Singapore in the economies of Johor and Riau.

Singapore-Batam

The cumulative foreign investment in Batam is summarized in Table 3. It is evident that investment in Batam only took off in 1989, and more or less coincided with both the economic liberalization in Batam and the formation of the JSR growth triangle. Foreign investment in Batam rose by 65 per cent in 1989, 52 per cent in 1990, and 20 per cent in 1991. Total cumulative foreign investment in Batam stood at nearly $867 million in 1991, up from only $289 million three years earlier. It is also important to point out that Batam accounted for 2.2 per cent of total foreign investment in Indonesia in 1991, compared to only 1.4 per cent in 1988. Another estimate puts

Table 3. Cumulative Approved Foreign Investment in Batam by Origin

	1990 Value ($'000)	1991 Value ($'000)	1991 Share (%)	Indonesia 1991 ($ billion)	Batam Share in Indonesia (%)
Singapore	347,164	409,830	47.2	1,235.1	33.1
US	172,591	177,596	20.5	2,220.5	8.0
Japan	54,000	61,750	7.1	10,343.6	0.6
Hong Kong	14,500	38,500	4.4	3,954.0	1.0
Netherlands	18,950	34,574	4.0	49.5	32.9
UK	22,066	22,066	2.5	1,036.8	2.1
Sweden	16,300	16,300	1.9	49.5	32.9
Bahamas	6,443	6,443	0.7	31.2	20.7
Panama	3,000	3,000	0.3	420.5	0.7
Others	69,725	96,725	11.7	18,543.1	0.5
Total	724,737	866,656	100.0	37,782.2	2.2

Source: Ahmad (1992).

Batam's share in total foreign investment in Indonesia at 4.2 per cent in 1990, up from about 2.5 per cent in 1988 (Pangestu, 1991). In any case, it is clear that in the last three years, investment in Batam rose significantly, as did its share of total foreign investment in Indonesia. Much of the absolute growth in investment is without doubt the result of the policy shifts of the Indonesian government, but certainly much could be attributed to Batam's participation in JSR.

The sectoral distribution of foreign investment in Batam is also revealing (see Table 4). While in the past investment activity was largely confined to the production of oil manufacturing equipment, the industry sector has now diversified, with electronics manufacturing emerging as an important subsector. Real estate and tourism, however, have been by far the largest recipients of foreign investment.

Singapore is the largest investor in Batam. With a total cumulative investment of more than $490 million between 1980 and 1990,

Table 4. Cumulative Approved Foreign Investment in Batam
by Sector in Selected Years
($'000)

	1985	1988	1989	1990	1991 Value	Per Cent
Electronics	0	500	500	26,000	88,198	10.2
Chemicals	3,495	3,495	3,495	3,495	3,495	0.4
Oil/Mining Equipment	108,925	108,925	113,425	113,425	113,425	13.1
Steel and Iron	76,465	77,465	125,465	127,665	131,965	15.1
Plastic and Paper	0	0	0	5,600	11,535	1.3
Food and Agriculture	0	17,300	43,600	53,600	53,600	6.2
Real Estate	0	1,500	1,500	193,225	222,849	25.7
Tourism	31,564	73,629	134,129	187,129	221,329	25.6
Equipment Services	2,000	6,000	6,000	8,600	9,600	1.1
Toys and Others	0	0	48,000	6,000	10,660	1.2
Total	222,448	288,814	476,114	724,739	866,656	100.0

Source: Ahmad (1992).

Singapore accounts for 47 per cent of total foreign investment in the island. About one-third of Singapore's investments in Indonesia are in Batam Island. Of particular relevance, too, is the growing volume of Singaporean investments since 1989. It is not clear from the data whether the investments from Singapore were by Singaporean companies or by subsidiaries of MNCs based in Singapore.

Either way, the investment-led economic boom in Batam is evident in the indicators shown in Table 5.

Table 5. Batam: Main Economic and Growth Indicators

	Population	Local Workers	Foreign Workers	Arriving Flights	Ship Calls	Tourists
1973	6,000	--	--	--	--	--
1983	43,000	--	--	481	5,029	--
1985	58,000	6,159	230	1,545	5,592	60,161
1988	79,400	9,478	153	2,887	9,066	227,981
1989	90,500	11,041	140	3,511	10,258	359,497
1990	106,800	16,085	251	6,487	37,802	579,305
1991	107,600	22,942	295	8,003	54,341	606,251

Source: Batam Industrial Development Authority.

Singapore-Johor

Singapore accounts for only about 2.5 per cent of total foreign investment in Malaysia, well behind Japan, the US, and Taipei,China (see Table 6). In 1992, Singapore was the ninth largest source of foreign investment in Malaysia, after ranking sixth in the previous year. But the role of Singapore as a source of investment flows into Johor is dramatically different. Singapore has for many years been the second largest investor in the state after Japan (see Table 7). In 1990, investment flows from Singapore accounted for one-fourth of all foreign investments in Johor.

Table 6. Approved Projects with Foreign Participation in Malaysia, 1992

	Approved Projects	Potential Employment	Foreign Equity (M$'000)	Foreign Investment (M$'000)[a]
France	5	1,076	826,250	4,085,980
US	41	6,286	568,444	3,298,200
Japan	150	24,184	584,208	2,635,553
Australia	19	1,691	462,141	2,119,517
Taipei,China	137	17,189	584,281	1,505,814
United Kingdom	19	1,851	1,007,475	183,997
Ireland	1	570	750,000	750,000
Indonesia	4	2,136	131,453	480,188
Singapore	186	20,982	200,503	440,543
Netherlands	6	1,425	43,170	141,004
Korea, Rep. of	23	2,576	46,214	99,365
Hong Kong	39	6,452	49,047	83,472
Switzerland	7	712	51,196	80,916
Germany, Fed. Rep. of	11	810	36,928	72,836
India	9	769	12,646	52,541
Sweden	2	62	5,100	25,050
Finland	2	164	13,875	22,873
Canada	9	673	15,378	22,258
Philippines	4	455	18,300	18,300
Denmark	3	61	5,516	14,775
China, People's Rep. of	6	808	6,872	9,572
Luxembourg	1	33	3,500	8,000
Cyprus	1	108	1,625	2,252
Thailand	3	160	1,037	1,526
New Zealand	1	8	416	1,516
Italy	2	80	1,000	1,000
Spain	1	15	626	800
Pakistan	2	497	30	125
Saudi Arabia	1	40	0[b]	0[b]
Others	65	6,437	219,255	462,893
Total	[c]	[c]	5,610,487	17,724,139

[a] Foreign Investment = Foreign equity + loans attributed to foreign interest. Loans attributed to foreign interest are provisionally determined according to the percentage of the foreign share in the equity of each project.

[b] Expansion of manufacturing capacities of additional products not involving further capital.

[c] Approvals and employment figures are not added to avoid double counting.

Source: Malaysian Industrial Development Authority.

Juxtaposing Singapore's investment in Johor with its total investment in Malaysia, there can be no doubt that Johor is the most important destination among the Malaysian states for Singaporean investors. In any assessment of the volume and pattern of investment from Singapore to Johor, it must be borne in mind that Singapore investors had already started to relocate to Johor well before the launching or formal endorsement of JSR. Thus, the size of Singapore's investment in Johor most likely has as much to do with Malaysia's liberalized investment climate since 1986 as with the geographical proximity of the two territories.

Trade Linkages

Trade generated by JSR is much more difficult to quantify than investment, mainly because adequate data are simply not available.

Table 7. Foreign Equity in Approved Projects in Johor, 1982-1991
(M$ million)

	1982	1983	1984	1985	1986	1987	1988	1989	1990	1991 (Jan-Nov)
Taipei,China	--	0.5	1.1	5.5	0.7	54.4	98.3	98.9	212.4	395.7
Korea, Rep. of	--	0.3	0.7	--	--	--	7.5	18.3	89.2	307.5
Singapore	4.8	9.2	22.1	17.6	42.6	41.7	101.9	131.5	406.9	294.5
Japan	0.3	1.4	9.9	2.9	28.5	43.6	49.8	282.7	507.7	221.1
Hong Kong	0.0	1.1	2.4	3.2	6.4	6.5	19.1	36.3	74.0	65.6
Europe	36.2	0.6	8.0	2.1	1.0	6.2	65.2	92.1	111.4	54.7
US	5.3	0.7	0.4	--	0.5	10.5	123.8	15.6	125.1	32.0
Indonesia	--	--	--	--	--	--	4.8	1.4	21.1	24.3
Thailand	0.3	--	--	--	--	--	10.2	0.3	--	--
Philippines	--	--	--	--	--	--	--	--	13.0	--
Others	5.3	18.6	26.5	19.2	22.3	36.8	77.0	8.6	36.8	722.9
Total	52.1	32.3	71.0	50.5	102.1	199.7	557.6	685.7	1,617.6	2,118.3

Note: Europe includes the United Kingdom, Netherlands, France, W. Germany, Sweden, Belgium, Italy, Switzerland, Austria, and Denmark. "Others" includes Australia, India, PRC, Canada, Sri Lanka, New Zealand, and Saudi Arabia.

Source: Johor State Economic Development Corporation.

Yet it is safe to say that the growing volume of Singaporean and other foreign investments has very likely led to a greater dependence on the part of Batam and other Riau islands on the port and maritime facilities of Singapore, which is the load center and container traffic hub for Southeast Asia. As Batam and the Riau islands develop their manufacturing base, it is likely that their operations will be increasingly bound up with the transport facilities of Singapore.

The situation with respect to Johor is somewhat more complex. As part of an explicit government policy to achieve a higher degree of self-sufficiency in port services, the Malaysian government has, among other measures, built Johor port to ensure that Malaysia's exports and imports will be shipped through its own ports. The policy has not been very successful, however. About one-fifth of Malaysia's exports and imports are still being transported to or from Singapore. The equivalent ratios for the state of Johor are higher.

Whether this means that trade links between Singapore and Riau and between Singapore and Johor are growing is not wholly clear. There are certainly substantial volumes of trade between Singapore and both areas, and as investment flows gain momentum trade volumes should increase. Now, however, trade linkages mainly involve cargo for transshipment, and as long as Johor and Batam continue to serve as export platforms for Singaporean investors, trade links in the growth triangle will remain superficial.

Tourism

There is a growing volume of tourist traffic between the three constituent parts of the growth triangle. Singaporeans constitute the largest group of tourists in Batam, followed by Malaysians (Pangestu, 1991). Although there are no firm figures on the number of tourists from Singapore to Johor, it has been estimated that Singaporeans make 980,000 visits to Johor Bahru in an average month, spending M$320 million (Devadason, 1992). This volume of tourist traffic is large by any standard.

Tourist linkages in the JSR growth triangle can be expected to grow. Some observers even expect that joint development of the tourist potential of the growth triangle will make it competitive with the Caribbean.

CONCLUSIONS

The basic premise of the growth triangle concept is complementarity. Full exploitation of complementarity requires the free movement of goods, services, and people (Pangestu, 1991). For there to be free movement of goods, the entire area must be duty-free, and there must be harmonization of customs procedures. For the area to be regarded as a single investment location, there must be harmonization and simplification of investment rules, taxes, land laws, and other regulations. Finally, for there to be free movement of people in the triangle, immigration regulations must be harmonized and simplified. The JSR growth triangle is well on its way to achieving such a high degree of harmonization. Still, it is useful to review a few of the triangle's strengths and weaknesses.

There is strong but uneven support for JSR among its members. Support is strongest in Singapore, as evidenced by its growing literature on the growth triangle (see particularly Chia and Lee, 1992; Kumar and Lee, 1991; Lee, 1992; Toh and Loh, 1992; and Wong, 1992, all of which wholeheartedly support the growth triangle). Indonesian scholars are not very enthusiastic about the triangle (Ahmad, 1992; Pangestu, 1991), and the Malaysians (as typified by Kamil et al, 1991) are even less so. The general perception of the Indonesians and Malaysians is that Singapore is likely to derive the largest benefits from the subregional economic grouping. Part of the explanation for the Malaysian and Indonesian perception has to do with complex intranational distributional issues emanating from the participation of Johor and Riau in the growth triangle.

The weakest link in the triangle is the Johor-Riau islands segment. There are no investments from Johor in Riau, and except for an Indonesian proposal to develop tourist facilities in Johor, planned and actual investment flows from Indonesia to Johor are minimal. The same situation holds with trade links, as both Johor and Riau are capital-importing members of the triangle. Moreover, entrepreneurs in Johor and Malaysia, unlike their counterparts in Singapore, are not quite ready for the regionalization of their activities. It is unlikely that investment and trade linkages will develop in the near future between Johor and Riau because they lack complementarity and are distant from each other.

A number of labor issues need to be highlighted. The first is that Riau is not a labor-abundant province. Laborers for islands such as Batam have to be brought in from outside Riau province. Johor, too, is experiencing a severe labor shortage. Latest estimates show that Johor is short of 30,000 workers (*Straits Times,* 12 February 1992). Skill upgrading is another problem, although this is one area where Singapore could play a very useful role. Johor wants to upgrade its industry sector, and expects Singapore to play a role in the training of its manpower. Laborers from Johor employed in Singapore at wages higher than those in Johor also create complications for industrial planning in Johor.

Of the three constituent parts of the JSR growth triangle, Johor appears to be the least able to play an active role. Its status as a state in a federal structure gives it little authority to act unilaterally on important economic issues. Proposals to give Johor more freedom to participate in the growth triangle are now being studied by the Federal Ministry of International Trade and Industry, however (*Business Times,* 8 January 1992).

As for the value of growth triangles at a time when formal trade links between Asia-Pacific countries are strengthening, it should be noted that growth triangles are investment-led and not trade-led, and thus do not detract from regional cooperation. On the contrary, more growth triangles (including multiple and overlapping triangles) should eventually facilitate cooperation on a regional basis.

Endnote:

1.   Professor, Faculty of Economics and Administration, University of Malaya, Kuala Lumpur, Malaysia.

Bibliography

Ahmad, Mubariq, "Economic Cooperation in the Southern Growth Triangle: An Indonesian Perspective," paper presented at the Conference on Regional Cooperation and Growth Triangles in ASEAN, organized by the National University of Singapore, Singapore, 23-24 April 1992.

Ariff, Mohamed, "Ensuring That Triangles Grow," in *The Star*, 2 November 1992.

Batam Industrial Development Authority, "Development Data up to 31 December 1991," 1992.

Business Times, "Investment in Growth Triangle Pays Off," 7 October 1992.

Business Times, "Proposal to Give Johor more Freedom in Growth Concept," 8 January 1993.

Damodaran, R., "ASEAN's Golden Triangle," in *Malayan Business*, 16-31 January 1991.

Davidson, A., "An Economic Law Perspective," paper presented at the Conference on Regional Cooperation and Growth Triangles in ASEAN, organized by the National University of Singapore, Singapore, 23-24 April 1992.

De Melo, J., and A. Panagariya, "The New Regionalization," in *Finance and Development*, December 1992.

Devadason, R., "Johor's Boon and Bane," in *Malaysian Business*, 16-30 April 1992.

Ganesan, H., "Conceptualizing Regional Economic Cooperation: Perspectives from Political Science," paper presented at the Conference on Regional Cooperation and Growth Triangles in ASEAN, organized by the National University of Singapore, Singapore, 23-24 April 1992.

Hady, H., "The Northern Growth Triangle in ASEAN: An Indonesian Perspective," paper presented at the Conference on Regional

Cooperation and Growth Triangles in ASEAN, organized by the National University of Singapore, Singapore, 23-24 April 1992.

Kamil, Yuhanis, Mari Pangestu, and Christina Fredericks, "A Malaysian Perspective," in Lee Tsao Yuan, ed., *Growth Triangles: The Johor-Singapore-Riau Experience*. Singapore: Institute of Southeast Asian Studies and Institute of Policy Studies, 1991.

Kumar, Sree, and Lee Tsao Yuan, "A Singapore Perspective," in Lee Tsao Yuan, ed., *Growth Triangles: The Johor-Singapore-Riau Experience*. Singapore: Institute of Southeast Asian Studies and Institute of Policy Studies, 1991.

Lee Tsao Yuan, "Regional Economic Zones in the Asia-Pacific Region. A Conceptual Overview," paper presented at the Conference on Regional Cooperation and Growth Triangles in ASEAN, organized by the National University of Singapore, Singapore, 23-24 April 1992.

Liwgaemsan, W., "The Northern Growth Triangle: Thailand's Perspective," paper presented at the Conference on Regional Cooperation and Growth Triangles in ASEAN, organized by the National University of Singapore, Singapore, 23-24 April 1992.

Naidu, G., and Mokhtar Tamin, "Private Sector Led Development and the Role of the Government of Malaysia," paper presented at the Korea Development Institute, Seoul, Korea, October 1992.

Pangestu, Mari, "An Indonesian Perspective," in Lee Tsao Yuan, ed., *Growth Triangles: The Johor-Singapore-Riau Experience*. Singapore: Institute of Southeast Asian Studies and Institute of Policy Studies, 1991.

Salleh, Ismail Muhd., "Economic Cooperation in the Northern Triangles," paper presented at the Conference on Regional Cooperation and Growth Triangles in ASEAN, organized by the National University of Singapore, Singapore, 23-24 April 1992.

Scalapino, Robert A., "The United States and Asia: Future Prospects," in *Foreign Affairs*, Winter 1991/92, pp. 19-40.

Tan, Clifford, "Growth Triangles from Several Angles: A NIE Perspective based upon Hong Kong-Guangdong Industrialisation," paper presented at the Conference on Regional Cooperation and Growth Triangles in ASEAN, organized by the National University of Singapore, Singapore, 23-24 April 1992.

Toh, Mun Heng, and Linda Loh, "ASEAN Growth Triangles: Experiments in Cooperation, Complementarity or Competition?" Paper prepared for International Centre for the Study of East Asian Development (ICSEAD) Model Comparison Conference on Trade Development and Regional Groupings in East and Southeast Asia, Kitakyushu, 30-31 July 1992.

Tsuruoka, Doug, "Johor Plays the Angles," in *Far Eastern Economic Review*, 3 January 1991.

Vatikiotis, Michael, "Search for a Hinterland," in *Far Eastern Economic Review*, 3 January 1991.

Wong Poh Kam, "Economic Cooperation in Southern Growth Triangle: A Long-term Perspective," paper presented at the Conference on Regional Cooperation and Growth Triangles in ASEAN, organized by the National University of Singapore, Singapore, 23-24 April 1992.

Yeo Nai Meng, "Singapore and Malaysia Tourism: Development, Trends and Prospects in the 1990's," paper presented at the International Conference on Tourism: Development, Trends and Prospects in the 90's, organized by the Department of Urban and Regional Planning, Faculty of Built Environment, Universiti Teknologi Malaysia, 16-18 September 1991.

Northeast Asian Regional Economic Cooperation

■ Hiroshi Kakazu[1]

INTRODUCTION

An important recent trend in the Asia-Pacific region has been the emergence of new forms of regional economic cooperation, such as the Asia-Pacific Economic Cooperation forum (APEC), the East Asian Economic Caucus (EAEC), and the ASEAN Free Trade Area (AFTA). These regional groupings are apparently encouraged by (i) the rapid economic integration of the European Community (EC); (ii) problems with the multilateral trading system under GATT's principles of free trade; and (iii) a new movement toward regionalism based on market-led principles (Kakazu, 1991).[2]

Aside from formal regional cooperation schemes, various "subregional economic zones" or "growth triangles" have emerged in Asia. These include the Southern China Growth Triangle, the Johor-Singapore-Riau Growth Triangle, the Baht Economic Zone, and the Tumen River Delta Economic Zone (see Figure 1). These zones have the following common features: (i) they are being formed more or less spontaneously in response to market forces; (ii) they are mostly located within free economic and trade zones (FETZs) established by governments to promote economic development in selected regions; (iii) they are designed to be export-oriented and to attract foreign capital; (iv) they possess comparative advantages either in location, labor endowment, or natural resources; and (v) their development has been pursued as part of the national or provincial development policies of the governments concerned.

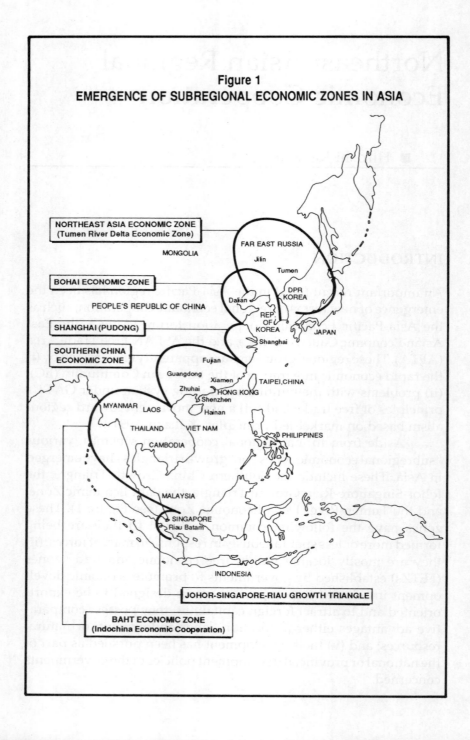

Figure 1
EMERGENCE OF SUBREGIONAL ECONOMIC ZONES IN ASIA

This paper will discuss (i) the concept of regional economic cooperation in Northeast Asia (NEA); (ii) the comparative advantages of the NEA region; (iii) the origin and concept of the Tumen Delta development; (iv) strategies and constraints in developing the Tumen Delta triangle; and (v) financing for the Tumen Delta projects.

TOWARD NORTHEAST ASIAN ECONOMIC COOPERATION

The Northeast Asia region includes Jilin, Liaoning, and Heilongjian provinces in the People's Republic of China (PRC), the Republic of Korea (hereafter South Korea), the Democratic People's Republic of Korea (hereafter North Korea), Far East Russia, Mongolia, and Japan (particularly the Japan Sea littoral prefectures of Niigata, Toyama, Yamagata, Akita, Isikawa, and Hokkaido). The idea of NEA economic cooperation was first publicly proposed in a speech of then Soviet President Mikhail Gorbachev in Vladivostok in July 1986. Gorbachev declared that the Soviet Union was an Asia-Pacific nation intending to link its economy with the dynamic market economies of the region, particularly Japan, South Korea, and the PRC. In a September 1988 speech in Krasnoryarsk, Gorbachev made detailed proposals to open up the USSR's regional economies to the outside world and to disarm eastern Russia. After these two landmark speeches, the political and economic curtains which separated eastern Russia from the rest of Asia were opened with sensational speed.

Era of Opening

As a political gesture, Gorbachev visited Beijing in May 1989. This was followed by (i) the establishment of diplomatic relations between the Soviet Union and South Korea in 1990; (ii) efforts to resolve territorial disputes with Japan; and (iii) the opening in 1992 of the Vladivostok military ports (closed since 1911) to commercial activities. On the economic front, Gorbachev made clear the necessity of multilateral regional economic cooperation in place of existing bilateral arrangements to strengthen regional economic autonomy and encourage foreign investment through joint venture projects.

In the late 1980s, the PRC launched an open door policy with neighboring countries. The resulting thaw in Sino-Soviet relations after more than 30 years of antagonism led the Soviet Union to reopen the Tumen River to the PRC in 1991. To the surprise of the international community, diplomatic relations between the PRC and South Korea were normalized in August 1992, as a consequence of which the PRC's northeastern provinces began vigorously promoting the development of the Tumen Delta area.

South Korea and North Korea meanwhile signed a mutual non-aggression pact after nearly four decades of hostilities, and began negotiations that could lead to unification. Both are interested in regional cooperation on the Tumen Delta basin development. South Korea is interested in the natural resources and potential markets in the region, while North Korea needs outside capital and technology to reconstruct its ailing, debt-ridden economy.

Mongolia, whose economy depended heavily on the USSR in the past, must now find new partners who can provide capital, technology, and markets. For Mongolia, as for the other countries, Japan is a welcome partner in development.

Finally, the Japan Sea littoral prefectures (particularly Niigata) are enthusiastic about the Tumen Delta basin development, as they have long considered their own needs to have been neglected by the Japanese government.

First Steps Toward Cooperation

NEA regional cooperation was first discussed internationally at an East-West Center conference in Changchun in 1990. This was followed by a conference in Pyongyang in 1991 sponsored by the United Nations Development Programme (UNDP). This conference, among other things, proposed that (i) a commission consisting of the six regional countries plus UNDP be set up to manage the regional projects of the Tumen Delta area; (ii) four subcommissions (on trade and logistics; telecommunications; banking and industry; and infrastructure and investment) be established under the commission; (iii) under the supervision of the commission, project planning be conducted for the above four areas; (iv) intracountry trade in the Tumen Delta area be promoted, with the participants sharing data, selecting priority products, resolving existing obstacles to trade (e.g., legal, institutional, financial, and infrastructure problems), and establishing a joint banking facility to replace the barter system for trade finance; (v) in light of the inadequate telecommunications facilities in the region, a temporary microwave system be installed immediately; (vi) new infrastructure projects be implemented under a coordinated overall development plan; (vii) investment promotion and incentive strategies be coordinated; and (viii) a thorough assessment of the environmental impact of the proposed projects be made.

The UNDP report concluded that "the resources of the region of Northeast Asia and their complementation reinforces the concept of the Tumen Delta area as a future Hong Kong, Singapore or Rotterdam with the potential for entrepot trade and related industrial development akin to theirs."

Although other proposals were put forward in various conferences after the UNDP report (Cho, 1992), politico-economic uncertainties in Russia and North Korea, a general lack of coordination, and the low priority given to the Tumen Delta project by the countries concerned have delayed their implementation. Further, Japanese investors have acted cautiously with respect to the Tumen project owing to sensitive, unresolved political issues compounded by worsening domestic economic conditions.

NEEDS AND ENDOWMENTS IN THE NEA REGION

As can be seen in Table 1, the NEA region contains highly diverse economies, with Japan's being 1,500 times as large as that of Mongolia in 1990. Populations, densities, and export-import ratios also vary widely. These differences translate into different advantages and different needs.

National Priorities

Land-poor South Korea and Japan need to promote land-saving industrialization and manufacturing exports so they can import land-based products such as fuel, minerals, timber, and agricul-

Table 1. Leading Indicators of the Northeast Asian Economies, 1990

	Population (million)	Area ('000 sq km)	Population Density (per sq km)	GNP or GDP ($ billion)	Per Capita GNP ($)	Exports ($ million)	Exports/GNP (per cent)	Imports ($ million)	Ratio of Exports to Imports
Total	298.0	9,169	325.0	3,243.7	10,885	361,715.3	11.2	304,368.3	1.19
Japan	123.5	378	326.7	2,942.9	25,430	286,768.0	9.7	231,223.0	1.24
South Korea	42.8	99	432.3	236.4	5,400	64,837.0	27.4	69,585.0	0.93
North Korea	21.7	125	173.6	21.0	987	1,095.0	5.2	1,899.0	0.58
Mongolia	2.1	1,565	1.3	1.7	522	297.4	17.5	359.3	0.83
Northeast China	99.9	787	126.9	41.7	417	7,434.0	17.8	1,302.0	5.71
Liaoning	39.7	146	271.9	20.2	509	5,588.0	27.7	695.0	8.04
Jilin	24.8	187	132.6	8.2	331	732.0	8.9	201.0	3.64
Heilongjiang	35.4	454	78.0	13.3	375	1,114.0	8.4	406.0	2.74
Far East Russia	8.00	6,215	1.3	n.a.	n.a.	1,283.9	n.a.	n.a.	n.a.
Primorskii Krai	2.20	166	13.3	n.a.	n.a.	445.0	n.a.	n.a.	n.a.
Khabarovsk	1.85	824	2.2	n.a.	n.a.	335.0	n.a.	n.a.	n.a.
Amour	1.10	364	3.0	n.a.	n.a.	112.9	n.a.	n.a.	n.a.
Sakhalin	0.72	87	8.3	n.a.	n.a.	68.7	n.a.	n.a.	n.a.
Magadan	0.53	1,199	0.4	n.a.	n.a.	66.7	n.a.	n.a.	n.a.
Kamchatka	0.47	472	1.0	n.a.	n.a.	12.4	n.a.	n.a.	n.a.
Yakut	1.10	3,103	0.4	n.a.	n.a.	243.2	n.a.	n.a.	n.a.

Sources: World Development Report 1992; Statistical Yearbook of China; Economic Almanac of the Russia Far East (1991); Ogawa and Murakami (1991); and Olzvoy (1992).

tural products. South Korea relies heavily on exports because of its relatively small domestic market and its competitive strength in international markets. But the recent slowdown in the world economy has highlighted the need for industrial restructuring. Both Japan and South Korea need to continue relocating their relatively labor-intensive industries to labor-rich countries such as the PRC and North Korea, while the other countries must dismantle their capital-intensive, state-owned industries to make better use of their growing labor forces and scarce capital resources.

While Japan can offer foreign direct investment (FDI), official development aid, advanced technology, management know-how, and a large market, it lacks natural resources and labor. Far East Russia (Primorskii Krai, Khabarovsk, Amour, Sakhalin, Magadan, Kamchatka, and Yakut provinces), with one-fifteenth the population and 16 times the land area of Japan, is endowed with abundant untapped natural resources such as petroleum, coal, metals, forests and fisheries. Yet it is critically short of capital, technology, and human resources.

Northeast China accounted for 8.7 per cent and 11.3 per cent of the PRC's total population and GNP, respectively, in 1990. At 1,995 yuan, the per capita GNP of the area is considerably higher than the national average of 1,558 yuan (see Table 2). Liaoning is the most populated and industrialized province in Northeast China, with a per capita GNP (2,316 yuan) that is higher than that of booming Guangdong province . The area is endowed with a vast land mass suitable for agricultural and industrial development, and a huge, largely unskilled labor force. It should be noted that the PRC has begun exporting labor and bidding for overseas construction contracts (Kim, 1992). There are about 15,000 Chinese workers, mainly from Heilongjiang, in Far East Russia at present.

North Korea is also rich in natural resources (especially mineral ores and timber), but it has been suffering from a dearth of capital, energy, modern technology, and industrial and marketing know-how. South Korea is becoming a major supplier of capital and intermediate technology which may be more appropriate to the region than the high-technology exports of Japan, but it lacks natural and agricultural resources, markets, and the most advanced basic technology.

Table 2. Indicators for Northeast China, 1990

	Total PRC	Northeast Provinces	Liaoning	Jilin	Heilongjiang
Population (million)	1,143.3	99.9	39.7	24.83	35.4
Per Cent Share	100.0	8.7	3.5	2.2	3.1
Land Area (per cent)	100.0	8.1	1.5	1.9	4.7
Population per Km²	189	79	272	132	78
GNP (billion yuan)	17,686	1,994	965	394	635
Per Cent Share	100.0	11.3	5.5	2.2	3.6
Per Capita GNP (yuan)	1,558	1,995	2,432	1,586	1,792
Agricultural Output					
Billion Yuan	7,662	708	274	189	245
Per Cent Share	100.0	9.2	3.6	2.5	3.2
Per Capita Food Output (kg)	390	–	377	824	653
Industrial Output					
Billion Yuan	23,924	3,023	1,607	552	864

Source: *Statistical Yearbook of China*, various issues.

Finally, Mongolia prides itself on having the highest per capita arable land in the region, with great potential for agricultural and livestock development. Yet, in addition to a critical shortage of capital and technology and a small domestic market, the country is landlocked and distant from the Asian growth centers. Economic complementarity in the Tumen Delta region is schematically presented in Figure 2.

Factor Endowments

Figure 3 and Table 3 depict the relative factor (resource) endowments among the countries in the NEA region. The vertical axis shows the capital-labor ratio (or capital intensity), and the horizontal axis shows the relative resource endowments (derived from the land-population ratio) (Campbell, 1992). As might be expected, Japan has the highest capital-labor ratio, while Mongolia has the lowest. Far East Russia has the highest relative resource endowment, while South Korea's is lowest. There is a clear division of

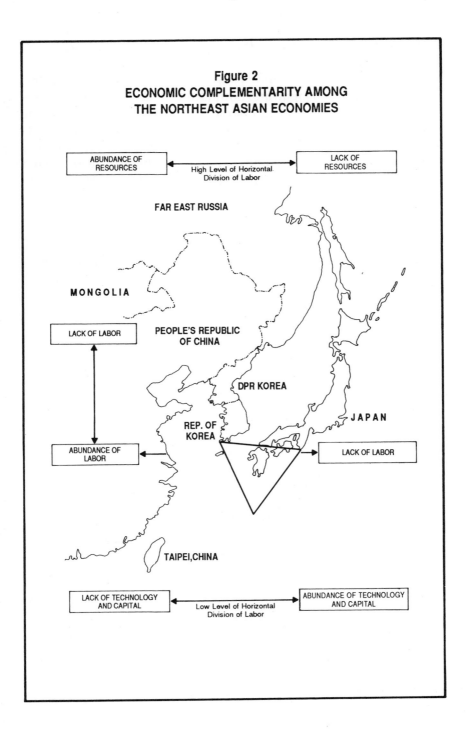

Figure 2
ECONOMIC COMPLEMENTARITY AMONG
THE NORTHEAST ASIAN ECONOMIES

factor endowments between the resource-poor, capital-rich areas
(Japan and South Korea) and the capital-poor, resource-rich areas
(Russia, Mongolia, PRC, and North Korea). The different capital-
labor ratios between Japan and South Korea indicate a complementary division of labor in industrial products, where the former
exports the most advanced capital goods in exchange for standardized, high quality products from the latter. South Korea exports
standardized capital goods and consumer products to the rest of the
region, while PRC exports either resource-based products or labor-

Figure 3
FACTOR ENDOWMENTS OF THE NORTHEAST ASIAN ECONOMIES, 1990

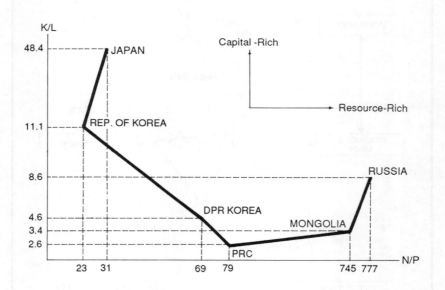

Notes: K/L = capital/labor ratio; capital stock estimates were derived by summing real investment data
        provided on World Bank data tapes. Labor supply estimates are from the same source. N/P = natural
        resources endowments are in terms of land area (km^2) per 100,000 population. Due to lack of data,
        Russia is used for Far East Russia.

Sources: Table 1 and Campbell (1992).

intensive, light manufactured products. Northeast China, in particular, has a comparative advantage in producing labor-intensive products along with agricultural products.

Relative factor endowments, and the capital-labor ratio in particular, should be carefully interpreted for the four currently and formerly centrally planned economies, which in the past tended to pursue more capital-intensive industrialization than they would have had their economies been based on market principles. Factor endowments may be useful as an indicator of potential cooperation only when they reflect relative factor scarcity or relative opportunity costs through a competitive demand and supply mechanism. Mongolia and the PRC have substantially departed from central planning, but deep-seated remnants of their previous systems remain. For example, heavy industry in Northeast China, particularly in Liaoning province, is still dominated by state-owned enterprises which have been operating at a loss (Shimakura, 1992).

Resource-rich Far East Russia and Mongolia show promise, but they are unable to exploit their resources because they lack needed infrastructure. Poor transportation facilities, labor shortages, bureaucratic inefficiencies, highly volatile exchange rates, political uncertainties, and severe winter weather all pose problems.

CHANGES IN INTRAREGIONAL TRADE

The wide variety of needs and endowments provides a perfect starting point for economic exchange based on the traditional Heckscher-Ohlin model. But it must be realized that the traditional theory of comparative advantage has been losing its relevance as barriers come down between countries and between industries. The concept of economic resources has dramatically changed in recent years. Such resources need not be location-specific, and they can be created, transported, transformed, and transacted wherever and whenever potential profit opportunities arise. Untapped natural resources in Siberia, for example, are worthless unless they can find competitive markets. This means that the mere existence of resource complementarities, including natural and human resources, does not spontaneously and naturally evolve into mutual economic

254   Growth Triangles in Asia

Table 3. Factor Endowments and Comparative Advantages Among the Northeast Asian Economies, 1990

	Japan	S. Korea	N.E. China	F.E. Russia	N. Korea	Mongolia
Agricultural Resources/Labor	3	3	2	1	3	1
Arable Crop Land	3	3	2	3	3	3
Mineral Resources	3	3	2	1	3	2
Labor Force Size	1	2	1	3	2-3	3
Physical Capital per Worker	1	2	3	2	3	3
Basic Human Capital per Worker	1	1	2	1	2	2
Advanced Human Capital per Worker	1	1	3	2	3	3
Labor-Intensive Production	3	2	1	3	1	2
Physical-Capital-Intensive Production	1-2	1	2-3	3	2-3	3
Human-Capital-Intensive Production	1	1	2	2	3	3
Economic Efficiency	1	2	3	3	3	3
Market Size (population)	1	2	1	3	3	3
Market Size (GNP)	1	2	3	2	3	3

Rankings: 1=above world average; 2=about world average; 3=below world average.
Source: Campbell (1992).

exchanges, a point which is demonstrated by the paucity of trade and investment among the Tumen Delta countries.

Nonetheless, that trade has been growing. Total intraregional trade (exports and imports) in the region (excluding Mongolia and including all of Russia due to the lack of data on Far East Russia alone) amounted to over $1 billion in 1990, representing an increase of 67 per cent from 1985 (see Table 4) (Imai, in Shimakura, 1992). Yet intraregional trade accounted for 12.7 per cent of the region's total trade, much lower than the comparable figure from the Asia-Pacific region. There are, however, wide variations in regional trade dependency.

Structure of Trade

North Korea traded about 80 per cent within the region, while Russia traded less than 10 per cent. South Korean intraregional trade increased from 20 per cent in 1985 to 25 per cent in 1990, with the bulk of the increase accounted for by its trade with the PRC. As expected, Japan's trade with South Korea recorded a large surplus, but this was more than offset by deficits in its trade with the region's resource-rich countries. The PRC is the country with the largest trade surplus in the region. Liaoning province, where the port of Dalian is located, is now the second largest exporting province after Guangdong. The province accounted for 83 per cent of total trade in the Chinese part of the Tumen Delta region. Japan is the dominant trading partner of Liaoning, while Russia is the number one partner of Heilongjiang, reflecting their geographical proximity.

Since North Korea has not published its trade statistics, figures must be derived from those released by its trading partners. Russia had been a dominant trading partner of North Korea, accounting for 58.9 per cent in 1990, followed by Japan, the PRC, and South Korea. It should be noted that North Korea's trade with South Korea has become visible only in recent years. After the collapse of the Soviet Union, its trade volume with Russia shrank substantially. Trade with the PRC, which has been conducted on a barter basis, has also been shrinking due to the PRC's shift to hard currency trade. One important aspect of North Korean trade is the rapid increase in relations with South Korean firms based in Japan (Ogawa and Komaki, 1991).

Table 4. Intraregional Trade Among the Northeast Asian Economies, 1985 and 1990

($ million)

	Japan	South Korea	North Korea	PRC	Russia	Total Intra-regional Exports	Total Exports	Share of Intra-regional Exports (%)
1985								
Japan	-	7,159	249	12,590	2,772	22,770	177,189	12.9
South Korea	4,144	-	0	683	n.a.	4,827	30,972	15.6
North Korea	177	-	-	223	485	885	1,082	81.8
PRC	6,534	609	239	-	1,037	8,419	27,329	30.8
Russia	1,438	n.a.	787	924	-	3,149	87,281	3.6
Total	12,293	7,768	1,275	14,420	4,294	40,050	323,853	12.4
Total Intraregional Imports	12,293	7,768	1,275	14,419	4,294			
Total Imports	130,516	31,667	1,542	42,480	90,023			
Share of Intraregional Imports (%)	9.4	24.5	82.7	33.9	4.8			
1990								
Japan	-	17,499	176	6,145	2,563	26,383	287,687	9.2
South Korea	11,743	-	5	1,585	519	13,852	63,225	21.9
North Korea	298	20	-	142	1,094	1,554	1,857	83.7
PRC	12,057	2,268	367	-	1,774	16,466	71,746	23.0
Russia	3,370	370	1,585	1,886	-	7,221	109,172	6.6
Total	27,468	20,157	2,133	9,758	5,850	65,476	533,687	12.3
Total Intraregional Imports	27,468	20,157	2,133	9,757	5,950			
Total Imports	235,307	71,359	2,920	60,217	131,333			
Share of Intraregional Imports (%)	11.7	28.2	73.0	16.2	4.5			

Notes: Russian rubles were converted to US dollars based on UN conversion rates. All trade data are in terms of FOB.

Source: Imai (1992).

In the past, Mongolia's trade had been mostly with socialist countries. The USSR alone accounted for more than 90 per cent of the total. Soviet-Mongolian trade fell from $1,234 million in 1990 to $472 million in 1991, however, due to the collapse of the Soviet economy. In place of Russia, the PRC rapidly emerged as an important trading partner for Mongolia.

Japan's trade with North and South Korea, the PRC, and Russia illustrates the actual comparative advantages of Japanese commodities (see Table 5). Japan mainly exports advanced industrial products such as machinery, transport equipment, chemicals, and metallic products, while importing foodstuffs, mineral fuels, raw materials, and light industrial products. As already noted, intra-industry trade between Japan and South Korea has been on the rise in recent years, while Japan's trade with the PRC, Russia, and North Korea is still dominated by vertical exchange: Japan mainly exports manufactured goods in exchange for raw material imports.

Table 6 shows that more than 90 per cent of South Korean exports are industrial goods such as machines, clothing, and textile products. South Korea, whose technology is not yet on a par with that of Japan, exports more resource-oriented and labor-intensive products to Japan than to the rest of the world. The PRC's export structure, on the other hand, has rapidly shifted from primary goods such as foodstuffs, raw materials, and mineral fuels to industrial goods such as chemicals, textiles, clothing, and light machines (see Table 7). It should be noted that although primary

Table 5. Japan's Trade by Major Commodity Groups with Selected Northeast Asian Economies, 1990
(per cent)

	South Korea		PRC		Russia		North Korea	
	Exports	Imports	Exports	Imports	Exports	Imports	Exports	Imports
Foodstuffs	0.3	12.6	0.4	16.1	0.4	9.6	0.0	19.0
Textiles	4.1	0.0	9.9	2.6	5.7	1.0	9.1	9.3
Mineral Fuels, Raw Materials	0.0	2.3	0.0	30.2	0.0	35.5	0.0	38.3
Chemicals	14.0	4.9	12.3	5.4	10.7	1.9	1.7	0.0
Metallic Products	11.0	0.4	19.5	0.3	18.3	1.9	5.1	7.7
Machinery, Transport Equipment	57.6	18.0	46.2	4.3	52.3	0.4	7.4	0.0
Others	13.1	57.8	11.7	41.1	13.9	49.7	0.0	0.0
Total Value ($ million)	17,457	11,707	6,130	12,054	2,563	3,351	176	300

Source: Ministry of Finance (1990).

good exports to Japan still accounted for 56.3 per cent of the total in 1989, the proportion of industrial good exports has jumped from 21.1 per cent to 43.7 per cent in the past four years. This lends credence to the assumption that the PRC will export more and more value-added industrial products, changing the nature of intraregional trade from vertical to horizontal.

Liaoning province accounted for 83 per cent of exports in the Chinese part of the Tumen Delta region. Although detailed trade data are not available, Liaoning's exports are highly resource-intensive compared to the national average. Jilin and Heilongjiang provinces export even more resource-intensive goods than Liaoning.

Exports from Far East Russia are dominated by resource-oriented goods such as forestry products, fishery products, and fuels (see Table 8). Although total exports steadily increased after 1975, it

Table 6. South Korea's Exports by Major Commodity Groups, 1985 and 1989
(per cent)

	1985		1989	
	World	Japan	World	Japan
Primary Goods	8.2	34.3	6.2	18.4
Industrial Goods	91.8	65.7	93.8	81.6
Chemicals	3.1	4.1	3.2	3.4
Raw Materials	23.4	21.3	22.3	24.4
Textiles	8.4	7.6	8.6	5.2
Steel	4.4	9.7	6.0	12.1
Machinery	37.6	18.3	37.8	19.1
Industrial Machines	2.0	1.8	3.4	2.3
Office Machines	1.9	0.6	4.4	1.3
Communication & Audio Equipment	6.5	2.4	9.7	5.0
Electrical Machines	6.4	6.0	11.4	8.4
Transportation	4.1	5.3	6.0	2.1
Ships, Boats	16.6	2.2	2.9	0.1
Other Industrial Goods	27.7	21.8	30.2	34.5
Clothing	14.7	13.4	14.8	23.3
Footwear	5.1	2.5	5.6	2.8

Sources: United Nations, *International Trade Statistics,* various issues; Imai (1992).

Table 7. PRC's Exports by Major Commodity Groups, 1985 and 1989
(per cent)

	1985		1989	
	World	*Japan*	*World*	*Japan*
Primary Goods	50.5	78.8	28.6	56.3
Foodstuffs	14.4	13.2	12.3	17.8
Non-Food Raw Materials	10.2	11.6	8.2	14.9
Mineral Fuels	25.9	54.1	8.1	23.6
Industrial Goods	49.5	21.1	71.4	43.7
Chemicals	5.0	3.7	6.1	6.0
Raw Materials	16.5	7.9	20.8	15.6
Textiles	11.9	6.3	13.3	9.7
Clothing	7.6	6.1	11.7	14.1
Machines, Transport Equipment	2.8	0.2	7.4	1.1
Misc. Manufactured Goods	0.0	0.1	0.0	0.0

Sources: United Nations, *International Trade Statistics,* various issues; Imai (1992).

is doubtful whether this trend was maintained after the collapse of the Soviet economy. Far East Russia has very poor infrastructure, and because of this handicap, the region cannot yet capitalize on its export potential. Primorskii Krai and Khabarovsk provinces accounted for more than 60 per cent of the region's exports because of relatively well-developed trading facilities. Forestry products are exported heavily by Khabarovsk and Amour, while 67 per cent of coal exports come from Yakut, where there are ongoing natural gas and oil joint development projects with Japan (see Table 9).

Mongolian exports have been slowing down since 1988. Measurement of recent declines in exports has been made difficult by the collapse of the ruble economy (ADB, 1992). The latest statistics show that the country exported $34 million worth of products in 1991 (see Table 10).

Border Trade

After the collapse of the Soviet economy and the implementation of economic reforms in the PRC, informal border trade flourished in

Table 8. Far East Russia's Exports by Type, Various Years
(per cent share)

	1975	1980	1985	1990
Forestry Products	61.1	51.0	43.5	43.2
Logs	46.9	35.6	35.0	33.3
Sawn Timber	6.6	7.7	6.0	5.0
Paper & Pulp Products	7.5	7.7	5.0	4.9
Fuel	6.0	5.6	18.2	18.0
Crude Oil	0.2	0.4	0.4	0.5
Petroleum Products	3.8	3.1	6.1	6.0
Coal	2.0	2.1	12.0	11.5
Fishery Products	22.1	24.7	19.5	19.0
Machinery and Apparatus	1.8	2.4	2.5	2.4
Chemical Products	2.5	2.0	1.6	1.9
Construction Materials	0.6	0.9	1.2	1.1
Metal Products	1.0	0.8	1.7	1.9
Hides and Animal Skins	3.6	9.8	5.6	4.9
Light Manufacturing Products	0.5	1.0	0.7	0.6
Others	0.9	0.8	4.3	5.2
Total Exports (million rubles)	486.1	588.4	827.2	1,283.2

Source: Academy of Sciences Russia (Japan), *Economic Almanac of Far Eastern Russia* (in Japanese) (1991).

the Tumen Delta region. Chinese merchants brought commodities ranging from electric appliances to agricultural products in exchange for Russian furs, military watches, binoculars, toys, and local agricultural products. Most of the transactions were conducted using rubles and yuan. The border trade has also been active along the PRC-North Korea border, the Mongolia-Russia-PRC border, and the Japan-Russia border.

Border trade is an important step toward more formal, freer trade in the region because it is conducted spontaneously. Such trade takes on particular significance for previously centrally

Table 9. Exports of Far East Russia Provinces, 1990

	Total Exports		Forestry Products		Coal	
	Value (million rubles)	Per Cent Share	Cubic Meters ('000)	Per Cent Share	Tons ('000)	Per Cent Share
Total	1,283.2	100.0	11,210	100.0	18,281	100.0
Primorskii Krai	445.4	34.7	1,535	13.7	898	8.3
Khabarovsk	335.0	26.1	6,044	53.9	1,511	8.3
Amour	112.9	8.8	2,859	25.5	2,442	13.4
Sakhalin	68.7	5.4	139	1.2	0	0.0
Magadan	66.7	5.2	0	0.0	397	2.2
Kamchatka	12.4	1.0	408	3.6	709	3.9
Yakut	243.2	19.0	225	2.0	12,324	67.4

Source: Academy of Sciences Russia (Japan), *Economic Almanac of Far Eastern Russia* (in Japanese) (1991).

Table 10. Mongolia: Major Commodity Exports, 1991

	Value ($'000)	Per Cent Share
Total	161,349	100.0
Copper Concentrate	7,942	4.9
Molybdenum Concentrate	12,618	7.8
Fluorspar Concentrate	8,489	5.3
Fluorspar	1,800	1.1
Cashmere Tops	3,009	1.9
Processed Cashmere	3,281	2.0
Raw Cashmere	3,150	2.0
Washed Wool	375	0.2
Camel Wool	149	0.1
Animal Hair	480	0.3
Hides and Skins	819	0.5
Cashmere Camel Wool Knitwear	295	0.2
Carpets	1,289	0.8
Velour Coats	3,047	1.9
Furs	302	0.2
Meat	9,479	5.9
Live Animals (not including horses)	9,558	5.9
Horses	4,605	2.9
Casings	547	0.3
Other Goods (including Border Trade)	34,357	21.3

Source: Olzvoy (1992). Data from Ministry of Trade and Industry of Mongolia.

planned economies, where controlled trade, or autarky in the case of North Korea, has been the norm. In Russia, for example, regional trade is still strictly controlled by the central government and there is virtually no regional trading organization to facilitate foreign trade. Border trade is also important because it is conducted by small-scale traders and manufacturers who play a major role in the formation of regional business linkages (Sekiguchi, 1992). A boom in such trade will pave the way for the creation of FETZs in the Tumen Delta region.

STRATEGIES FOR THE TUMEN DELTA TRIANGLE

If a growth triangle is defined as an area comprised of three riparian countries with great economic potential and a clear desire to work closely together based on common economic interests, the Tumen Delta triangle may not qualify. Although Russia, the PRC, and North Korea do share borders, no clear-cut and consensual concept has emerged on how the triangle should be formed.

FETZs as Catalysts

As discussed earlier, the three Tumen Delta riparian countries can complement each other in terms of labor, natural resources, and markets. The required capital and technology can be supplied mainly by Japan and South Korea under an NEA economic cooperation scheme. Yet a key step toward developing the triangle would be the creation of free economic trade zones, which could help the participants harmonize regulations and procedures, thus facilitating the inflow of foreign capital for joint development (Kong and Zhou, 1992).

One approach is to establish one or more FETZs in each country through administrative and policy coordination among the contiguous countries. A second approach is to develop one FETZ in the region whose site borders the territories of the other participating countries. A third option is to establish a free trade zone which would be administered jointly by the three contiguous countries. These countries would, in effect, create a jointly owned and managed agency to be responsible for ports, power, road and rail facilities, etc., that may be required for the establishment of industrial parks, stand-alone manufacturing plants, office and housing complexes, etc. (UNDP, 1991).

UNDP has suggested two possible FETZs in the region. One is a small triangle of 1,000 sq km in the PRC's Hunchun, North Korea's Rajin and Russia's Posyet areas (see Figure 4). The other is a larger area of 10,000 sq km covering Yanji in the PRC, Chongjin in North Korea, and Vladivostok in Russia. Since UNDP made its proposal, Hunchun, which had a population in 1991 of 175,000 and which sits on the Russian border, has become a booming city. In March 1992, the Chinese government designated Hunchun as an "open border city" in which foreign investors would be granted more preferential treatment than their counterparts in Shenzhen and Xiamen. A Hunchun export processing FETZ, including a 5.6 sq km industrial estate, is now under construction. The zone, which will soon be linked to Tumen City by rail, seeks to attract light manufacturing industries making such products as textiles, food, construction materials, consumer goods, and electronics. Land in the Hunchun FETZ will be leased to foreign investors for 70 years at the price of 20 yuan per square meter, compared to 4,000 yuan in Shenzhen and 700 yuan in Dalian (Kan, 1992). By the end of June 1992, Hunchun had received about 250 applications from foreign investors.

Yanji, the capital city of Jilin province, is the core Chinese city of the larger of the two proposed triangles. Yanji's provincial government designated four areas in its territory as "special economic zones for minorities" in May 1992. More than one million Chinese-Koreans live in these areas. There are now more than 100 foreign investors, mostly from South Korea, operating in the special zones. South Korea succeeded in establishing an industrial zone in the region after normalizing relations with the PRC in August 1992. A joint car assembly project between the Kia Motor Company and the Yanji city government will start soon. Another big South Korean project would establish a cattle ranch that could be the largest of its kind in Asia.

Following the UNDP proposal, North Korea designated the 612 sq km Rajin-Sonbong area, which is near the borders with Russia and the PRC, as a free trade zone in December 1991. The FETZ will be developed not only as an export processing zone but

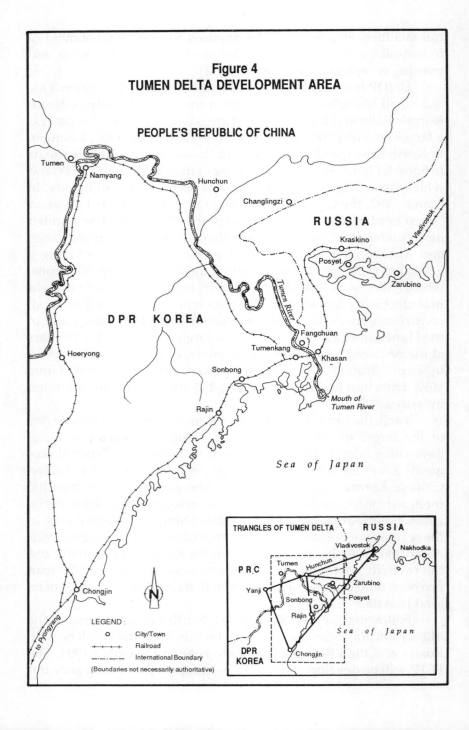

Figure 4
TUMEN DELTA DEVELOPMENT AREA

as an international tourist zone as well (Kobayashi, 1992). The Rajin-Sonbong FETZ allows 100 per cent foreign-owned enterprises in the fields of high technology and export-oriented activities. Foreign investors can lease FETZ land for a maximum period of 50 years, and they will be required to pay a 14 per cent income tax (compared with 25 per cent for enterprises located in non-FETZ areas). The area has relatively well-developed infrastructure, including ports, rail and road networks, electric power, and water for industrial development. The port of Rajin, which has a capacity of 3 million tons per year, is projected to have a capacity of 10 million tons in the future. Furthermore, the population in the Rajin-Sonbong area is expected to grow rapidly from its present level of 180,000. Chongjin, at the core of the large triangle, has also been designated a free trade zone, and North Korea has been attempting to establish metal, chemical, machinery, shipbuilding, and light industries in this zone by inviting foreign investors.

North Korea was reluctant to develop the Tumen Delta jointly with its neighboring countries until the second Programme Management Committee (PMC) meeting on Tumen River Area Development Programme (TRADP), which was held in Beijing in October 1992 and attended by the PRC, North Korea, Russia, South Korea, and Mongolia. North Korea, PRC, and Russia agreed to develop the region jointly, based on a leasing system developed by UNDP. Under this system, the three countries are to offer land for a special economic zone to be administered jointly by them, as well as by South Korea and Mongolia. Although this is a step forward, there are still daunting tasks to be completed, such as the drafting of an overall development plan and feasibility studies, project prioritization, coordination of financing, resource mobilization, and harmonization of various legal and institutional systems.

The Russian government designated 11 FETZs in 1990, of which four are in eastern Russia. The most promising is the Greater Vladivostok Free Economic Zone (GVFEZ), which stretches from the east near Vostochny to the west at Khasan, bordering on North Korea and the PRC. A study plan for the FETZ was completed by the Engineering Consulting Firms Association of Japan under the auspices of the United Nations Industrial Development Organization (UNIDO) in 1991, but the Russian government has not yet approved the scheme.

At the International Development Seminar on Tumen Delta Development Cooperation held in Hunchun on 27-28 July 1993, the PMC member countries agreed to establish a joint land development corporation to implement the various Tumen Delta projects (*Niigata Nippo*, 30 July 1993).

Financing the Tumen Delta Projects

Japanese FDI and ODA

Japan and South Korea are regional suppliers of capital, including FDI, loans, and official development assistance (ODA). With the appreciation of the yen as a stimulus, Japan's FDI in Asia, on an application basis, has surged from $1.4 billion in 1985 to $56.9 billion in 1990. The FDI declined to less than $40 billion in 1992, however, due mainly to Japan's recession. The Asian NIEs took 47 per cent of the total cumulative Japanese FDI in Asia in 1990, followed by the Southeast Asian countries (46 per cent) and the PRC (5 per cent). In terms of individual countries, Hong Kong (25 per cent), Indonesia (16 per cent), and Singapore (12 per cent) accounted for 53 per cent of the total FDI. There has been a marked shift in Japanese FDI from the NIEs to the ASEAN countries and the PRC in recent years.

The PRC is the number two recipient country of Japanese ODA after Indonesia, accounting for about 10 per cent of the total. Japanese ODA to Mongolia began in 1977, but it was only in 1991 that substantial yen project loans started. South Korea is no longer a recipient of Japanese ODA, having become a donor country. For political reasons, Japanese ODA project loans are not flowing into North Korea and Russia, which are the two countries that need them most.

With its rich natural resources and abundant labor force, the Tumen Delta region (and Northeast China in particular) is attractive to Japanese investors. Although Japanese FDI in South Korea sharply declined from $696 million (54.2 per cent of the total FDI in South Korea) in 1988 to $236 million (29.4 per cent of the total) in 1991, the FDI in the PRC and Russia increased by 32.2 and 168.4 per cent, respectively, during 1989-1991 (see Table 11). Japan was third (behind Hong Kong and Macao) in total FDI in the PRC in 1990 on an actual investment basis, accounting for 14.4 per cent. The greatest amount of Japanese FDI went to the Shanghai region (38 per cent), followed by Bohai (25.6 per cent), Tumen Delta (13.2 per cent), and South China (12.8 per cent) (Fukagawa, 1993). Of the total FDI in the Tumen Delta region, Liaoning accounted for 84 per cent, followed by Jilin (10.6 per cent) and Heilongjiang (5.3 per cent). Liaoning province, due mainly to its proximity to and historical ties with Japan, has recently become as attractive a site for Japanese investors as Shanghai. This also reflects the fact that the province has the PRC's largest foreign trade port (Dalian), a large labor force, and a well-established industrial base.

By number of projects, Japanese FDI in Far East Russia accounted for 20 per cent (89 projects) in 1992, after the US (21 per cent), and followed by the PRC (17 per cent), North Korea (5 per cent), and South Korea (3 per cent) (Murakami, 1993). Khabarovsk and Sakhalin were major areas for Japanese FDI, together accounting for 66 per cent of the total. This is due largely to the relatively high development of infrastructure in both areas, to their proximity to Japan, and to their rich forestry and fishery resource endowments.

Table 11. Foreign Direct Investment from Japan and South Korea to PRC and Russia, 1989-1991

	To PRC		To Russia	
	Number of Projects	$ Million	Number of Projects	$ Million
From Japan				
1989	126	438	12	19
1990	165	349	15	25
1991	246	579	18	51
From South Korea				
1989	12	10	2	0.5
1990	38	54	3	9
1991	112	85	10	11

Sources: Japanese Ministry of Finance; Central Bank of ROK; *Economic Trade Almanac of China;* and Fukagawa (1993).

Once the remaining politico-economic problems are resolved (particularly those related to disputes over territories claimed by both countries), it is expected that the influx of Japanese FDI to Russia will be greatly accelerated. Investments in natural resources such as oil, gas, and forestry products are highly attractive to Japan in view of its policy of diversifying the procurement of natural resources. Although reliable statistics are not available, Japanese investors are also attracted to service-oriented businesses such as hotels, transportation, and communications in Far East Russia.

Japanese FDI in Mongolia and North Korea is not yet visible. Mongolia, whose economy depended heavily on foreign savings in the past (and especially on the former Soviet Union), has been anxious to obtain Japanese FDI and ODA since it launched its open door policy in 1990. Although various possible projects have been discussed, Japanese private investors are cautious about investing in the country due mainly to the lack of a transportation system, weak economic institutions (including the foreign exchange system) and the lack of a trained labor force. Feasibility studies on resource endowments have also not been adequately undertaken. The situation is very similar in North Korea, although opportunities for Japanese FDI are apparently greater there than in Mongolia. Tense political relations between North Korea and Japan have been the single most important reason for the sluggishness of Japanese FDI. Reflecting the increasing political uncertainties in North Korea, investment from ethnic Koreans residing in Japan has also slowed down.

South Korean FDI and ODA

South Korean FDI has been rapidly shifting from its major destination, North America, to Asia. Although still small, South Korean FDI in the PRC and Russia has sharply increased in recent years. South Korean FDI in the PRC has been channeled into labor-intensive manufacturing industries such as textiles and electrical machinery. South Korea has an advantage over Japan in the Tumen Delta region not only because of its geographical proximity and its more appropriate technological products, but also because of nearly 2 million readily available Chinese and Russian-Korean workers who can speak the Korean language. Nonetheless, there is still a long way to go before South Korea can invest in North Korea.

With its growing economic influence in the Asia-Pacific region and its balance-of-payments surplus from 1986 to 1989, South Korea has started its own version of ODA. It has committed $3 billion in loans to Russia since resuming normal relations in 1991, and about half this amount has been disbursed so far. Trade between the two countries has increased sharply, due largely to these loans (Komaki, 1992).

Chinese Investment

The northeastern Chinese provinces (particularly Heilongjiang) have begun to invest in the neighboring Amour province of Russia. As indicated earlier, cross-border trade between Northeast China and Far East Russia has been growing, and Chinese investments are mainly intended to support this activity.

It appears that the PRC is in the best position to secure project funds both internally and externally. The country has been accumulating foreign reserves ($13.7 billion in 1991) which can be used to finance the foreign components of its development projects, such as machinery and essential intermediate goods. As noted before, the northeastern provinces, and Liaoning in particular, have recorded continuing surpluses in their external trade. These reserves can also be used to finance the Tumen projects. External funds, both private and public, are also flowing into the northeastern provinces. Foreign borrowing in Liaoning jumped from $16 million in 1986 to $470 million in 1990, or a 29-fold increase. Liaoning alone accounted for 22.8 per cent of Chinese external borrowing in 1990, followed by Guangdong (21 per cent), Shanghai (7.1 per cent), Hunan (6.1 per cent), and Beijing (5 per cent).

Multilateral Sources

There are many public channels through which the Tumen Delta projects could be financed, including multilateral financial institutions such as the Asian Development Bank (ADB) and the World Bank. A large proportion of the UNDP-proposed Tumen Delta projects (amounting to $30 billion over 20 years) must be financed through external public sources. In financing the infrastructure projects, the Tumen Delta developing countries expect a particularly significant role for Japan, now the largest among all ODA donor countries, with about $10 billion in ODA in 1991.

A linked economic cooperation scheme originally proposed by then Japanese Prime Minister Miyazawa could be very effective. Japanese and South Korean ODA, together with funding from other sources including ADB, the World Bank, and UNDP, could be used to finance Chinese projects in the Tumen Delta. The PRC, in turn, using its own funding sources, would be in a position to finance the projects on the Russian and North Korean sides. In fact, Russia has agreed to lease out Zarubino through its own financing. This linked cooperation scheme would also be useful in breaking the political deadlock in the region, and in enhancing relations between South Korea and Japan as well.

The cooperation scheme could also be applied to the regional division of labor. Because of geographical proximity and historical ties, South Korea is in a better position to invest in Heilongjiang, particularly in construction activities. At the moment, South Korean manufacturing technologies are more appropriate there than those of more capital-intensive Japanese concerns. On the other hand, Japan has superior expertise in developing a range of processing industries.

There is a plan to establish a Northeast Asian Development Bank to assist in the economic development of the Tumen Delta region (Park, 1992). However, a more realistic scheme would be the establishment of a Northeast Asia Development Fund (NEADF) within ADB or the World Bank.

CONCLUSIONS

Although Japan has revised its longstanding view that political issues and economic issues cannot be separated, the territorial dispute between Japan and Russia continues to be the most important obstacle to further economic cooperation. Aside from political issues, there are also mounting institutional and economic issues that need to be resolved before the Tumen Delta projects can take off.

First, despite two PMC meetings on Tumen Delta economic cooperation, no comprehensive joint development goals and strategies have emerged. Some important issues to be resolved under the PMC are: (i) identification of the comparative advantages of each participating country or region; (ii) determination of the locational priorities of infrastructure projects based on identified comparative advantages; and (iii) identification of ways to mobilize resources including finance, labor, raw materials, and technology.

Second, it is important to realize that all PMC countries do not yet recognize the Tumen Delta development as a national priority. The Russian central government, for one, has not given the go signal for the projects on its territory. It is also highly uncertain whether Chinese and North Korean projects will get the nod from their respective central governments. The Russian central government has been tightening its grip on the provincial governments, as demonstrated by restrictive measures to deter the importation of right-hand drive vehicles (mainly from Japan), the nationalization of fishery resources, and the abolition of preferential measures for promoting joint ventures with foreign investors (Murakami, 1993). In the case of the PRC, high priority is presently being given to the Pudong area in Shanghai. South Korea and Japan are obviously more interested in the Bohai economic zone than in the Tumen Delta. Mongolian interest probably diverges most from that of other PMC countries due to its distant location. It will be difficult to secure ODA funds to finance the Tumen Delta projects unless or until national investment priorities are clearly established.

Third, economic, market, and institutional conditions in Mongolia, North Korea, and Russia are in a state of flux. A degree of stability will be needed if multiregional cooperation is to be viable. It has been pointed out, for example, that the legal system and risk aversion mechanisms in Russia and North Korea are still incompatible with an open market economy. Even if laws or rules were to exist, the local authorities may not be granted the necessary power to conduct business with foreign concerns (Zimbler, 1992). This is a major obstacle to market-driven development.

Fourth, there has been a lack of coordination among donor countries and agencies, reflecting their different interests. In the European Community and the United States, there is little support for using public funds for Tumen Delta projects. Although the Japan Sea littoral prefectures, notably Niigata, have been enthusiastic about the projects, the central government has never officially made any commitment. Japanese officials would like to see the private sector take the initiative, but the latter strongly believes that public funds should be committed first to induce private investments. The best solution under current conditions is to begin with small-scale businesses, making full use of existing infrastructure. Foreign exchange earned through such businesses could then be used to modernize existing facilities. It should also be noted that UNDP's idea of Tumen Delta development has not always been consistent with UNIDO's idea of the Greater Vladivostok Free Economic Zone. Coordination between these two UN agencies is absolutely necessary.

Fifth, the establishment of a production-based free trade zone must be consistent with global demand conditions. The current worldwide recession has not been wholly conducive to the establishment of new export-seeking FETZs, especially as Japan's import capability has been rapidly eroded. Japan has played a very important role in accelerating the intra-industry division of labor in the region, particularly after the 1986 Plaza Accord led to an appreciation of the yen. This trend needs to be continued in order to develop viable regional economic cooperation in this area.

D espite the daunting difficulties facing Tumen Delta regional cooperation, there have been signs of progress. The PMC countries finally agreed to proceed with the leasing system proposed by the UNDP. The powerful Japanese Keidanren (Federation of Economic Organizations) has decided to commit itself positively to the Tumen Delta projects (*Japan Economic Journal*, 29 January 1993). Although uncertainties remain, North Korea has offered more attractive incentives to foreign investors, including wholly-owned foreign ventures.

Tumen Delta development is significant not only as a test of regional multicountry economic cooperation, but also as a potential "growth pole" to help convert formerly centralized economies into more dynamic market economies. The market dynamism created in the Tumen Delta should spread quickly through North Korea and eastern Russia, thus benefiting all the NEA countries.

Endnotes:

1. Dean and Professor, Graduate School of International Relations, International University of Japan.

2. This study is based on the author's field missions to the Southern China Triangle, the Johor-Singapore-Riau Growth Triangle, and the Tumen River Delta Economic Zone in 1992. The author would like to express his deep gratitude to Dr. Mubariq Ahmad, Center for Policy & Implementation Studies, Indonesia; Mr. Herbert Behrstock, UNDP; Mr. Aage Holm, UNDP consultant; and to Messrs. Myo Thant and Min Tang for their very useful comments on an earlier draft of the paper.

Bibliography

Asian Development Bank. *Mongolia: A Centrally Planned Economy in Transition*. New York: Oxford University Press, 1992.

Campbell, Burnham O., "Regional Comparative Advantage in Northeast Asia: Determinants of the Present Structure and Some Future Possibilities," draft paper presented at the Vladivostok Conference on Northeast Asian Regional Cooperation, Vladivostok, 24-28 August 1992.

Fukagawa, Yukiko, "The Role and Position of South Korea in the Japan Sea Rim Economic Cooperation," paper presented at the Niigata International Forum on the Japan Sea Rim '93, Niigata, Japan, 19 February 1993.

Imai, Kenichi, "Regional Trade and Interdependence in the Northeast Asian Region," in Tamio Shimakura, ed., *Tohoku Ajia Keizaiken no Shido*. Tokyo: Institute of Developing Economies, 1992.

Kakazu, Hiroshi, "Post Hong Kong: Economic Frontiers in the Asia-Pacific Region under the Tumultuous World," in *Economics and Society*, Vol. 8 (July 1991).

Kan, Yonji, "Bakuhatsu teki na Ikioi no Kanchu Keizai (A Bursting Trend in China-South Korean Trade)," in *Asia* (11 November 1992), pp. 12-15.

Kanamori, Hisao, "Economic Cooperation in Northeast Asia," in Won Bae Kim, Burnham O. Campbell, and Mark Valencia, eds., *Regional Economic Cooperation in Northeast Asia.* Honolulu: East-West Center, 1992.

Kim, Won Bae, "Population and Labor in Northeast Asia," paper presented at the Vladivostok Conference on Northeast Asian Regional Cooperation, Vladivostok, 24-28 August 1992.

Kim, Won Bae and Burnham O. Campbell. *Proceedings of the Conference of Economic Development in the Coastal Area of Northeast Asia (Changchun, China, 29-31 August 1992).* Honolulu: East-West Center, June 1992.

Kobayashi, Shoichi, "Free Economic Zones in the North-East Asia Region," paper presented at the Vladivostok Conference on Northeast Asian Regional Cooperation, Vladivostok, 24-28 August 1992.

Komaki, Teruo, "Prospects for the Northeast Asia Economic Zone," in *Asian Trends,* Vol. IV, No. 60 (1992), pp. 65-75.

Kong, Deyong and Zhou Yuan, "The Implementation of the Development Strategy of the Tumen River Region: Constriction and Progress," in Won Bae Kim, Burnham O. Campbell, and Mark Valencia, eds., *Regional Economic Cooperation in Northeast Asia.* Honolulu: East-West Center, 1992.

Kumar, Sree, "JSR Triangle: A Model of Joint Cooperation," paper presented at the ADB-IUJ Workshop on Growth Triangles in Asia, Asian Development Bank, Manila, 24-26 February 1993.

Lee-Jay, Cho, ed. "The Pyongyang International Conference and Field Trip," Pyongyang, 29 April-4 May 1992. August 1992 (draft).

Murakami, Takashi, "Rosia Kyokuto Chiiki no Gobenkigyo no Genjo to Tenbo (Problems and Prospects of Joint Ventures in the Russia Far East)," paper presented at the Niigata International Forum on the Japan Sea Rim '93, Niigata, Japan, 19 February 1993.

Ogawa, Kazuo and Teuro Komaki, "Kan Nihonkai Keizaiden (Japan Sea Rim Economic Zone)," in *The Japan Economic Journal,* 1991.

Ogawa, Kazuo and Takashi Murakami. *Mezameru Soren Kyokuto* (The Awakening Soviet Far East). Tokyo: Nihon Keizai Hyoron Sha, 1991.

Olzvoy, Khumbgyan, "Mongolia: Developmental Efforts and Possibilities for Closer Economic Cooperation with Countries of Asia and the Pacific," paper presented at the Vladivostok Conference on Northeast Asian Regional Cooperation, Vladivostok, 24-28 August 1992.

Park, Sung Sang, "The Korean Experience and the Potential Role of Financial Policy in Northeast Asian Regional Cooperation", in Won Bae Kim, Burnham O. Campbell, and Mark Valencia, eds., *Regional Economic Cooperation in Northeast Asia*. Honolulu: East-West Center, 1992.

Planning and Coordination Division, Niigata Prefecture, ed. *The Niigata International Forum on the Japan Sea Rim '91*. Niigata, Japan, February 1991.

_____. *The Niigata International Forum on the Japan Sea Rim '92*. Niigata, Japan, February 1992.

Sakiyama, Teruji, "Development and Environment in Northeast Asia," paper presented at the ADB-IUJ Workshop on Growth Triangles in Asia, Asian Development Bank, Manila, 24-26 February 1993.

Sekiguchi, Sueo, "Industrial Complementation in the Northeast Asia," paper presented at the Vladivostok Conference on Northeast Asian Regional Cooperation, Vladivostok, 24-28 August 1992.

Shimakura, Tamio, ed. *Tohoku Ajia Keizaiken no Shido* (Birth of a Northeast Asian Economic Zone). Tokyo: Institute of Developing Economies, 1992.

Shiode, Hirokazu, "Multilateral Development Focusing on the Tumen River Area," paper presented at the ADB-IUJ Workshop on Growth Triangles in Asia, Asian Development Bank, Manila, 24-26 February 1993.

UNDP, "Tumen River Area Development," mission report by M.

Miller, A. Holm, and T. Kelleher presented at the Pyongyang International Conference, Pyongyang, 16-18 October 1991.

Zimbler, Brian, "Legal Problems Facing Western Investors in Russia," seminar paper presented to the Center for East Asian Studies, Monterey Institute of International Studies, Monterey, California, 12-13 June 1992.

Tumen River Area Development Programme: The North Korean Perspective

■ Hirokazu Shiode[1]

INTRODUCTION

In the Asia-Pacific region, where there are no formal trade arrangements akin to Maastricht or the North American Free Trade Agreement (NAFTA), various alternative economic cooperation schemes have begun taking root. The Southern China and Johor-Singapore-Riau growth triangles are the most advanced of these schemes. Both are market-led and open to outside participants in terms of trade and investment.

In Northeast Asia (see Figure 1), schemes such as the Yellow Sea Growth Triangle, the Kyushu-Ryukyu Growth Triangle, and the Sea of Japan Rim Growth Triangle (a component of which is the Tumen River Area) have existed for some time, although none have progressed beyond the planning stage. This region is arguably more politically and culturally diverse than Southeast Asia and other parts of East Asia, and (with the exception of Japan) it lacks a large domestic market. Nonetheless, potential economic complementarity within Northeast Asia is significant and there is scope for regional economic cooperation.

The Tumen River marks the border between the Democratic People's Republic of Korea (North Korea hereafter) and the People's Republic of China (PRC), except for the last 15 km to the sea. The Tumen River estuary, which is located on the border of North Korea and Russia, flows into the Sea of Japan (see Figure 2). Since

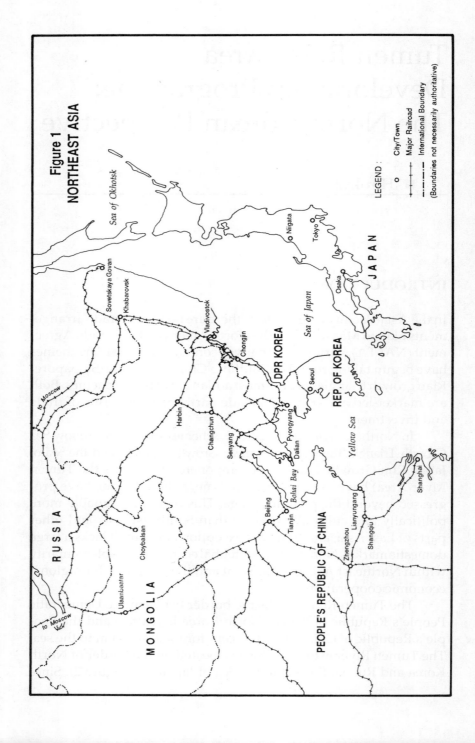

Figure 1
NORTHEAST ASIA

LEGEND :
o   City/Town
+–+–+ Major Railroad
––––   International Boundary
(Boundaries not necessarily authoritative)

1990 many international seminars and conferences have been held to discuss development plans relating to the Tumen River Area, which includes Russian, Chinese, and North Korean territories. In July 1990, the PRC expressed its interest in the development of the area at the first Northeast Asia Economic Development Conference held in Changchun, PRC. In June 1991, at a seminar in Tokyo, Ding Shicheng, the head of Jilin province's Science and Technology Commission, released a Chinese plan for the development of the area (Ri, 1992).

That same year, following discussions with the United Nations Industrial Development Organization (UNIDO), the Soviet Union presented a plan to designate three international ports (Nakhodka, Vladivostok, and Posyet) as the "Greater Vladivostok Free Economic Area." This area covers some 15,200 sq km and is populated by 1.4 million people. North Korea released its own proposal in 1991 for the development of the areas near the Tumen River. As a first step, the North Korean government designated the Rajin-Sonbong area, covering 621 sq km, as its first free economic and trade zone (FETZ).

The United Nations Development Programme (UNDP) officially adopted the idea of multilateral development cooperation in the Tumen River Area in July 1991 on the basis of agreements reached with the governments of North Korea, Republic of Korea (South Korea), PRC, Japan, and Mongolia, with Russia joining later.

This paper discusses the North Korean perspective on the Tumen River Area Development Programme (TRADP). The first section reviews the state of the North Korean economy. The second section discusses the Tumen River program, and the last section identifies the multilateral initiatives that could be taken to further develop the area.

THE NORTH KOREAN ECONOMY

North Korea has had a centrally planned economy for more than 40 years. With economic assistance from the Soviet Union and the PRC, the economy showed satisfactory performance, especially in heavy industry, until about the mid-1970s. Since the late 1980s, however, the North Korean economy has been ailing.

In 1991, the country's total population was estimated at 22 million and the per capita GNP at about $1,000 (Rhee, 1992a). The North Korean government, however, claimed its per capita GNP to be over $2,500 in the same year (see Table 1 and Hiraiwa, 1991). At present, North Korea is suffering from serious shortages of energy and food. Imported petroleum obtained through barter trade with the Soviet Union and the PRC was for a long time its main source of energy. The collapse of the Soviet Union, however, resulted in a sharp decrease (from 440,000 tons in 1990 to 41,000 tons between January and July 1991) in North Korea's imports from the former Soviet republics. The PRC's oil exports to North Korea (about 1 million tons annually) have been more stable, but since 1991 the PRC has insisted that North Korea pay for its oil in hard currency instead of through barter trade. Given its shortage of hard currency, this has proved very difficult. An increase in domestic coal production could provide North Korea with energy for domestic industries, but the amount and quality of the country's coal cannot meet the domestic demand at present.

Grain imports also drain North Korea's foreign reserves. It is estimated that North Korea imported at least 1.6 million tons of food in 1991, but even this large amount was unable to meet the country's food requirements.

North Korea has been experiencing trade deficits on its balance of payments since 1986 because of heavy imports of grain and crude oil. At the end of fiscal year 1989 its foreign debt was estimated at $6,780 million (*Korea Reference*, 1993).

As a result of the decrease in energy supply from abroad and the shortage in domestic food production, the industrial output of North Korea recorded negative growth rates in the 1990s. Even the food rationing system established as a response to the shortage does not work well.

The North Korean government has decided to drastically change its foreign policy in response to the poor state of its economy and changing international circumstances. In November 1990, it initiated talks with Japan with a view toward establishing normal bilateral relations. It also joined the United Nations in September 1991 together with South Korea.

Trade between North Korea and South Korea has been on the rise. In 1991, North Korea imported rice, sugar, and color television

Table 1. Selected Indicators of Northeast Asian Countries and Regions, 1991

	South Korea	North Korea	Mongolia	PRC Inner Mongolia	Liaoning	Jilin	Heilongjiang
Area (sq km)	98,480	120,540	1,565,000	1,183,000	146,000	187,000	453,000
Population ('000)	44,149	22,227	2,305	21,460	39,460	24,660	35,210
GNP ($ million)	281	23	2	–	–	–	–
Per capita GNP ($)	6,498	1,050	911	–	–	–	–
Exports[a] (FOB) ($ million)	65,016	1,890	829	325	5,600	752	1,086
Imports[a] (CIF) ($ million)	69,844	2,925	1,458	465	6,295	953	1,492

[a]1990.

Sources: Asia Trend Yearbook 1992; The World Factbook 1992; Statistical Year Book for Asia and Pacific 1990; Hirata (1992); and Izumi (1992).

sets from South Korea, while South Korea imported coal from North Korea (Rhee, 1992a). The total volume of trade between the two countries was estimated at about $200 million in 1991. In 1992, however, North Korea's imports from South Korea dropped by 56 per cent to $11 million, while its exports increased only slightly to $199 million (*Nihon Keizai Shimbun*, 15 January 1993).

Changes in economic policy began earlier than these foreign policy shifts. Since 1984, there has been a restructuring of economic organizations and a reshuffling of economic bureaucrats. Young technocrats have been appointed as corporate managers of key sectors such as energy and light industries. Some decentralization of corporations has taken place, with the managers now having more power to decide how to use profits and to design investment projects. The country's policy changes have, however, been very selective, and its pursuit of an economic open door policy has been limited compared to that of the PRC. From time to time, the importance attached to central control and political consciousness has been reasserted. Nonetheless, it is clear that North Korea accelerated its economic reforms, particularly in its external economic relations, with the enactment of many relevant laws in 1992 and 1993 (see Appendix 1).

Despite these changes, impediments to closer economic and foreign relations with neighboring countries remain. Although the PRC maintained relatively close political and economic relations with North Korea while establishing relations with South Korea, it decided in early 1991 to stop barter trade with North Korea within a few years. Both countries are also still at odds over the Paekdo San Mountain (Changbai Shan in Chinese) at the upper end of the Tumen River. Russia, meanwhile, has been too absorbed with its own pressing domestic problems to support North Korea substantially. Furthermore, Russia has also established closer relations with South Korea in order to obtain economic aid.

North Korea has been trying to establish better relations with the US, but its withdrawal from the Nuclear Non-Proliferation Treaty (NPT) on 12 March 1993 proved to be an impediment. North Korea decided to suspend its withdrawal from NPT in June 1993, but the International Atomic Energy Agency and the US were not satisfied with the North Korean response to the international requirement to inspect its nuclear facilities. However, in July 1993, the

US and North Korea agreed to convert the latter's controversial graphite-moderator type reactor to a light water type reactor, which would make it more difficult for North Korea to produce nuclear weapons. This has opened the way for North Korea to establish a new channel of communication with the US.

Relations between North Korea and other international organizations have not been encouraging. Although North Korea expressed its interest in joining the Asian Development Bank (ADB), its admission was not included in the agenda of ADB's 1993 annual general meeting. After the Tokyo summit and the US president's visit to South Korea in July 1993, security talks on the Asia-Pacific region took place through several regional groupings, including the Association of Southeast Asian Nations (ASEAN) and the Asia-Pacific Economic Cooperation (APEC) forum, but North Korea was again not invited to the meetings.

TUMEN RIVER DEVELOPMENT

Recent Progress

North Korea submitted a study report on the Rajin-Sonbong (sometimes called Najin-Sonbong) Free Economic and Trade Zone to the Northeast Asia Sub-Regional Program Meeting of UNDP held in Ulaanbaatar, Mongolia, on 6-7 July 1991. In that meeting, representatives from the then People's Republic of Mongolia (now Mongolia), PRC, and South Korea agreed with North Korea's proposals for developing the Tumen River Area (UNDP, 1991). The Tumen River Area Development Programme's Programme Management Committee (TRADP-PMC) established the Tumen River Economic Zone (TREZ, or "small triangle") and Tumen Economic Development Area (TEDA, or "large triangle") during its first meeting in February 1992. The TREZ, which is located within a radius of 40 to 50 km from the estuary of the Tumen River, includes Sonbong, Rajin, Hunchun, and Posyet. The larger TEDA includes the TREZ as well as the cities of Vladivostok, Chongjin, and Yanji, which are all located within 80 to 120 km of the estuary (see Figure 2).

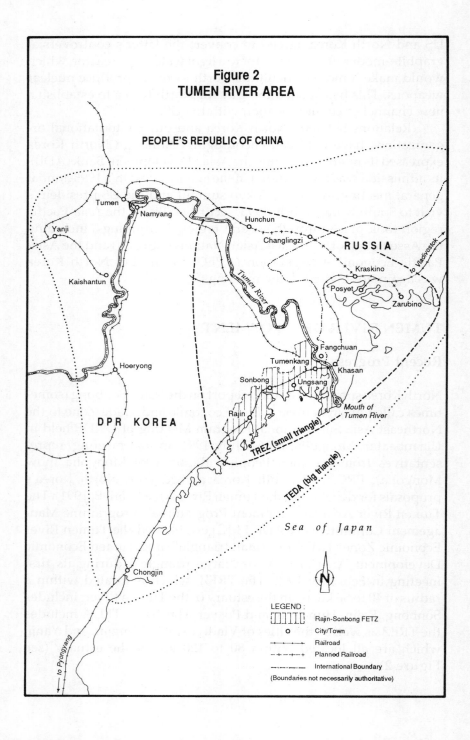

Figure 2
TUMEN RIVER AREA

PEOPLE'S REPUBLIC OF CHINA

Tumen
Namyang
Yanji
Hunchun
Changlingzi
RUSSIA
Kaishantun
Kraskino
Posyet
Zarubino
to Vladivostok
Hoeryong
Fangchuan
Tumenkang
Khasan
Sonbong   Ungsang
Rajin
Mouth of
Tumen River
DPR KOREA
TREZ (small triangle)
TEDA (big triangle)
Sea of Japan
Chongjin
to Pyongyang

Tumen River

N

LEGEND :
Rajin-Sonbong FETZ
City/Town
Railroad
Planned Railroad
International Boundary
(Boundaries not necessarily authoritative)

The small North Korean port of Sonbong lies about 20 km west of the estuary of the Tumen River. The port, which has an oil refinery, has been used for importing crude oil, mainly from the former Soviet Union and Iran. Sonbong's annual capacity is 3 million tons of oil but in 1992 it was not able to operate at this level.

North Korea's major ports near the Tumen River are Rajin and Chongjin. Rajin City, which is located about 30 km west of the Tumen River estuary, has a population of about 10,000. Rajin port has three terminals and ten quays with a total length of 2,525 m and a revetment of 640 m (Democratic People's Republic of Korea, 1992). Its berths, which are about 13 m deep, are capable of accommodating 10,000-ton ships. The port has a rated capacity of 3 million tons per year but its facilities are very old, having been built during the Japanese colonial period. Since about half of the facilities have long been unuseable, available capacity at the end of 1992 was estimated at only 1.2 to 1.5 million tons.

Chongjin City, in North Hamgyong province, is about 80 km southwest of the Russian border. The port of Chongjin is divided into the East Port and the West Port, which are approximately 5 km apart. The East Port has three terminals with a total quay length of 2,138 m, while the West Port has four terminals with a total quay length of 1,384 m. Berths at the port with a depth of 10 m can accommodate vessels of up to 5,000 tons size. North Korean officials have rated Chongjin port's full cargo capacity to be 8 million tons, but its true capacity may be only 2.5 to 3 million tons. The port has a terminal with a railway connection that can handle 200,000 tons of grain annually. This is currently being used for exports of Chinese grain.

There is a triangular railroad link between Sonbong, Chongjin, and Namyang. The North Korean railway system is connected to the Russian railway system at Tumen Kang-Khasan and to the Chinese railway system at Namyang-Tumen. Since the gauge of the North Korean railway is 1,435 mm and that of the Russian railway is 1,520 mm, the railroad from Khasan to Rajing is thus a double-gauge track (*Railway Journal*, March 1992).

Within the small triangle (TREZ), Russia has two small ports: Posyet and Zarubino. Posyet, which is located about 40 km north-east of the North Korean border, has two piers that are 6 to 7 m in depth. Its annual handling capacity is 1.5 million tons. The port of

Zarubino, which is smaller, has a depth of about 12 m. In 1992, the PRC and Russia agreed to build a railway from Hunchun to Kraskino via Changlingzi, and it is anticipated that in 1994 this will connect the seaports of Posyet and Zarubino to the Chinese railway system. A major Japanese business organization has reportedly agreed to finance this project, while the PRC promised to invest more than $100 million. Nineteen representatives from the Japan-China Northeast Development Council, a business organization established by major Japanese trading and construction companies, visited the PRC and Russia in March 1993 to discuss this railway and port project. They also consulted with UNDP officers while they were in Beijing. As a result, Japanese representatives and their Chinese counterparts agreed to establish a joint committee on Tumen River Area development.

Jilin province had already established a joint corporation to build and operate the railway and port that will link it with Russia. Construction of the cross-border railway from Hunchun to Kraskino began in April 1993. As mentioned above, the plan is to connect this railway to the Russian railway system by June 1994, and the whole project (including Zarubino port extention) is expected to be completed in 1996. The route will be provided with both Chinese and Russian gauges to eliminate the need for the transfer of goods from one car to another at the border. It is expected that 3 million tons of goods will be transported via the railway annually and that some 3,000 people per day will travel between the Russian port which will have links to Japanese ports and the major cities in the northern part of the PRC.

The railway and port project will shorten the distance to Japan by more than half. Two inland Chinese provinces (Jilin and Heilongjiang) will benefit from the activity that will be generated by the new routes. Chinese exports from Jilin to Japan (mainly food and consumer goods) currently go through Dalian port and thence around the Korean peninsula, since the condition of the Far East Russian railway and its connection to the PRC is not satisfactory. Jilin plans to export 2 million tons of grain to Japan and other countries in the Asia-Pacific region. With the opening of this cross-border route, Russia should also find a substantial new market for its raw materials.

Policies and Perspectives

In December 1991, the North Korean Administration Council (the cabinet) issued a decree designating a 621 sq km area (including a part of the city of Rajin and a part of the county of Sonbong) as a free economic and trade zone. The government also declared Rajin, Sonbong, and Chongjin as free ports open to vessels from all countries where handling fees would be lower than international rates (see Figure 3).

The salient points of the decree are as follows:

(i)   A 621 sq km area consisting of the 14 *dongs* (townships) and *ris* (villages) of the city of Rajin and 10 *ris* of the county of Sonbong constitutes the FETZ;

(ii) Equity and contractual joint ventures, as well as wholly foreign-owned enterprises, will be permitted to operate within the zone;

(iii) Investors from any country will be allowed to operate in the zone;

(iv) The state shall, under the law, protect the capital and assets invested by foreigners in the zone, as well as the income to be derived from them;

(v)   Rajin and Sonbong ports, which are inside the zone, and Chongjin port, which adjoins them, will be free trade ports; and

(vi) A number of incentives will be granted to investors in the zone, including exemption or reduction of enterprise income tax.

The North Korean government considers the Rajin-Sonbong area to be an important logistical hub in Northeast Asia. To develop this hub, North Korea promulgated seven relevant laws. These are the Law on Equity Joint Venture, the Law on Foreigners' Invest-ment, the Law on Foreign Enterprises, the Law on Contractual Joint

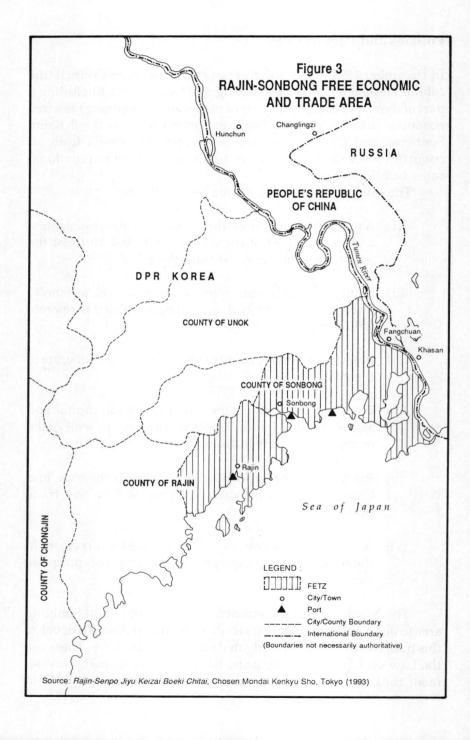

Figure 3
RAJIN-SONBONG FREE ECONOMIC AND TRADE AREA

RUSSIA

PEOPLE'S REPUBLIC OF CHINA

DPR KOREA

Tumen River

Changlingzi

Hunchun

COUNTY OF UNOK

Fangchuan

Khasan

COUNTY OF SONBONG

Sonbong

COUNTY OF RAJIN

Rajin

Sea of Japan

COUNTY OF CHONGJIN

LEGEND :

▯▯▯▯▯▯ FETZ
○ City/Town
▲ Port
------- City/County Boundary
-·-·-·- International Boundary
(Boundaries not necessarily authoritative)

Source: *Rajin-Senpo Jiyu Keizai Boeki Chitai*, Chosen Mondai Kenkyu Sho, Tokyo (1993)

Venture, the Law on Free Economic and Trade Zone, the Law on Foreign Exchange Administration, and the Law on Foreign Investment-Business Enterprises and Foreign Individual Tax. These laws allow foreigners within the FETZ to invest in manufacturing, agriculture, construction, transportation, telecommunication, science and technology, tourism, commerce, finance, service, or any other kind of industry or business. They also allow the operation of full subsidiaries of any of these concerns (Imu, 1993).

North Korea has extended special tax treatment for future foreign investors in the area. While foreign investors in other parts of North Korea are required to pay a 25 per cent income tax, investors in the FETZ are required to pay only 14 per cent. For the first three years of operation after their businesses show a profit, foreign investors are exempted from paying income taxes, and for the following two years the tax rate is only 7 per cent. Investors of leading industries will be eligible for further tax concessions, although it is not known yet what kinds of industries are to be included in this category. Foreign investors within the FETZ can lease land for up to 50 years and can transfer the lease. Duty-free imports and exports, as well as foreign remittance of profits, are also to be allowed.

In late 1992, the government appointed a large group to conduct a feasibility study for the entire FETZ. The main objective in the first stage (1993-1995) is to strengthen the role of the zone as an international cargo transit point by rebuilding and upgrading its existing infrastructure (railways, roads, ports) and creating a favorable climate for foreign investment. The main objective in the second stage (1996-2000) is to ensure that the zone eventually becomes a trade center in Northeast Asia. The program for the second stage includes plans to (i) increase the ports' annual cargo handling capacity from about 10 million tons in 1992 to 50 million tons in 2000, (ii) set up districts specializing in different industrial activities, and (iii) establish an export-oriented economic zone through large-scale investment. The plan also includes proposals to develop the zone into an international tourist center. The main objective in the third stage (2001-2010) is to construct a comprehensive, modern international trade center (Imu, 1993).

The establishment of a free economic and trade zone by North Korea in December 1991 was the culmination of the change in its economic policy which began when it passed the Law on Equity Joint Venture in 1984. Although the process proceeded slowly and policy objectives were not very clearly spelled out, it is evident that North Korea plans to become more open and less isolated than it once was. The establishment of the FETZ was in part designed to help North Korea keep pace with the global trend toward developing international economic cooperation and exchange areas, and in part is a response to the UNDP's proposal for a Tumen River Economic Zone (Imu, 1993). The FETZ was also intended to help the country reform its national economy while preserving the existing political structure.

Official policy is still that the path of the North Korean economy shall be towards "self-reliance."[2] However as Vice Premier Kim Dal Heon stated in April 1992, self-reliance should not mean isolation from the world economy. North Korea seems to be following the Chinese example in opening up and reforming its economy; its pace, however, is much slower. The future of North Korea's open economic policy will depend largely on its participation in TRADP, which is its first significant international undertaking.

MULTILATERAL COOPERATION

In the late 1980s, the PRC and North Korea both realized that they needed some kind of international support to develop the Tumen River Area to its full potential. This assessment was based on a number of factors. First, while the Tumen River itself traverses three riparian countries, some inland areas could also benefit from its development. These include Jilin and Heilongjiang provinces of PRC, Inner Mongolia (an autonomous region of the PRC), Mongolia, and Far East Russia, most of whose seaports are closed during winter.

Second, the riparian countries and provinces are perennially short of capital. The cost of developing the Tumen River Area as a major international trade center has been roughly estimated by UNDP at $30 billion. In Northeast Asia, only Japan and South Korea, with support from international organizations, can afford to finance a project of such magnitude.

The area has many logistical advantages and exploitable resources (see Table 2). Japan and Korea will benefit from the project

Table 2. Economic Complementarities in Northeast Asia

Country/Region	Market	Capital	Transportation	Skilled Labor	Quantity of Labor	Technology	Fuel and Mineral Resources	Marine Resources	Forestry Resources
North Korea	5	5	5	4	2	4	2	2	3
South Korea	2	2	2	2	3	1	4	3	4
Far East Russia	4	5	4	3	4	3	1	1	2
Northeast China	2	3	Liaoning 3; Jilin and Heilonjiang 4	3	1	4	2	4	3
Japan	1	1	West side 3; East side 2	2	5	1	5	3	4
Mongolia	5	5	5	5	4	5	1	–	4

Legend: 1 Very rich/more than sufficient   4 Poor/insufficient
         2 Rich/sufficient   5 Very poor/quite small
         3 Medium   6 None

Source: Ishikawa (1992).

in terms of cheaper and faster transportation of goods to and from the inland areas of Northeast Asia, and even to and from Europe in the future.

From the 8th to the 10th century, the Sea of Japan played an important role as a safe route between Japan and the Asian continent (Ueda, 1992). The Tumen River Area can assume such a role once a reliable cargo port and a railway connection to mainland Asia and Europe are opened. Undeveloped natural resources, especially in mineral-rich Mongolia, can be harnessed and transported to industrialized nations via the Tumen River Area.

The Tumen River delta could take advantage of the 13,000 km Siberian railway, which connects Vladivostok with Rotterdam, and which has long served the Far East and Europe. An 11,000 km alternative route, via Lionyungang port and Kazakhstan, was opened by the PRC in 1992. The use of the ports of North Korea and of the rail route in Northeast China (built in the 19th century) should help revive the Siberian route. A new short-cut via Northeast China and Mongolia could also shorten the Siberian route by about 1,000 km. Furthermore, this new route could take advantage of the natural resources of Mongolia, which needs to import industrial products to maintain the living standards of its people and modernize its economy.[3]

Finally, although the PRC and South Korea resumed normal relations in 1992, Japan and North Korea still have not, and are not likely to do so in the near future. Relations between Japan and Russia are also still hindered by a longstanding territorial dispute. Given these problems, an international response may have greater chance of success than bilateral initiatives.

The Role of UNDP and TRADP-PMC

UNDP is one of the few international organizations to which North Korea belongs. By 1987, the Programme had provided more than $20 million in aid for the modernization of North Korean agriculture and industry.

UNDP has played a significant role in the Tumen River Area Development Programme. At the UNDP Northeast Asia Sub-Regional Program Meeting held in Ulaanbaatar, Mongolia, in July 1991, North Korea, South Korea, Mongolia, and the PRC asked

UNDP to provide support for their efforts to develop the areas proximate to the Tumen River and to invite Japan and the then Soviet Union for consultation. In August and September 1991, the Northeast Asia Economic Development Conference was held in Changchun, Jilin province, PRC, so that representatives from the countries concerned could discuss matters of common interest. In the next UNDP consultative meeting, held in Pyongyang on 16-18 October 1991, Mongolia, North Korea, South Korea, and the PRC agreed to establish the Tumen River Area Development Programme and its Programme Management Committee (PMC). Japan and Russia attended this meeting as observers. At the first meeting of the PMC, held on 27-28 February 1992, representatives of the four governments and UNDP, as well as of Japan and the Russian Federation, agreed that there was potential economic complementarity in Northeast Asia, particularly in the Tumen River Area, with opportunities to achieve greater benefits through intercountry cooperation. Cooperation through TRADP was seen to benefit not only the riparian countries or the provinces bordering the Tumen River, but also the rest of Northeast Asia, and even beyond.

The PMC clarified the role of TRADP, as well as its structure and timetable. As agreed upon at the first meeting, cooperation should (i) pave the way for the preparation of practical regional plans; (ii) provide a forum for the drawing up of specific proposals for development and investment; (iii) establish close linkages and explore opportunities for cooperation with international financial institutions, as well as with shipping, trading, industrial, and construction companies; and (iv) achieve harmonious cooperation among participants not only in the Tumen River Area but in the larger economic area as well. The PMC noted the urgency of achieving concrete results by late 1993, including the securing of governments' decisions crucial to TRADP and the preparation of "bankable" project proposals. The UNDP was asked to facilitate regional discussions and to provide financial assistance. Delegates also decided to invite Russia as a full member of PMC, and Japan and ADB as observers.

The PMC established three suborganizations. The first, a Working Group composed of national team leaders and selected members of the national teams, was to review plans and monitor progress. The

Finance Consultative Group (FCG), composed of senior members of the national teams, was instructed to interact with the international financial community while taking directions from the PMC. The third group, composed of UNDP-recruited advisors and a program manager, was set up to support the technical work of the national teams and to help in intergovernmental activities and meetings. The program manager acted as the leader for all other UNDP inputs and also provided secretariat services to the PMC.

In a meeting held in Beijing on 27-29 April 1992, program documents, work plans, and other papers prepared by the UNDP advisors were reviewed and finalized. The Russian Federation became a full-fledged member of TRADP-PMC during a meeting in Beijing on 9-11 October 1992. Senior government officials from the five member countries participated in this meeting, while representatives of the Japanese government, ADB, and the World Bank attended as observers. The member countries signed an agreement on the 18-month preinvestment phase of TRADP, to be implemented under a UNDP-administered project valued at $4.5 million, with $3.5 million to be provided by UNDP and $1 million by the government of Finland.

During this meeting, the PRC withdrew its insistence that the Tumen River be dredged to accommodate the construction of a port at Fangchuan. Earlier the UNDP Mission Report had concluded that dredging the river would be too costly and would benefit the PRC only.

After careful deliberation, PMC agreed on the following principles: (i) governments would retain sovereignty over the territory leased for use in the TRADP; (ii) land leases would be negotiated according to the sovereign investment laws of individual countries; (iii) the program would be subject to international management; and (iv) attractive incentives would be offered for international investment.

The second PMC meeting focused principally on the institutional structure for TRADP. It was agreed that a two-tier institutional structure might work well (see Figure 4). The first tier is an intergovernmental coordinating commission composed of member countries and observers. The second tier, consisting of two institutions, would focus specifically on the development and management of the Tumen River Economic Zone and its immediate sur-

Figure 4
TUMEN RIVER AREA INSTITUTIONAL ARRANGEMENTS

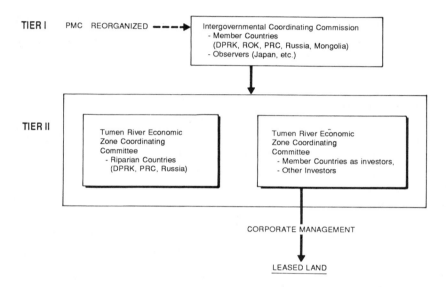

rounding area. One institution is a coordinating committee, composed of representatives from the three riparian countries, which would supervise the activities of the other institution, which would be a corporation. The corporation would be charged with developing the land leased from the three riparian countries for infrastructure projects such as ports, railroads, and an international airport. The program manager and the secretariat of the PMC were charged with preparing detailed recommendations on the institutional structure for presentation at an interim Working Group meeting and for submission to the PMC meeting scheduled in April 1993. As for infrastructure development, the secretariat was further instructed to prepare a master plan for the transportation sector which covers railroad network development, highway upgrading, air transport facilities, and the construction of major ports. A study of the overall economic prospects of the Northeast Asia Regional Development Area/Tumen Economic Development Area will also be undertaken. In May 1993, North Korea, the PRC and Russia agreed, in principle, to lease their land around the estuary of Tumen River for 70 years to an international corporation which would be established in Bermuda and be responsible for the development of the leased land. The treaty was to be concluded in April 1994. This is a major breakthrough for TRADP.

CONCLUSIONS

Despite the recent progress, there remain a number of impediments to the realization of effective multilateral cooperation. The characteristics of the Tumen River Area are very different from those of other growth triangles in Asia. For one, market forces (both domestic and international) in the area are weak. Some bilateral relations are not congenial. The future of the Tumen River Area Development Programme is highly dependent on the political situation in the countries concerned. Multilateral cooperation may be achieved if the governments can maintain a sense of tolerance and keep issues in perspective over the long term.

It may be difficult to ensure amicable relations among the countries concerned. For example, North Korea has not yet given up its policy to "liberate" South Korea in order to effect unification between them. The South Korean government, on the other hand, will provide economic assistance to North Korea only if the latter will accept the former's government and guarantee that any assistance it may give will not be used for military purposes (Rhee, 1992b).

The normalization of diplomatic relations between North Korea and Japan is still a long way off for at least two reasons. First, North Korea denied inspectors from the International Atomic Energy Agency access to its two nuclear facilities in 1993, and did not completely accept mutual nuclear inspection with South Korea (*The Asian Wall Street Journal,* 11 February 1993). Japan and other countries are very concerned about North Korea's nuclear facilities. Second, the Ministry of Foreign Affairs of Japan is quite reluctant to accelerate the process of negotiation due to domestic political problems involving key persons who initiated the dialogue with North Korea.

The instability in Russia is another impediment. The economy of Far East Russia requires a huge infusion of capital and further reform. However, the Japanese government is not willing to provide full support to Russia because of the territorial dispute over the southern Kuril Islands.

There are many different political and economic systems in the region, adding to the complexity of cooperative efforts. Most of the East Asian economies are still under state control or guidance. They are neither completely market-led economies like Hong Kong nor centrally planned economies like the former Soviet Union. Only North Korea's economy is still completely state-controlled, and the country's leadership has not yet opted for wide-ranging internal reforms, although it did implement a very selective economic reform process.

The Japanese political system is highly centralized. A reformation of this system, which will grant more financial independence to prefectural governments, is now underway, albeit slowly. The prefectures located on the Sea of Japan (Akita, Niigata, Toyama, Ishikawa, etc.) are interested in TRADP, while the central government is not yet particularly keen on the project. Most of the large companies in Japan are also headquartered in Tokyo. Lately, however, some trading companies have moved parts of their international business operations from Tokyo to Niigata City.

As for Japan's supposed major stake in the transport business generated by the development of the Tumen River Area, Japanese ports along the Sea of Japan handle only about 3 per cent of the country's total cargo. Japan would have to develop coastal areas along the Sea of Japan before it could fully utilize the Tumen River Area's potential. Furthermore, most airports on the Sea of Japan's coastal prefectures cannot handle many international flights because of short runways and poor customs facilities. The transportation network in this part of Japan is backward compared to that supporting airports in Fukuoka, Osaka, Tokyo, and Sapporo.

Although the Tumen River Economic Zone, leased from the three riparian countries, will be managed as a single entity by one development corporation, sovereignty over the original territories will remain with the respective countries. It will be very difficult for the TREZ Coordinating Committee or the Development Corporation to resolve judicial disputes among the riparian countries, since each of them has vowed to keep its national sovereignty within the leased land.

Duplication of investment is also a problem, particularly for major capital-intensive projects such as international airports or main ports linked to the international railway system. Each government wants to set up large-scale infrastructure within its territory. North Korea is planning to start renovating its ports in 1993, while the PRC and Russia have already agreed to build a new railway from Jilin to Kraskino and Zarubino in Russia (Nihon Keizai Shimbun, 29 October 1992). For a more rational distribution of investment, the development corporation should be given a stronger hand in coordinating development projects. But before this happens, bilateral cooperation in a number of small-scale projects (e.g., the improvement of existing cross-border transportation facilities) would help reduce mutual distrust and build confidence.

The PRC's economic decentralization and Mongolia's market reforms are good ingredients for multilateral cooperation, barring any political instability that they might engender. The Chinese central government has been concentrating on the development of the Shanghai and Changjiang areas since 1992. In the case of the Mongolian economy, liberalization has only been partial, but the desire to enter the international market is very strong.

Cooperation in the Tumen River Area has begun with the building of a cross-border railway between the PRC and Russia with the support of Japan. In the talks on TRADP, UNDP has been acting as a liaison and a catalyst for the nations concerned. The UNDP's assistance is especially important for North Korea, which does not have an effective communication channel with many countries. UNDP can only provide a small amount of seed money, however, since it is not an investing body. For the project to materialize, other international organizations, including financing agencies, must contribute to the multilateral cooperation. The next step is to determine the extent of North Korea's commitment to TRADP. Although one purpose of multilateral cooperation in TRADP is to foster understanding, stability, and peace throughout the region, difficult negotiations will be necessary if the participants are to formulate mutually beneficial economic agreements. Only then can the Tumen River Area become a part of dynamic East Asia.

Much will also depend on North Korea's sustained commitments to liberalization. After the collapse of the Soviet Union in December 1991, North Korea once again insisted on state control and a single and pure ideology (*Korea Reference*, 1993). This left the strategic position of TRADP with respect to North Korea unclear. Nonetheless, the ideological preparation or popular education for an open economy or for any kind of change in economic life has started (Suzuki, 1993). North Korea's 1992 constitution has in fact eliminated the phrase "Marxism-Leninism" and instead stressed original thought or *chuch'e* (self-reliance). But change will take time.

Appendix 1

Chronology of Significant Events

1979   North Korea joins UNDP.

1984   Law on Equity Joint Ventures enacted by North Korea.

1988 Dec   First counselor-level talks between US and North Korea.

1989 May   Soviet Union allows PRC to use Tumen River.

1990 July   First Northeast Asia Economic Development Conference held in Changchun, PRC.

     Nov   First government-to-government talks between Japan and North Korea held in Beijing.

1991 May   North Korea expresses desire to join United Nations.

     June   Plan to develop Tumen River announced by Jilin province at seminar of Japan-China Northeast Development Association held in Tokyo.

     July   Greater Vladivostok Free Economic Area proposal presented by Russia and UNIDO.

     July   At UNDP Northeast Asia Sub-Regional Program Meeting in Ulaanbaatar, Mongolia, four countries agree to cooperate in the Tumen project.

     Aug   Northeast Asia Economic Cooperation Conference held in Shenyang, PRC.

     Aug-   Second Northeast Asia Economic Development Conference in Changchun, PRC.
     Sep

     Sep   Simultaneous admission of North Korea and South Korea into UN.

     Oct   Agreement reached on Programme Management Committee for TRADP.

     Nov   Taipei,China permits direct trade with North Korea.

     Dec   PRC opens Hunchun to foreigners.

     Dec   North Korea and South Korea sign "Non-Aggression Agreement."

1992 Feb   First Meeting of Programme Management Committee of TRADP held in Seoul, South Korea.

	May	Third Northeast Asia Economic Development Conference held in Pyongyang, North Korea.
	June	Direct passenger train service begins between Urumqi, PRC and Alma Ata, Kazakhstan.
	Aug	Fourth Northeast Asia Economic Development Conference (Northeast Asia Economic Forum) held in Vladivostok, Russia.
	Sep	Direct container service begins between Lianyungang, PRC and Alma Ata, Kazakhstan.
	Oct	Second Meeting of TRADP-PMC held in Beijing.
	Oct	Law on Foreigners' Investment, Law on Contractual Joint Venture, and Law on Foreign Enterprises enacted by North Korea.
1993	Jan	PMC Telecommunications Sub-Group Meeting held in Seoul, South Korea.
	Jan	Law on Foreign Investment-Business Enterprises and Foreign Individual Tax, Law on Foreign Exchange Administration, and Law on Free Economic and Trade Zone enacted by North Korea.
	Mar	North Korea claims to withdraw from NPT.
	Apr	Hunchun (PRC) - Kraskino (Russia) Railway construction starts.
	May	North Korea, PRC and Russia agree to lease their land to an international corporation.
	June	North Korea suspends withdrawal from NPT.
1994	Feb	North Korea and US agree on inspection by International Atomic Energy Agency of some of North Korea's nuclear facilities.

Endnotes:

1.   Researcher, Research Institute of Asian Development, International University of Japan.
2.   For instance, Kim Jong Wu, chairman of the Committee for the Promotion of External Economic Cooperation, is quoted as saying on 1 October 1992, "Our national principle is self-reliance .... South Korean foreign trade is over $130 billion and that of the North is only $11 billion. This proves that we produce food, clothes, and houses domestically.... Our people are satisfied and self-confident."
3.   More than 90 per cent of Mongolia's international trade had been with COMECON countries, especially the former Soviet Union. In 1989, COMECON countries' share of total Mongolian exports was 89.8 per cent, while for imports it was 92.5 per cent (Aoki and Hashimoto, 1992). Because of the failing economies of the COMECON countries, Mongolian exports declined from $829 million in 1988 to $279 million in 1991, although the country had export potential for coal, copper, tin, molybdenum, tungsten, fluorite, and many kinds of dairy products. Exports fromMongolia are transported either through the Russia-Mongolia-PRC railway and the port of Tianjin or via the Choybalsan-Siberian railway and the port of Nakhodka. The first route is not efficient since the gauges of the Mongolian section are different from those of the Chinese section. The Choybalsan-Siberian route is indirect. Once a short-cut via Inner Mongolia, Jilin, and the Tumen River Area is opened, resource-rich eastern Mongolia will have easier access to its potential markets.

Bibliography

Aoki, Shinji, "Country in Great Pain Today: A Message to Japanese and Mongols," in Shinji Aoki and Masaru Hashimoto, eds., *Mongolia for Beginners* (in Japanese). Tokyo: Heigensha, 1992.

Central Intelligence Agency. *The World Factbook 1992*. Washington, D.C., 1992.

Democratic People's Republic of Korea, Committee for the Promotion of External Economic Cooperation. *Golden Triangle Rajin-Sonbong*. Pyongyang, 1992.

Hiraiwa, Shunji, "Democratic People's Republic of Korea: Economy," in *General Review of China 1992* (in Japanese). Tokyo: Kazankai, 1991.

Hirata, Mikio. *Data Book of Contemporary China*. Tokyo: Kokonshoin, 1992.

Imu, Tedoku, "On the Creation of Rajin-Sonbong Free Economic Trade," in *Higashi Asia Review* (in Japanese), January 1993.

Institute of Developing Economies. *Asia Trend Yearbook 1992*. Tokyo, 1992.

Ishibe, Kimio, "Industry: Restructuring and Forming of Legal System," in Shinki Aoki and Masaru Hashimoto, eds., *Mongolia for Beginners* (in Japanese). Tokyo: Heigensha, 1992.

Ishikawa, Kazuo, "Present Condition and Prospects of the Japan Sea Rim Economic Zone Concept," in *RIM Pacific Business and Industries*, Vol. 3 (1992).

Izumi, Mitsuo, "Foreign Trade–Present Situation and Issues," in Shinji Aoki and Masaru Hashimoto, eds., *Mongolia for Beginners* (in Japanese). Tokyo: Heigensha, 1992.

Kantaiheiyomondaikenkyusho, ed. *Korea Reference 1993* (in Japanese). Tokyo: Harashobo, 1993.

Rhee, Sang-Woo, "North Korea in 1991: Struggle to Save Chuch'e Amid Signs of Change," in *Asian Survey*, Vol. 32 (January 1992a).

_____, "Inter-Korean Relations in the 21st Century," in *Korea and World Affairs* (Spring 1992b).

Ri, Tetsuchin, "Sonbong Economic Trade Zone Plan Starts," in *United Review* (in Japanese), No. 319 (January 1992).

Suzuki, Masayuki. *North Korea: Resonance Between Socialism and Tradition.* Tokyo: University of Tokyo Press, 1993.

Ueda, Takeshi. *Mystery of Bohaiguo* (in Japanese). Tokyo: Kodansha, 1992.

United Nations. *Statistical Yearbook for Asia and Pacific 1990.* Bangkok, 1990.

Authors and Affiliations

1. MIN TANG
   Economist
   Economics and Development Resource Center
   Asian Development Bank

2. MYO THANT
   Economist
   Economics and Development Resource Center
   Asian Development Bank

3. EDWARD K.Y. CHEN
   Director, Center of Asian Studies
   The University of Hong Kong

4. ANNA HO
   Assistant Research Officer
   Centre of Asian Studies
   The University of Hong Kong

5. POCHIH CHEN
   Professor, Department and Institute of Economics
   National Taiwan University

6. CHEN DEZHAO
   Member, Executive Board
   China Center for International Studies
   People's Republic of China

7. YUE-MAN YEUNG
   Director, Hong Kong Institute of Asia-Pacific Studies
   The Chinese University of Hong Kong

8. WANG JUN
   Professor, Department of Economics
   Lingnan (University) College
   Zhongshan University, People's Republic of China

9. SREE KUMAR
   Fellow
   Institute of Southeast Asian Studies, Singapore

10. G. NAIDU
    Professor of Applied Economics
    Department of Economics
    University of Malaya, Malaysia

11. HIROSHI KAKAZU
    Dean and Professor
    Graduate School of International Relations
    International University of Japan

12. HIROKAZU SHIODE
    Researcher and Lecturer
    Research Institute of Asian Development
    International University of Japan